OPENING THE WAY

Memoirs of a Cuban exile:

Political prisoner. Brigade 2506. First Cuban elected to public office in the United States in the 20th century. International Presence. Builder and family man.

COLECCIÓN CUBA Y SUS JUECES

EDICIONES UNIVERSAL, Miami, Florida, 2023

Manolo Reboso

OPENING THE WAY

Memoirs of a Cuban exile:

Political prisoner. Brigade 2506. First Cuban elected to public office in the United States in the 20th century. International Presence. Builder and family man.

Copyright © 2023 by Manolo Reboso

———

First edition, 2023

EDICIONES UNIVERSAL
P.O. Box 450353 (Shenandoah Station)
Miami, FL 33245-0353. USA
(Since 1965)

e-mail: ediciones@ediciones.com
http://www.ediciones.com

Library of Congress Control Number: 2023946012

ISBN: 978-1-59388-338-6

Edited by Julio Estorino
Translated by Tere Estorino Florin

Text composition: María Cristina Zarraluqui

Cover design: Luis García Fresquet
On the cover: The fortress of La Cabaña and the Morro Lighthouse

All rights reserved. No part of this book may be reproduced
or transmitted in any form or by any electronic or mechanical means,
including photocopying, recording, or computerized
systems, without the written permission of the author,
except in the case of brief quotations incorporated
in critical articles or in journals.
For information, please contact
Ediciones Universal.

To my children Alex, Roberto Luis, Irma, Noreen, Melissa and Manny.

To Nadia, my wife.

So that you may know a little more about what my life has been and what my life is, a life in which you are the most important thing.

Table of Contents

Thank you 11

Prologue 13

Preface 17

Chapter 1 The Two Islands 21

Chapter 2 A New World – My Baptism into the Art of Politics 31

Chapter 3 Return to a Sinking Cuba 39

Chapter 4 A Young Conspirator – The Trap 49

Chapter 5 Fidel Castro, Prison and the Miracle 57

Chapter 6 Say Goodbye to the Palm Trees 67

Chapter 7 Rendezvous with Duty: Brigade 2506 73

Chapter 8 Playa Girón: The Sad Reality 81

Adendum Nº 1 93

Chapter 9 Robert F. Kennedy – The Rescue of the Brigade Members . 109

Chapter 10 One Make Mistakes in Life… Death of the Kennedys 123

Chapter 11 New Directions – Florida Politicians 133

Chapter 12 The First Cuban in State Government 143

Chapter 13 From Florida to Latin America 153

Chapter 14 The First Cuban Commissioner 161

Chapter 15 The New Mayor 171

Chapter 16 The First Cuban Elected in Miami 181

Chapter 17 "The Cuban-Born Commissioner" 195

Chapter 18 The Fourth Power 205

Chapter 19 More than 20,000 Votes – The "Dialogue" 215

Chapter 20 Anastasio Somoza and Carlos Andrés Pérez 225

Chapter 21 The Resignation and the Pact – Tragedy is Repeated 235

Chapter 22 A Hispanic Mayor – The Cuban American National Foundation 247

Chapter 23 Ronald Reagan – Politics and Politicians in Miami-Dade 257

Chapter 24 Return to Nicaragua – The Two Statues 267

Chapter 25 Politics, Yesterday and Today 275

Chapter 26 Family and Friends – Leaders, Past and Present 283

Chapter 27 Cuba and its Exile – Democrats and Republicans 303

Chapter 28 Miami's Future – Necessary Changes 313

Chapter 29 Fidel Castro and Donald Trump 323

Chapter 30 The 2024 Elections: A Prediction 329

Index 333

Thank you

I would like to acknowledge and thank Roberto Rodríguez Tejera, great journalist and best friend, for convincing me that I should write this book about my life and the events that I have lived through in the course of it, because of their historical value.

To Julio Estorino, an excellent human being, intelligent and good friend, thanks to whose cooperation and talent this book has been possible.

And to my wife, Nadia, who helped me gather details to complete this project.

To them, my sincere gratitude.

Prologue

Here is this man, now approaching 90 years of age, who, every morning, half an hour before breakfast, drinks 12 ounces of warm water mixed with a whole squeezed lemon, a large spoonful of honey and a teaspoonful of apple cider vinegar; and, in spite of the vinegar and lemon at the beginning of the day, he is an absolute optimist.

Not only this, but, as if that were not enough, every day, religiously, summer or winter, he takes a bath that ends with a "Scottish shower," which is nothing more than starting with a lukewarm shower, and, little by little, lowering the water temperature until it becomes a cold shower, C-O-L-D, for the last two or three minutes. In these times and in our hedonistic society, this can be considered either an act of extreme bravery or a masochistic ritual.

According to him, these tortures help immunize the body and keep it in optimal conditions, and if we judge by him – healthy, agile and alert-minded – we must conclude that, as Cecilia Valdés would say, "he must be onto something."

Of course, since not everything has to be rigorous, the reward comes at noon, every noon, which is when this gentleman, with equal discipline, takes a refreshing nap of one or two hours, depending on his schedule, which is still that of a person who has no time to get bored.

Like all the smart people in the world, our protagonist seeks inspiration in the great and the wise. A faithful admirer of Joe DiMaggio since he was a child playing baseball at school and in his neighborhood, he began to fasten his belt, in imitation of the baseball star, not below his navel like the rest of us mortals, but on the left side of his waist, a ritual that he maintains to this day.

A disciplined man – as I've already said – who also firmly believes in the value of discipline, he once heard Admiral William H. McRaven, military chief of the team that put an end to Osama Bin Laden's diabolical life, recommend that, as a rule of life, no man should leave his room in the morning without first leaving his bed meticulously made up, and he immediately adopted the practice for himself. You don't have to be a psychologist to decipher what his self-imposed rituals tell us about his personality.

If you think the life of someone like that should be interesting, wait until I tell you the rest: he was an early conspirator against Fidel Castro's dictatorship in Cuba; he knew the ordeal of political imprisonment; he lived as a fugitive for a short time, no less risky for it being a short time; he was part of the first waves of exiles in Miami; he participated in the Bay of Pigs Invasion in Cuba. He was friends with people of great relevance such as Robert F. Kennedy, Manuel Artime, José Miró Cardona, Tony Varona, Bob Graham and Reubin Askew.

He was the first Cuban elected to public office in the United States in the 20th century. Together with Maurice Ferré, he was one of the creators of the Miami we see today, and when everything indicated that he could become the first Cuban mayor of the "Capital of Latin America," he distanced himself from active politics. He participated in some episodes of high diplomacy, rubbing shoulders with politicians such as Anastasio Somoza, Jr., president of Nicaragua, and Carlos Andrés Pérez, president of Venezuela, and lived more than one historical milestone, not only in Cuba and in exile, but also in Central America.

All this and much more, Manolo Reboso tells us in this book, his memoirs, which, yes, narrates his life since he was born until the present. However, what's shared here isn't only a biography; it's also the history of South Florida, of Miami and of the Cuban exile community, and also much of what has touched us and continues to touch us most about politics in the United States, in addition to his interesting vision of life.

When, at the beginning of 2022, I met with Manolo for the first time so that he could tell me about this project, about his desire to have a written testimony of his life, I wasn't sure that his story had the necessary elements to make it interesting and worthwhile for today's readers. He was offering to hire me as the editor of his book, the person who would put in writing what he would provide verbally, and I hadn't decided what answer to give him.

I had never met Manolo Reboso before. Of course I knew who he was and, to a certain extent, I remembered his presence and activity in Miami's political life, but I didn't begin practicing journalism until many years after his retirement from the political scene. We had greeted each other once, but nothing more. I said to myself: "I'm going to meet with him; I know that a couple of conversations will be enough to know if the effort is worthwhile. If he doesn't convince me, I will politely decline, and that's the end of it."

The first work meeting we had was more than enough for me to become enthusiastic about the project. The diversity of details and circumstances, the different stages of his life, the protagonist's own vision of himself and his history, all the aspects of the experiences narrated here, are extremely interesting, informative and useful and will satisfy the reader.

I'm not the right person to judge the way in which this story, the multifaceted life of Manolo Reboso, is written. I can only say that I have endeavored to fill these pages with absolute fidelity to what he has told me and to the opinions he has expressed. My mission has been to give coherence to the story and polish the language without altering what he has said. I have only transferred the words from his voice to paper.

I thank God for having allowed me to be part of this work and Manolo Reboso for trusting me with such a special task. Thanks also to all who read this.

Julio Estorino, Miami, August 2022

Preface

> *At this point in my life, I'm not looking to be part of a tale with a happy ending; I'm just looking to be happy without so many tall tales.*
> Anonymous

It was the sad days after the failure of the Bay of Pigs Invasion, days in which we all wondered how the fateful outcome we had never believed possible *had* been possible.

It was also the days when, within the Kennedy administration, everything concerning the ill-fated military operation that had left the prestige of the United States so battered was being debated.

It was John F. Kennedy himself who put an end to the internal debate and the burning questions of the press and of the adversaries and enemies of his administration. In a speech delivered at the Statler Hilton Hotel in Washington, D.C., during a banquet of the American Society of Newspaper Editors, three days after April 17, 1961, the president addressed the matter, implicitly taking responsibility for what had happened.

A short time later, I was invited to participate in a television program that aired in New England, where a panel of four journalists dissected what had happened. One of them asked me who, in my opinion, was responsible for that tremendous disaster: "President Kennedy has already taken responsibility," I replied. "However, I believe that a large part of the blame falls on the thousands of military-age Cubans who stayed 'patrolling the streets of Miami' and did not go to the camps."

I have wanted to begin this account of my life, my memoir, in this way, because for me and for all Cubans of my generation and those who have come after, Cuba's political evolution marked our lives strongly and in such a defining way, and in that political evolution nothing was so shocking, so devastating, nor of such profound consequences as the failure of the Bay of Pigs Invasion, an operation that should have put an end to the then-incipient communist dictatorship of Fidel Castro and, on the contrary, ended up consolidating it in power, to the disgrace of Cuba and its children. Therefore, when putting into perspective each of our own histories, we are obligated to refer to something so important, so heroic and so unfortunate at the same time.

I think that, if we Cubans want to find a sure path of freedom for Cuba, and if we exiles want our presence and participation in all aspects of life in this other homeland that has welcomed us to be as transparent as it should be, we must begin by owning our mistakes. And the absence of many exiles of that time in the ranks of those who participated in the Bay of Pigs Invasion to seek Cuba's freedom, was, as a people, one of our most serious faults, perhaps the most serious of all.

Of course, this doesn't diminish the Kennedy administration's responsibility in the unfortunate event, which it bears, and to a great extent. But I think it will do us all good and will be helpful to remember always, in discussing this and any other subject, that those who live in glass houses should not throw rocks.

And since we are talking about President Kennedy's administration, and without trying to diminish his mistakes in terms of U.S. policy toward Cuba, which I've pointed out in the previous paragraph, it seems to me that it would be good for our morale and would focus our history better if we ended what seems to be the obsession of some who blame JFK for every blunder that has been committed in Washington with respect to the Cuban regime, not realizing or not wanting to remember that the biggest mistake, the fundamental mistake and the most ill-advised decision made by the United States with respect to Cuba rests entirely on the shoulders of the previous president, Republican Dwight D. Eisenhower.

Dwight D. Eisenhower was, without a doubt, an American patriot, who won acclaim with his valuable participation in World War II as Supreme Commander of the Allied Expeditionary Force in Europe and years later, as president, had great successes in the White House. However, his administration's policy toward Cuba was plagued with failures, especially in the last days of Fulgencio Batista's government, in which his State Department forced Batista out of power, without taking the necessary measures to prevent that power from going directly into the hands of Fidel Castro, despite the evidence indicating the true communist nature of the 26th of July Movement.

This is no secret. It was clearly and civilly denounced by Earl E. T. Smith, former U.S. ambassador in Havana during those turbulent years, in his well-documented book, *The Fourth Floor: An Account of the Castro Communist Revolution*, where he chronicles the twisted efforts of some State Department officials to ensure not only that Batista would leave power, but also that he would be replaced by Fidel Castro and no one else.

Had this not happened, had Batista's departure not been mediated without the necessary safeguards to prevent Cuba from falling into the hands of known Marxists, such as the Argentine Ernesto Guevara and Raul Castro, Fidel's own brother, the lives of millions of Cubans, like myself, would not have been sadly tinged by the typical horrors of communist regimes, from executions without due process to the tearing apart of families that all exile provokes. The attempt to free Cuba at Playa Giron, where the Bay of Pigs Invasion occurred, would not have been necessary.

My life, then, and that of so many other compatriots, would not have an open wound for more than six decades, a wound that can only heal the day Cuba is free.

With a conscience free of this burden, let's remember that life goes on. Please join me in visiting my memories, which is not only the story of my life, but also, to a great extent, the story of Miami, the story of the Cuban exiles in South Florida and, equally, the story of how the Cuban-American identity was forged.

Manolo Reboso

Chapter 1
The Two Islands

There is no coming to heaven with dry eyes.
Thomas Adams

I am more than 3,800 miles from Miami, my small homeland in the United States of America, and I have before me a spectacular landscape, where a beautiful conjunction of land, sea and sky invite reflection. I am at the foot of enormous volcanic peaks, in front of an incredible natural pool Mother Nature carved out of the rock. The gentle breeze envelops everything with the typical smell of laurel forests.

And I think: nobody would ever want to leave here.

But from here, the island of El Hierro, one of the smallest of the Canary Islands archipelago, Spanish land on the African coast, my paternal grandparents, José Reboso Padrón and Casilda Brito Mérida, left one day at the end of 1911, accompanied by Maximina, their four-year-old daughter, and their little boy, Manuel, who would become my father, and who was then just over a year old. Luckily for them, they were going to another distant and different island, but one no less paradisiacal.

They were going to Cuba, the so-called "Pearl of the Antilles," the young republic that only nine years earlier had broken the ties that bound it to Spain, seeking its independence, and that in those early years of the 20th century was receiving waves of Spanish immigrants who knew they would be welcome, since the political rupture had had no repercussions on the emotional ties between Spaniards and Cubans.

Upon their arrival in Cuba, the Reboso-Brito family settled in Esmeralda (Spanish for "emerald"), a small town on the northern coast of Camagüey province, which at that time wasn't even considered a municipality. The number of inhabitants in those days was barely more than 3,000, most of whom lived in the countryside. They were *guajiros*, in the vernacular. That countryside possessed a wild beauty that had no reason to envy the already-remote island of El Hierro.

Parallel to the coast and separated from it by a narrow stretch of sea were Jardines del Rey, islets full of wildlife and fierceness. On Cayo Romano, for example, lived herds of untamed horses descended from the first ones that arrived in America with the conquistadors. Several rivers watered the terra firma of Cuba; to the south, low mountains and across almost all the surface, abundant sugar cane and small fruit plantations; there were, additionally, forests where precious woods abounded.

Once there, and in spite of the natural homesickness of those who leave their beloved places, it's certain that my grandparents thought the same as I've thought when contemplating the beauty of El Hierro: that no one who lived in Esmeralda would ever want to leave. The landscape confirmed what the name described: Esmeralda was a jewel.

The town grew and experienced a remarkable boom as a result of the opening, in 1921, of a sugar mill like no other. A gigantic sugar factory, the largest in Cuba and the world, the Central Jaronú (Jaronú sugar mill) was owned by the United States and had a milling capacity of 12,500 tons every 24 hours. My grandfather, who in the Canary Islands had been a furniture manufacturer, got a job in the modern sugar mill, and there he spent the rest of his working life in Cuba.

By then, when he started working at the sugar mill, José Reboso, Casilda Brito, Maximina and Manuel already felt at home in Cuba. They had even gotten used to the fact that the Cubans, affable as they were, called the Canary Islanders specifically "islanders," as if they, the Cubans, were not themselves also islanders.

What they cannot have imagined is that, just as they had to leave their beautiful island of El Hierro because life there was made impossible by the economic conditions, one day, almost half a century later, their son and grandchildren would have to leave this other beautiful island, the one that now opened its doors to them, not because of its economic conditions, but because its politics would make it impossible for them to live there as well.

I spent only two days in the Canary Islands and was able to fulfill my old dream of visiting the land of my ancestors. On the long flight back to Miami, I pondered on what had been the life and history of those islanders and on what has been my life, that of another islander, Cuban, American...

And I started to remember:

My father, Manuel Reboso Brito, was born in the village of Valverde, El Hierro's capital, on July 30, 1910. As I have already mentioned, he arrived in Cuba when he was not yet two years old, so all his life experience was Cuban, and he felt Cuban from head to toe.

My father
Manuel Reboso Brito

He spent his childhood and adolescence in the quietness of Esmeralda, but when he turned 18, he decided to look for wider horizons than those he could glimpse from his small Camagüey town. The year was 1928. The aspirations of Gerardo Machado Morales, then-President of the Republic, to be reelected bitterly permeated the Cuban political scene. The role that the armed forces could play in what was already pointing towards an institutional crisis was a cause for conjecture, since in Cuba, as in all Latin America, the military were seen as arbiters of power and they saw themselves that way, too.

Despite these unsettling circumstances, Dad moved to La Habana and enlisted in the Army. He later studied at the Air Force Academy, where he graduated as a lieutenant. That was the beginning of what would become an outstanding military career, which was not negatively impacted by the violent fall of the Machado government on August 12, 1933.

On the contrary, when, as a result of the subsequent political instability, Fulgencio Batista burst onto the national scene, leading the so-called *Revolución de los Sargentos* (Sergeants' Revolt, or, more commonly, the Revolution of 1933) of September 4 of that same year, greater opportunities for advancement opened up for those in uniform, which confirmed to Lieutenant Reboso what he considered his wisdom in enlisting in the Army.

During World War II, the Cuban government sent him to take flying lessons in different airplanes in the United States. Thus, he received training in places such as Randolph Field and Waco, Texas and Fort Benning, Georgia.

He was Chief of the Cuban Army Air Force Cadet School and in 1956, he was appointed military attaché of the Cuban embassy in Washington, D.C., a position he held until Fidel Castro came to power.

Dad was a man of good bearing and keen intelligence. Of medium height, with a broad forehead, penetrating blue eyes and wide-ranging knowledge, he could, when he wanted to, be a good conversationalist, despite his tough and introverted character. He exuded confidence and perhaps it was this that most impressed Esperanza, the young woman who captured his attention from the first time their eyes met.

Esperanza Bello Álvarez was born in La Habana on January 10, 1913, the daughter of Francisco Bello and Belarmina Álvarez, both natives of León, Spain. She was a pretty woman, with well-proportioned features, very expressive brown eyes and an attractive figure. Her physical beauty, which was no small thing, was complemented by a splendid smile and a happy disposition. She was the typical extroverted and cheerful Cuban woman, always aware of the needs of others, always ready to help. And perhaps because of their opposite characters, because they complemented each other, love quickly took hold between the young woman from La Habana and that military man of Canary Island origins.

They were married in February 1933. He was on his way toward his 23rd birthday; she had just turned 20. I was the fruit of their honeymoon, born on November 26, 1933, on a Sunday, at two o'clock in the afternoon, and I was named José Manuel.

Eight years later Roberto, my only brother, was born.

My mother, Esperanza Bello, and my brother Roberto

I had a happy childhood. Our upbringing was good and well balanced. As in almost all families at that time, the father was the authority and exercised discipline without excesses; the mother provided protection and contentment; and the grandparents spoiled with affection and forgave all mischief. Despite the age difference, Roberto and I shared some games, and I enjoyed the role of older brother.

Roberto at first studied for a few years in a school that was right in our neighborhood, Ampliación de Almendares, and then continued his studies in the United States. He did high school in Maryland, as well as university, where he graduated with a degree in Economics. As an adult, still in Maryland, he was an administrator in a grocery store company, one of the largest in that state. He then came to Miami, where he married and had a daughter, my niece Michelle. In reality, he lived only a short time in Cuba; most of his life was spent in the United States. In Miami, he worked with Clerk of Courts Harvey Ruvin and spent about 20 years as the director of the marriage license bureau. Roberto was a great man, very loved by all who knew him, and he died relatively young, quite young. I loved him very much, and he loved me too.

Eventually, first my paternal grandfather and then my maternal grandmother, when they were both widowed, came to live with us, and this enriched our family life. My grandmother was so sweet; I was very attached to her. Once in La Habana, my grandfather dedicated himself to making wines that he later sold in the neighborhood. These were sweet wines that, according to him, were what they drank in the Canary Islands. He also made an artisanal rum with honey, which was more of a hobby for him.

We were a middle-class family who, without being rich, lived comfortably. Dad was an officer in the Air Force, where he worked his way up. He was a captain for many years; then he was promoted to commander; and later, as I mentioned before, he was appointed military attaché in Washington, D.C., when Colonel Ramon Barquín was dismissed from this post for his participation in the so-called *Conspiración de los Puros* (Conspiracy of the Pure), in which several military men were involved and whose objective was to overthrow President Batista.

Our house was spacious and beautiful, with two stories. We lived in the Ampliación de Almendares neighborhood in the municipality of Marianao, part of what today we would call "Greater Havana." It was a beautiful, clean and lively neighborhood, whose boundary, to the north, was La Habana's coastline with its famous beaches.

Near our house was the Metropolitan movie theater, whose owner was the great actor Federico Piñeiro, and who, with Alberto Garrido, formed the comedy duo "Chicharito y Sopeira," famous throughout Cuba. Roberto Goizueta, the Cuban who years later would become president of Coca-Cola here in the United States, lived in my neighborhood. I remember his sister, May Goizueta. The family of Alfredo Durán, my great friend since childhood, also lived there.

Also living in the neighborhood was another great friend, Tony Lamas, who got me out of La Cabaña prison, and thanks to whom I was able to escape from Cuba when Fidel Castro controlled everything in the country and my life was in danger. As it's easy to see, the friendships I made in my childhood and adolescence in Ampliación de Almendares, a neighborhood that reflected the prosperity of Cuba in the 50's and in which I felt truly happy, were very strong and very good.

I was also very fortunate in my parents' school of choice for my education. La Habana in particular, and all of Cuba in general, had excellent schools. Public education was free and very good, and the private schools, both religious and secular, strived and competed with each other in terms of the quality of their teachers and their advanced educational programs.

The Baldor School, owned by brothers Aurelio and Francisco Baldor, was for me and for the thousands of children who passed through its classrooms, a true forge of character and knowledge. In general terms, their teachers understood their work as a total dedication to the best education of their students, and that education included not only scientific and literary knowledge, but also the values and behavior that distinguish good people. Without being authoritarian, they instilled those values in their students who, for the most part, when they graduated and went on to other educational institutions, were well-prepared and well-trained men and women.

I especially remember Professor Fernando Guerra, who was my favorite teacher, as well as the principal, Aurelio Baldor, who was a renowned mathematician and whose textbooks continue to be used today in many countries. I think it was from him that I got my love for mathematics.

Something very important for me, since I was a child, was sports, especially baseball, *la pelota*, as we Cubans say. I had a baseball field one block from my house, and I enjoyed and learned a lot there, with the boys from my neighborhood. I played first base, and I think I was pretty good at it.

In high school, I played in the under-15 league, and later, in the under-18. We played against other schools like LaSalle, Candler College, and so on. We had a great time because we all put a lot of effort into winning. I don't know, maybe that shaped a competitive spirit in me, which would be very useful later in my life, in politics.

Another sport I practiced was rowing and canoeing, but to tell you about this, I must tell you about the Círculo Militar y Naval.

The Círculo Militar y Naval was like my second home and it was, in fact, not only for me, but for countless servicemen and their families who found there an active social life, fellowship, sports, and a very good ambience. Children and young people particularly enjoyed many opportunities for recreation there, and its lounges and events saw more than one romance blossom among its young associates.

The Círculo was one of the societies known in Cuba as "de instrucción y recreo" (for instruction and recreation). It had been founded in 1911, when General José Miguel Gómez was President of the Republic, and was originally located at the Columbia Camp. Years later, a permanent location was built on Marianao's beach, which added to the attractiveness of the place, since water sports such as swimming, water polo and regattas could be practiced there, as well as others like baseball, soccer, horseback riding, etc.

Although it was an institution created primarily for members of the armed forces and their families, it also admitted as members civilians, who participated in all activities. Members all paid a modest one-time initiation fee and a monthly fee, also very modest, with which its facilities were maintained, and its events paid for.

In its best times, the Círculo had more than a thousand members. In 1953, when I stopped attending due to continuing my studies in the United States, General Eulogio Cantillo chaired its Board of Directors.

At the Círculo, I participated, as a boy, in swimming competitions and also in canoeing. I was 12 or 13 years old when I was a coxswain, something I enjoyed very much and that allowed me to participate with the team members, almost all of whom were older than me. Later on, I started playing squash, a sport in which I excelled, because I really liked it and felt very comfortable playing it. My brother Roberto also excelled greatly in squash.

For adolescents, the Círculo also served, without that being its purpose, as a first source of knowledge of politics. It was logical and natural that, its members being military personnel and their families, as well as civilians who, in one way or another, were linked to them and to the government, and to political activity, many of the conversations that were heard there revolved around the country's political events and the opinions of different sectors within the armed forces. Although the children and adolescents didn't interfere in the grown-ups' conversations and discussions, much of what we heard stuck to us and formed our thoughts on the subject.

My family, then, was no stranger to Cuban politics. Dad was still a young soldier in 1933, when the September 4 coup led by Batista took place and which, in the opinion of many, had been the remedy for the chaos and power vacuum created when Gerardo Machado was overthrown in August of that year.

Batista therefore enjoyed the sympathy of most of the members of the armed forces, and my father was no exception. He had a great friendship with General Ignacio Galindez, who was one of the generals close to Batista and was my brother Roberto's godfather. It was a situation in which family circumstances, class factors and political loyalties were mixed.

And I can say that, contrary to the stereotypes created and engendered by Castro's propaganda, there were many military men who sincerely sought the best for Cuba.

Chapter 2
A New World – My Baptism into the Art of Politics

Anyone can teach, but only those who are a living example can educate.
José de la Luz y Caballero

I had finished my studies at the Baldor School. Nine years had passed since I had entered the school as a young boy, and I was leaving its classrooms as "a little man," in the words of my elders, and "a real man," according to my own vision of myself.

The year was 1949. I was to begin high school; that is to say, the preparation for, four years later, to be able to enter the university. The change of environment appealed to me, it was an important challenge for my young life, and challenges certainly excited me. However, I had not calculated that becoming a student at the Instituto del Vedado would mean a real-life change for me.

The Instituto was totally different from Baldor. As a private school, Baldor was much stricter, more disciplined. The students all came from the same type of families, all from more or less the same social class and with a very similar education. At the Instituto, we students had more freedom and came from different types of family backgrounds, both economically and in terms of education and values. There, I could talk to everyone without being noticed, I could come and go as I pleased, and everything was more flexible.

I quickly adapted to the new environment and tried to get along with everyone. I was part of the baseball team and traveled several times within Cuba for games with other youth teams. We went to Holguín, and to Santiago de Cuba, in Oriente, and other places.

One big difference was the expression of different political sympathies among the student body, which often led to violence. Among the older students, the juniors and seniors, for example, many belonged to different organizations, which competed with each other. That was something new to me.

In high school

Leonel Alonso, who, many years later would be involved in Miami politics, since his wife, Miriam Alonso, was a County Commissioner, attended the Instituto. There I also met my good friend Osiel Gonzalez, who, later in life, would become chief of La Habana's fire department.

It wasn't unusual for fights to break out between the different groups, and sometimes they were very violent. It was all very regrettable, because it was Cubans against Cubans, killing each other, with none of them realizing that, at the end of all that bloodshed, there would be only one beneficiary, Fidel Castro, the worst dictator that Cuba had ever suffered.

I, naturally, avoided all those matters of insurrectionary groups in the Instituto. I did not get involved in any of that, and I was able to weather the situation without major difficulties.

However, this didn't mean that I wasn't interested, nor that politics were foreign to me. Fulgencio Batista had been president of Cuba between 1940 and 1944. He had been democratically elected and, in the opinion of many, ran a good government then. He also democratically conducted the elections to choose his successor, who turned out to be the opposition candidate, Dr. Ramón Grau San Martín, of the Partido Revolucionario Cubano, known as the Partido Auténtico (Authentic Party). Batista handed over the presidency without any problems.

Batista came to the United States and settled in Daytona Beach, Florida. In Cuba, Grau was succeeded, in 1948, by Dr. Carlos Prío Socarrás, also from the Partido Auténtico, and when the presidential elections of June 1952 approached, Batista announced that he would run again for president of the Republic.

That announcement mobilized his supporters in Cuba, those who were members of his party, the Partido Acción Unitaria (United Action Party), known as PAU, which would later change its name to Partido Acción Progresista (Progressive Action Party), known as PAP. My father, as I mentioned before, like most of the members of the Cuban armed forces, sympathized with Batista, and in the Círculo Militar y Naval, the atmosphere was one of great enthusiasm for the possibility of a new presidency of the candidate who had come from their own ranks.

This was around 1951 and for me, at the age of 18, it was natural to join that political trend. I met one of my mentors, Rafael Díaz-Balart, who was a very intelligent and very eloquent man, and a very good political organizer. Batista had named him president of the PAU youth, and he named Joseito Saiff president of the youth in Marianao and the same for me in Ampliación de Almendares, which included neighborhoods like La Sierra.

That was my first political experience. It didn't last long, because Batista did not wait for the elections to become president again. On March 10, 1952, he staged a *coup d'état* that large sectors of the armed forces and many of his former political allies supported. It was very controversial, applauded by many and criticized by many. The people, however, accepted the *fait accompli* without great protest.

By then, my nascent political activities were very limited. I was about to begin my last year at the Instituto, and I dedicated myself to my studies with great zeal, since I was already sure of how I would move forward to try to reach my goals in what would become my profession.

I spent my last year at the Instituto del Vedado concentrating on my studies and in spite of the politically charged atmosphere that reigned in Cuba and the fact that most of the students were vehemently against Batista, I never had any problems, because I avoided political discussions and few there knew that I was the son of a military man.

At one time I had been tempted to study law and become a lawyer, but by the time I graduated with a Bachelor of Science degree, I had no doubt: I would be an architect. I was fascinated by mathematics and drawing, and I could clearly see that, for me, there would be nothing better than studying architecture.

Only, to achieve this, I would have to go through a change, a welcome one, but as abrupt or more than the transition from Baldor to the Instituto. University awaited me... in the United States.

It was already decided that I would do my college studies in "the North." Having received his training in different models of military aircraft in several U.S. Air Force bases in Texas and Georgia had given my father the opportunity to get to know the way of life and education in this country, and he greatly admired it. That was not uncommon among Cubans.

Contrary to what Castro's propaganda has spread, the Cuban people never had anti-Yankee feelings. It was only the few members of the Partido Socialista Popular (Popular Socialist Party), who were communists, who accused the United States of being an oppressive, imperialist country. Most Cubans in those days enthusiastically admired the "Giant of the North."

So, I was very much in agreement with coming to study here and, as that had been decided by my parents, I, for my part, decided to study at the Georgia Institute of Technology, or Georgia Tech, as it's commonly known.

Georgia Tech was founded in 1885 in Atlanta and from the beginning was defined as an institution of higher education, focused on the field of technology, especially mechanical engineering. It emerged in the post-Civil War era as part of the Reconstruction of the South, and from then on steadily and successfully grew and expanded its academic offerings.

I knew of this university's excellent reputation in technical and scientific studies, in everything we commonly call the exact sciences, a reputation it maintains to this day. I was especially enthusiastic about the distinction of its engineering and architecture graduates and did not even consider choosing any other university: Georgia Tech would be mine.

I was accepted for the semester that began in the fall of 1953. In September of that year, I came to this country, to a room already designated for me in the dormitories of Georgia Tech, in Atlanta, Georgia, the heart of the southern United States, something very different from my beloved Ampliación de Almendares.

Today I realize, more than I did then, the tremendous challenge I was facing. I was starting a new life, in a new country, with its particular way of life, in a very different environment and with a foreign language. With all this on my shoulders, I had to start studies that were difficult in themselves, and in which I could not fail. Perhaps it is because of this experience of my early youth that I have always felt a sense of empathy with all those who begin a new life in this country.

Language was the most immediate challenge I had to overcome. I arrived with very basic knowledge, that English from Professor Sorzano Jorrín's book that we learned in Cuba: "Tom is a boy, Mary is a girl," which helped somewhat, but was not remotely sufficient. But, with the help of teachers and classmates, I soon managed to understand and make myself understood.

Along with this, there was the challenge of adapting to the "American way of life."

The first thing that struck me was the fact that Cuba was practically unknown to most Americans, at least to my fellow students. There were more who had heard of La Habana, which to them was simply "Havana," than those who knew that it was the capital of Cuba, an island only 90 miles off the coast of the United States. Many did not even know where it was located.

Now, in all honesty, I must say that this ignorance did not mean contempt. I personally didn't experience any instance of offense or discrimination from my non-Hispanic teachers or fellow students. On the contrary, as we got to know each other, they were interested in knowing something about the country you came from, and they treated you cordially.

Of course, in those times of the early 50's, there was racial discrimination, the great division between white and Black people in this country. I came from Cuba, where I had black friends and where there was no discrimination, or at least, I didn't know what discrimination was, and I landed in a city where, two blocks from the university, was Martin Luther King Jr.'s church. He was arrested almost every week for not wanting to sit in the back of the buses. That was the civil rights movement, a crusade that seemed strange to me, because, as I said before, I came from Cuba, where none of that existed.

I was following these events in the *Atlanta Constitution*, the state's leading newspaper, where the protests by black people were continually covered. It seemed incredible to me that this was happening in the United States, that African Americans had separate bathrooms, that they could only sit in the back seats of the buses. They had so many restrictions that were terrible. We Hispanic students discussed this situation among ourselves, but, as foreigners, we did not get directly involved.

One thing that pleasantly surprised me, however, was seeing that Georgia Tech was a true house of learning. There was no political interference, and in that sense, it was easier to study there than at the Instituto del Vedado, even though I had no problems at the Instituto.

Here everything was different. One of the rules that caught my attention was that almost all universities in this country require that, in their first year of studies, all students have to live in the dormitories of the university itself. Well then, we lived there, and we had our groups, each of us with our own.

For example, there were about 50 of us Hispanics. Most of us were Cubans, then Venezuelans, and then other Hispanic nationalities, such as Colombians, but most of us were Cubans and Venezuelans. We would get together to go to The Varsity, the drive-in where we would buy hamburgers. Georgia Tech's Varsity was supposed to be the biggest drive-in in the country. And we also hung out at the Pan American Club, which I'll tell you more about later.

All of us students, especially the freshmen, were in the midst of our youth. Let's remember that I started my studies there in

1953, two months before my 20th birthday and just one year after Georgia Tech admitted female students for the first time. Before then, it had been an all-male university. As you might expect, student romances were happening left and right.

At Georgia Tech, Atlanta, with Alfredo Quintana from Caracas, Venezuela

Those times were different. Although young people enjoyed freedoms here that were not given to them in Cuba, everything was very wholesome; you didn't see the excesses that you see today. Today, girls of 18 or 19 already have tremendous experience; they don't have the innocence they had back then. For example, among the students there was no knowledge of drug use; it was a very pleasant environment, without the debauchery that we see today in many aspects of life.

On the other hand, I don't know if it's destiny, as some say, or if it's that, consciously or unconsciously, one ends up doing what one is attracted to or what is one's vocation in life. I could not say whether, at that stage of my life, it was me who got involved in politics, or it was politics that pursued me. What is certain is that my time at Georgia Tech also had its political side.

Chapter 3
Return to a Sinking Cuba

> *And in this treacherous world / there is neither truth nor lie: everything depends on the color / of the lens through which we look.*
> Ramón de Campoamor

The Pan American Club was already firmly established at Georgia Tech when I arrived there as a student in 1953. It was the socio-cultural organization for Hispanic students, and it was a great thing really, because it gave those of us from south of the Rio Grande and the West Indies the opportunity to meet, socialize, help each other and preserve our roots.

I quickly joined the club and enjoyed its activities. Most of the Hispanics, as I said before, were Cubans, followed by Venezuelans. There were also many Colombians and others who, in smaller numbers, came from almost every country on the continent. Cubans and Venezuelans, above all, we were always together, but we got along very well with everyone else. I don't remember ever seeing disputes or problems in the club due to nationality issues, although there was no lack of jokes among everyone, sometimes about the characteristics of each culture, but it was all in good fun.

There I shared many good times with Hilario Candela, whom we all called Lalo. He was also studying at Georgia Tech and would eventually become one of the most renowned Cuban architects, many of whose works can be admired in Miami, especially his favorite, which was the Miami Marine Stadium. He was an active member of the club and an excellent fellow student. He sadly passed away in Miami in early 2022.

In addition to Lalo Candela, there was a good group among the many Cubans at the university, and I shared many experiences with members of that group. I remember Willy Vals, Silvio Silveira, Julio Escribano, Rafael Huguet, Miguel Díaz, Manolo Gutiérrez, Gustavo Xirau and others. I remember them all with true affection.

The club was the main center of activity for us Hispanics. There we would meet to spend some time talking; to meet up to go out in groups, to have fun in the city; and to make plans for the parties we would throw. Now, when I remember those times, I realize that the Pan American Club at the university was for me similar to what the Círculo Militar y Naval had been in Cuba: an enjoyable place where friends had a good time.

When I was in my second year of studies, a sophomore, some friends began to tease me to go for club president. I was very popular with my classmates, and they had seen how enthusiastic I was about our activities. I was tempted by the idea, but I thought it would be very difficult because, by tradition, the presidents had always been seniors, or perhaps a third-year student.

The point is that I decided to run for president of the Pan American Club. It was the first time in my life that I aspired to be elected for an office, and I liked the idea. I had plans in my mind to revitalize our activities, and it seems to me that that experience at Georgia Tech was what definitely cemented in me my political vocation. I won the presidency by only one vote and was reelected the following two years. It was there that I learned the importance of *one vote* in an election.

I have very happy memories of those years as a student at Tech. Simply Tech, as we called the university when talking to each other. Those memories are all pleasant now, although there were a few occasions when we got into trouble, almost always because of youthful mischief or "wildness."

With that in mind, I remember very vividly a big mess in which we got into because of a party we had and in which we "forgot" some rules that we had to followed.

On that occasion, as was often done, we invited the girls from Brenau College (now Brenau University), a women's college not far from ours, to be at our party. Whenever they came, they were always accompanied by a chaperone, as it was a Catholic college. We went, I as president, with the board members, and asked the nuns to let the girls come to our party, and they did.

As usual, the girls came with their chaperone. Alcoholic beverages were forbidden in our activities, a rule that was strictly enforced in all fraternities, but it was not unusual for us boys to find a way around it. That party was not the exception, and we managed to slyly take some bottles of different drinks to the party. Almost all the partygoers enjoyed their contents, especially the Venezuelans, the Puerto Ricans and also us Cubans.

We were unlucky enough that the chaperone noticed and, without hesitation, put a bottle of booze in her purse, which was very large, to have proof of our violation of the rules. I remember it was February, a cold night when it was snowing, which was strange in Atlanta, since it almost never snows there. When the party was over, there were many who had had too many drinks and it showed. When we were leaving, someone shouted, warning that the chaperone was taking a bottle and things got very ugly, because some students ran after the chaperone to take the bottle, though I don't remember if they succeeded.

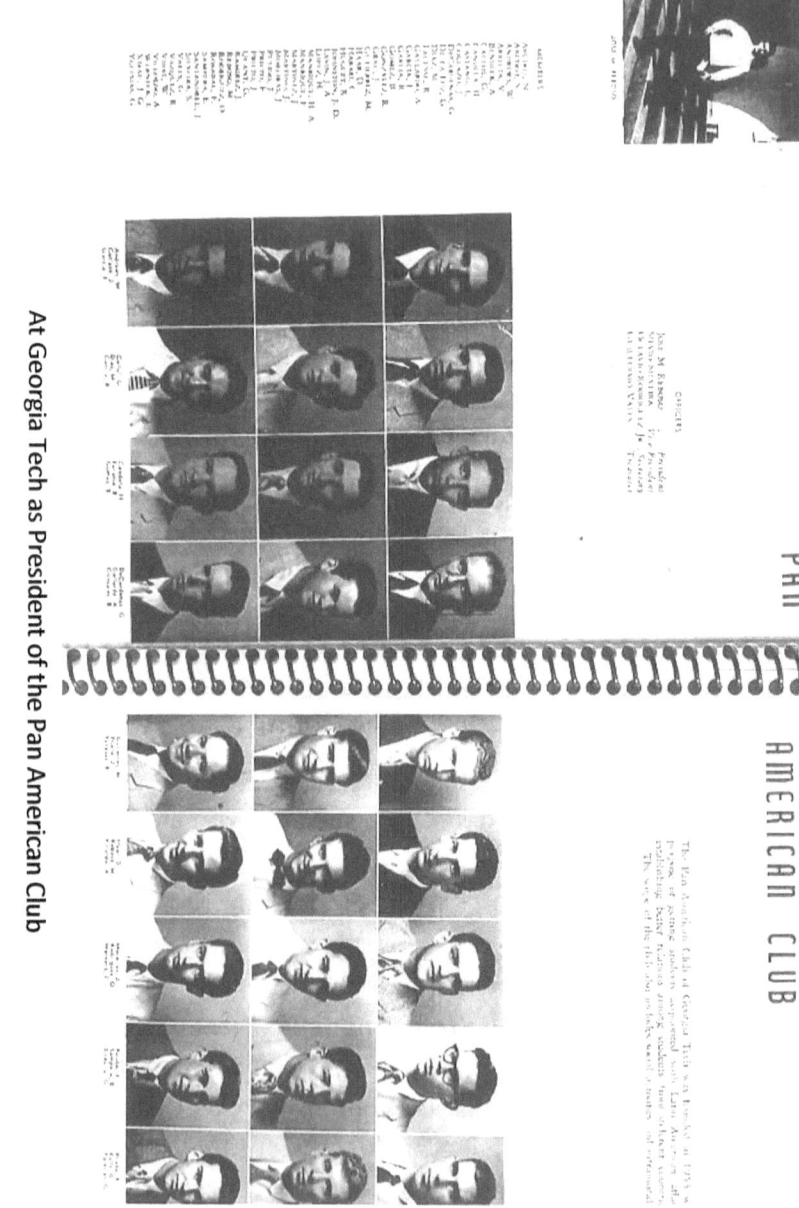

At Georgia Tech as President of the Pan American Club

As expected, the consequences were not pleasant. When we went to Brenau College again, this time to apologize to the nuns for what had happened, we were surprised, because the drinks were not the only problem. The nuns also accused us that when we had gone there before, to invite the girls, we had taken their totem pole, a staff that had symbolic meaning for them, as they began their sessions with a strike of this pole.

It was unbelievable. Dean Griffin, who was our dean, threatened us with expulsion if the totem pole did not appear. It turned out that it had been hidden in the nuns' library by Wilbur Andrews, one of our board members, whose father was the manager of the Woolworth's stores in La Habana. Wilbur confessed, told them where the totem pole was, and all that commotion ended in a sharp scolding and a big scare. But, after it was all over, we laughed as we recalled the incident.

In the meantime, my life continued as normal. I was doing well in my studies, I liked what I was doing, and I kept in touch with my family. I spent my summers in Cuba and enjoyed the beach and the activities of the Círculo very much. Things changed a little in 1956, when my father was appointed as military attaché in Washington, D.C. He and my mother moved there, and Roberto continued his high school studies in Maryland. My paternal grandfather and my maternal grandmother remained at home, in Cuba, and I spent the last summer of my student years with them.

It was precisely in that year, 1956, that I saw John F. Kennedy for the first time on television. He was campaigning to join the Democratic presidential nominee, Adlai Stevenson, as vice-president. He wasn't able to achieve this, as the convention decided in favor of Senator Estes Kefauver.

Virginia was the last state to be counted in the Democratic primaries that year, and knowing that he would not be vice-president, it was then that Kennedy said, "Four years from now, in 1960, I will be running for President of the United States," and sure enough, he did. Not only did he run, but he won the election that year, thus becoming the 35th president of the United States.

Living that electoral process in the United States, even in my simple position as a foreign student, awakened my interest. I found it exciting to follow the news about it. I was very far from thinking that, a few years later, I myself would be aspiring to an elected position and not in Cuba, but also here, in the United States.

Of course, many things would still have to happen, in my life and in the course of events in Cuba, before my political vocation could find its way in this great country.

In 1957, as I was finishing the fourth year of my career, important changes occurred for me. My good friend Alfredo Durán was studying agricultural engineering at Louisiana State University (LSU) and was about to graduate, since his career required only four years of studies, while mine, architecture, required one more year. Years later, after being freed with Brigade 2506, Alfredo studied law and became a lawyer. Alfredo and I were presented with a golden opportunity, and to take advantage of it, I had to return to Cuba quickly.

Alfredo's stepfather, Anselmo Alliegro, was the president of the Senate, and he would give us the contracts for the reconstruction of several schools; we also had a big project for the construction of a night club. These were opportunities we could not miss. I decided to return to Cuba and did just that, a year before graduating, intending to finish my degree at the Universidad de la Habana, as soon as possible.

Alfredo and I decided to found a construction company, which we named MANALF, S. A., a conjunction of our own names:

Man, for Manolo and Alf, for Alfredo. And we did tremendously well!

We started to earn a lot of money with our work and being as young as we were, this greatly influenced the fact that I postponed the completion of my studies – something that never happened.

Now that we're no longer young, when we look back at the circumstances of our return to Cuba in 1957, to start a business that was really our start in life as independent adults, some friends are astonished and ask if we were unaware of the real situation we would find on the island, where there was practically a civil war, with tremendous instability and the Batista government crumbling.

As the American saying goes, "hindsight is 20/20." Looking back, we realize there were mistakes we couldn't avoid in time, things that, had we known, we would've done it differently and would not have made the decisions that we'd regret later.

Our families, Alfredo's and mine, had access to privileged information that could provide a realistic assessment of what was happening in Cuba, which way the balance was tipping in the confrontation between the army and the guerrillas of the Sierra Maestra and Escambray mountains, and what position the United States had in that conflict. But the information we had then - today we can see it - was far removed from reality.

The prevailing impression in the armed forces and among the Batista's closest officials was that "the bearded ones" had everything to lose, that the government's candidate in the upcoming 1958 elections, Dr. Andrés Rivero Agüero, an honest and experienced politician, would win, take office and inaugurate a new era in which, in one way or another, everything would return to normal. Among the Batista loyalists, the possibility of Batista abandoning power and leaving Cuba, when he did and in the way he did, was never contemplated.

We felt so sure and so confident about the future that I decided to take a step that is transcendental in every person's life. My fiancée, Irma Mathews, and I had previously discussed the possibility of marriage and decided not to wait any longer. In September 1958, we were married and in time, we would have three children: Manuel Alejandro (Alex), Roberto Luis and Irma Teresa.

So, I was back in Cuba, happily working, newly married, satisfied with how well we were doing and full of dreams and projects. The awakening would be very abrupt. Things would change radically, from one day to the next, and it hit me very personally, thanks to something that happened during the construction of the nightclub.

The nightclub was the old Bambú, which would now be called Casino del Río and was located on the road to the Rancho Boyeros airport. Its new design had a lot of glass, which was very important. It also included a very large and beautiful swimming pool, close to the casino. The road leading to the casino was full of glass. It was a work of great architectural beauty.

Pedro Luis Díaz Lanz and his brother Marcos, who was a very good friend of mine, also lived in Ampliación de Almendares. Knowing about the project, Marcos, who represented a company that sold glass, came to see me and said: "Manolo, you have to give me the glass contract, because I need it." And I gave it to Marcos, without any bidding or anything like that. I gave it to him, moreover, without knowing that he belonged to the 26th of July Movement, or that Pedro Luis was in charge of the flights that took weapons to Fidel in the Sierra Maestra.

We were already finishing the Casino del Rio at the end of 1958. All we needed to do was put the glass in the last place that required it, which was on the road that led from the restaurant to the nightclub, over the water. The glass had already been delivered to us, but it wasn't all installed. When we were celebrating at our Christmas party in 1958, Marcos came to me and said, "Manolo, I need to give money to the employees. The glass is already here, the only thing I need to do is to put them in..." There was $25,000.00 left to pay, and he asked me to please give him the check, if I could give it to him in advance.

The Casino del Río, built in 1958 by MANALF S.A., company of Alfredo Durán and Manolo Reboso

I gave Marcos the check for the $25,000. This, remember, was on December 24, 1958. The following January 1, seven days later, Batista has left Cuba, the revolution triumphs, Fidel Castro comes to power... everything is turned upside down. Alfredo takes refuge in the Chilean embassy together with Alliegro, his stepfather, and that was the end, that was the end of the Casino del Rio project, that was the end of Cuba.

The worst thing, of course, was not the loss of that project and of the others we were carrying out; all that is insignificant. The worst thing was the loss of democracy in Cuba, an imperfect but perfectible democracy. A Cuba which, with all its problems and all defects, was a thousand times better than what came later.

What came after that hit me very hard.

Chapter 4
A Young Conspirator – The Trap

What's for you, no one can take away.
Titti Soto / Willy Chirino

My parents were in Cuba those last days of 1958, as they always went from Washington to La Habana to spend the Christmas season there. We would have a big dinner with the grandparents and other relatives, as was traditional in Cuban families, and we would bid farewell to the old year in the same way.

Remembering that Christmas Eve and New Year's Eve, so many years later, it seems inexplicable to me that we hadn't realized the seriousness of the political situation in Cuba, that we could not have foreseen what was coming, not only to us as individuals, but to the entire nation as a republic, as the homeland of all Cubans.

So, when we exchanged our best regards and congratulations at the stroke of midnight that signaled the arrival of 1959, the least we could've imagined was that, practically at that very moment, Fulgencio Batista, his relatives and some of his closest allies were boarding the planes that would take them to a golden exile, abandoning the island that had given them so much and leaving to their fate a legion of people committed to the regime he had headed up to that moment.

Everything took us by surprise, without any idea of what to expect. On January 2, the political prisoners who were in the Modelo prison in Isla de Pinos were released, among them Colonel Ramón Barquín, Commander Borbonet and other former military men who had participated in the so-called *Conspiración de los Puros*.

Let's remember that after Barquín was arrested in that conspiracy in 1956, my father had been appointed to replace him as military attaché in Washington, D.C. As soon as he was released from prison, Barquín, without consulting with Fidel Castro, proclaimed himself Chief of the Army, appointed Borbonet as Chief of the military fortress of La Cabaña and had my father arrested.

My father was taken to the military camp in Columbia as a prisoner. Fidel Castro had not yet arrived in La Habana. Credible rumors arrived in the capital of the military shootings that Raul Castro was ordering in Santiago de Cuba. We didn't know what to expect. My father had never abused anyone, but we were aware of the potential for evil that exists in political rivalries. I immediately began to take steps, the few that could be taken in those circumstances, to try to obtain his release.

Barquín's command at the head of the army was short-lived, only a few days, until Fidel gave orders appointing Camilo Cienfuegos, in Columbia, to this post, and sending Che Guevara as chief of La Cabaña in place of Borbonet. It was clear that Fidel Castro did not allow anything that would undermine his authority, nor did he recognize opponents of the Batista government other than those under his command.

I remember very vividly how that difficult situation the triumphant revolution put my father and, in fact, our whole family, in, came to an end.

We were still in the early days of January 1959; my father had been imprisoned for a few days. I was driving along Fifth Avenue in Miramar when I heard on the radio that Fidel had appointed Pedro Luis Díaz Lanz as head of the Air Force. Right then and there, I drove my car to the Air Force, which was very close, also in Ampliación de Almendares and, when I arrived, I was able to enter without difficulty because the former soldiers of the Constitutional Army were still there, most of whom knew me.

I walked in and met Marcos Díaz Lanz, dressed in olive green with the rank of commander, which surprised me. Marcos hugged me and was very happy to see me. He took me to Pedro Luis who, likewise, received me with great joy. They asked me why I was there, and I explained my father's situation. Without wasting any time, Pedro Luis called Camilo Cienfuegos and told him that he was sending a jeep for Reboso.

I only had to wait a short time. Sure enough, the jeep that Pedro Luis Díaz Lanz had sent arrived with my father on board. When my father arrived, Pedro Luis told me: "I want the old man to stay with me here, in the Air Force." Dad did not want to stay and told us: "I have to go back to Washington. Roberto, your brother, has to go back to school there."

At that moment a plane from Miami was landing right there at the Air Force. It was a plane that had been chartered by the son of José Manuel Alemán, a Cuban politician who had settled in Miami during Grau San Martín's presidency, under accusations of corruption in Cuba. The plane was bringing to Cuba a large number of exiles who saw the fall of Batista as the end of their exile and were returning to the island full of hope for the revolution that many of them had helped finance from the United States. The same plane was supposed to return to Miami to bring more exiles.

I explained to Pedro Luis that my father wanted to return to Washington for family reasons, such as taking care of the continuity of my brother's studies, etc. He ordered the plane to stop and ordered "that it not take off for the return trip until Reboso was ready."

My father went home; he bathed and shaved off his week-old beard. My brother packed his suitcase, all in a hurry, and I took them back to the Air Force. They boarded the plane and left for Miami without a hitch. My father had been accused as an accomplice to the March 10 coup d'état, because he was the duty officer in the Air Force when Batista staged the coup, and Colonel Carlos Cantillo then took command of the Air Force. But, thank God, that providential plane was their salvation. My mother would join them a few days later.

I could hardly believe that everything had been resolved so quickly, and since then I have felt a deep gratitude to the Diaz Lanz brothers who, shortly, would have to escape from Cuba into exile, like so many other Cubans of good faith who had believed in Fidel Castro's false promises.

The fate that awaited Cuba in the hands of Fidel Castro and his subordinates could be recognized very quickly, since they arrived imbued with an insatiable lust for power, a manifest thirst for revenge, a total disregard for legal norms and the rights of others, an unbridled hatred for the rich and the bourgeoisie and an ostensible anti-Yankee disposition, all of which was very easy to detect.

But, the vast majority of the Cuban people were as if bewitched by the Maximum Leader's skillful verbiage and, together with the hopes of social and political improvement that many good Cubans placed in the revolution, envy and resentment overflowed from many Cubans who saw in the political process that was beginning to develop a great opportunity to get the goods and achieve the status to which they could never have reached by their own merits – even if to achieve this, they had to step on other Cubans, including friends and relatives.

So, amidst the idealists' incredulity and the support of the opportunists, the absolute power of the little university gangster who now posed as the homeland's redeemer was quickly cemented. And I say that the hidden intentions of Fidel and the most enlightened *fidelistas* were easy to detect because those first months of the new regime were a repulsive orgy of executions and abuses of all kinds that contradicted the most elementary sense of justice and true patriotism.

On the other hand, many of the most prominent members of the team close to Fidel Castro showed a great lack of capacity, a great lack of preparation to govern. Castro had appointed as Chief of the Army Camilo Cienfuegos, who was a tailor, and as Police Chief Efigenio Ameijeiras, who was a car valet. There was tremendous disorganization in the ministries and other government agencies. We thought that this could not be maintained for long, that Fidel would have to hold elections sooner or later and a government would come to stabilize things. The people were in favor of the revolution, of Fidel Castro, but we understood that this fanaticism would be temporary.

Now, together with the conviction about the diabolical nature of Castroism that those of us who had never allowed ourselves to be captivated by the new caudillo's rhetoric had, another conviction took root: The United States would never allow the existence of a government that conflicted with its interests only 90 miles from its coasts; anything else would be unthinkable.

Therefore, we thought that Fidel Castro and his henchmen wouldn't be in power for long, if not because of internal struggles among the revolutionaries, then because of direct or indirect action by the United States. I don't remember having met a single one among the early anti-Castro activists with whom I spoke who was not convinced of the validity of that reasoning which, a few years later, disenchanted, we would have to rename "the myth of the 90 miles."

Those of us displaced by the revolution, not only those who were Batista's people, but also other Cubans who weren't happy with the course of events, soon began to get in touch with each other to exchange thoughts and see what direction to give to our lives under the circumstances of those times. We soon realized that those who didn't submit unconditionally to the new order would be in grave danger and could face either a firing squad or a long prison sentence. Something had to be done.

I often met with a friend whom I held in high esteem, a young ex-military man of proven courage, incapable of betraying his friends or renouncing his militancy: Renaldo Blanco Navarro.

Renaldo, only in his early twenties, had reached the ranks of army captain, fighting against the rebel guerrillas in the Sierra Maestra. He had defeated the forces commanded by Raul Castro in the battle of Guisa and without being boastful, he had repeatedly shown great personal courage, giving the impression that he knew no fear. He was also an intelligent person who expressed himself very well.

It didn't take us long to start conspiring at full speed against Fidel's nascent tyranny. Renaldo was the leader of the group, which included former military men like himself; businessmen like Armando Caíñas Milanés; Enrique Ovares, a former university leader; and politicians like former senator Arturo Hernández Tellaheche, of the Partido Autentico. Our group also included revolutionaries supposedly upset at having been excluded from power by Fidel Castro, such as the "comandantes" Eloy Gutiérrez Menoyo and William Morgan, chiefs of the Second Front of the Escambray, from where they had fought against Batista's government.

We were in an initial conspiratorial phase, contemplating different options ranging from a palace revolt to a new phase of guerrilla warfare, but with nothing concrete yet. We met very cautiously in a house in the La Sierra neighborhood, which, until December 31 of the previous year, had belonged to the engineer Alberto Vadía – the luxurious mansion he and his family had had to leave in haste, since his ties to Batista had forced him into exile. The "revolution of the poor" quickly seized the enormous residence and gave it to one of its own, Commander William Morgan, to live in.

Morgan was from the United State, an *americano*, as we say, who had joined, out of pure adventurism, the forces fighting

Batista's army in the Escambray, in the former Cuban province of Las Villas. He was in his early thirties when we began to meet. He was born in Cleveland, Ohio, and had left in his native country a past with no shortage of run-ins with the law, one of which had landed him in prison for two years. His military experience boiled down to his dishonorable discharge from the U.S. Army. Be that as it may, he had earned his star as a co-commander fighting against Batista and was one of the most popular people in the revolution.

On August 7, 1959, a Sunday, we were summoned to meet at what was then his home. The meeting was in the morning. Héctor Rodriguez, my childhood friend, picked me up at my house and we went in his car to Morgan's house. As soon as we got there, we were arrested by Commander Jesús Carreras and Aldo Sánchez, both from the Second Front. They had set a trap for us, and we had fallen into it.

We were prisoners.

Chapter 5
Fidel Castro, Prison and the Miracle

> *No man is good enough to govern another man without that other's consent.*
> Abraham Lincoln

We were imprisoned in that house where we had met so many times to plan the best way to get Cuba out of the worrying destiny that was taking shape as a result of the initial barbarities of the government which, under the absolute rule of Fidel Castro, was showing its criminal instincts and totalitarian leadership more and more aggressively every day.

Never before in the history of our young republic had conflicts and ambitions for power led Cubans to civil war. Never before had the victors in a political contest ordered mass executions of their adversaries. The fact that the great majority continued to support that barbarism, after half a year of bloodthirsty and despotic exercise of power, did nothing to change our opinion of the situation, since it was a fanaticism that, little by little, was beginning to lose followers. We were confident that most of those fanatics would eventually awaken from their rapture, as in the end they did.

In addition, we were somewhat reassured by the fact that notable anti-Batista revolutionary fighters, such as the prominent members of the Second National Front of the Escambray, who were part of the conspiracy, were willing to join ex-military men, their former enemies, in a project that I and many others involved saw as an effort to save our nation.

And we didn't distrust the former Escambray guerrillas, because we believed that they had more than enough reasons to be against the 26th of July Movement, the anti-Batista organization founded by Castro himself after the attack, in 1953, on the Moncada Barracks in Santiago de Cuba. They had been left out. Menoyo had sought to be mayor of La Habana, and they hadn't given him that position. They hadn't given important positions to the members of the Second Front, even though they had been part of the armed struggle against Batista.

Furthermore, Eloy Gutiérrez Menoyo had been very explicit in explaining all this to us. He said that he needed young military men who had fought, who had the experience of the war. I believe that Menoyo's idea was to show Fidel that he could be useful to him and that he could count on him, and to gain that trust, he gave him assets from Batista's army that could've damaged the revolution in the future.

The fact was that Menoyo, William Morgan, Jesús Carreras, Aldo Sánchez, Armando Fleites, all the former members of the Second Front who supposedly conspired with us, betrayed us and delivered us into the hands of Fidel Castro.

We were prisoners.

As I've already explained, that Sunday morning, as soon as we entered the house that had belonged to Vadía the engineer, we were caught by surprise and arrested, without having time to do anything and without understanding, at first, what was going on. Of course, that initial confusion was because of the unexpectedness of our new situation, and immediately afterwards, Hector and I realized that we'd been victims of an artful betrayal, of counterintelligence work between those who were arresting us and the highest levels of that government that the former had pretended to detest as much as we did ourselves.

They immediately stripped us of everything we had in our pockets and ordered us to hand over our shoes and belts. The same thing happened to the other members of the group, those who were not part of the Second Front, as they arrived at the house.

Not everything went smoothly. Apparently, Menoyo wanted to give himself the pleasure of personally arresting Renaldo Blanco Navarro. He made him go to the elegant office where Vadía previously worked and when he confronted Renaldo and told him that he was under arrest, the latter quickly took a letter opener from the desk and pounced on Menoyo, to whose shouts his guards came, and between them they all restrained the brave Blanco Navarro, who, sometime later, in a trial, would be sentenced to 20 years in prison.

In addition to being imprisoned and held incommunicado, we had to endure our captors' taunts. They continually laughed at us, crowed that they had deceived us and delighted in asserting that a firing squad awaited us.

"Look what dumbasses they are," they said among themselves, but so that we would hear them. "How timid, we caught them red-handed."

The hours went by, and we were unable to do anything, in silence most of the time and with an overwhelming uncertainty that grew as the day went by. Besides, they hadn't given us anything to eat.

As night was falling, our captors ordered some of us to sit down in the living room. Eddy Arango, Enrique Ovares and I sat on a sofa. The other imprisoned conspirators were scattered throughout the rest of the house. And then Fidel Castro arrived.

Fidel arrives, does not greet anyone, does not talk to anyone, does not look at anyone. He walks theatrically in front of us smoking a big cigar. Suddenly, Armando Fleites, commander of the Second Front, who was one of those guarding us, turned to him and said: "Fidel, what do you think? Enrique Ovares, so much swimming, and we caught him on the shore, conspiring with Trujillo."

Fidel continued unaffected. He didn't answer anything. He and Enrique Ovares, now his prisoner, had been friends in their days at university, when Enrique was president of the Federación Estudiantil Universitaria (University Student Federation) or FEU. It should be remembered that, in those times, in Cuba, anyone who used violence to confront the government in power was called a "revolutionary." These "revolutionaries," some of whom were simple thugs and others more like misguided idealists, were very proud to be so called and were enemies not only of the Cuban leaders, but also of the Latin American dictatorships and even participated in armed activities against them. Fidel Castro and Ovares, for example, had participated together in a violent riot in Colombia in 1948, popularly known as "el bogotazo," which we'll get into later. The "revolutionaries" took it as an unforgivable offense to be associated with figures such as Rafael Leonidas Trujillo, the Dominican dictator. Generally speaking, Cubans vehemently disliked Trujillo.

I met Enrique Ovares the day we were both imprisoned. That day, we exchanged a few sentences, more like introductions, and we didn't speak again until three days later, when, by pure chance and without having asked for it, we were put together in the same bunk in the 13th cell of La Cabaña prison; he slept in the lower bed and I in the upper one.

For two months and 21 days, we talked all the time and thanks to those conversations with Enrique, I was able to learn a lot about Fidel Castro's history and personality. That knowledge was broadened and deepened years later, thanks to my friendship with Dr. Rafael Díaz-Balart, who was, without a doubt, the person who had known and judged that despicable man best.

Enrique, as I already mentioned, was president of the FEU for three years. He was in the School of Architecture and Fidel Castro in the School of Law. They became friends and Enrique took him with him on some trips, all related to his anti-imperialist adventures. He took him to Puerto Rico, to an interview with Albizu Campos, the Puerto Rican independence leader; to the World Peace Congress in Mexico; to the Cayo Confites expedition; and the most notorious of all, to Bogotá, Colombia, in April 1948, where Enrique met with the presidential candidate of the Liberal Party, Jorge Eliécer Gaitán. When the latter was assassinated in an attack on April 9, the insurrection known as "el bogotazo" broke out; the Cuban university students who were there were involved.

The then-ambassador from Cuba in Colombia, Carlos Tabernilla, gave Fidel and Ovares asylum; they were accompanied by Alfredo Guevara and Rafael del Pino. Coincidentally, the Cuban delegation to the Ninth Pan American Conference, from which the Organization of American States (OAS) would emerge, was in Bogota. The diplomat Guillermo Belt headed the delegation, and one of its most prominent members was the diplomat and writer Guy Pérez Cisneros. The latter personally saw to the safe return of the four students to La Habana.

Guy Pérez Cisneros was married to Berta Barreto. Later in this story, we'll see how that gesture influenced Fidel Castro during the negotiations for the release of the members of Brigade 2506 imprisoned in Cuba.

As they had been such close friends, Fidel called Ovares "Flaco," and Ovares called Fidel "Guajiro." Fidel, as I said, remained silent, but Ovares, as soon as he heard Fleites associate him with Trujillo, jumped out of his seat, and told the Maximum Leader: "Guajiro, I am not going to allow him to link me to Trujillo. When he was still in diapers, I was already fighting Trujillo."

Fidel looked at him but stayed silent. He didn't answer him, turned his back to us and left.

That incident gave us a clue, which perhaps we didn't fully understand at the time, as to what was being plotted against us. We had no contacts or links of any kind with the Trujillo government. There was another group of anti-Castro Cubans that was linked to Trujillo, one of whose leaders was Luisito Pozo.

He was the son of La Habana's mayor during Batista's time, Justo Luis del Pozo, and had saved Eloy Gutiérrez Menoyo's life when he was wanted by the police. Luisito was in exile in the Dominican

Republic, where he and other Cubans, such as Roberto Martin Perez, were seeking help to try to overthrow Castro. Menoyo, as it was later learned, phoned Luisito and convinced him (and the others) to go to Cuba, where, upon landing, they were immediately captured by Castro agents who were waiting for them, thanks to Menoyo's treachery.

We didn't know anything, nor were we part of that group, but Castro, always skilled in evil ways, wrapped us all up in the same case, to stigmatize us as "the Trujillistas." Apparently, his main interest was to discredit a group of cattle ranchers headed by Caíñas Milanés, since it was well known in Cuba that they had cooperated with the revolution and had even created a voluntary tax on cattle to help the 26th of July Movement. The ranchers had turned against the revolution upon seeing its treacherous intents. Furthermore, in this way, he was also trying to stain Arturo Hernández Tellaheche, a very popular politician known for his honesty and for creating, when he was a senator, a law that made employers give all employees a Christmas bonus. That bonus was known throughout Cuba as "el Arturito" (the little Arthur, "Arturito" also being Hernández Tellaheche's nickname). In the end, they wanted to present us all to the public as a band of outlaws guided by their worst interests against the revolution.

Late that night, around eleven or twelve o'clock, they took us to the military camp Columbia, the Cuban armed forces' headquarters, which they now called "Ciudad Libertad" (Liberty City). Once there, they took us all to the movie theater located in the Army General Staff building, a movie theater that had been built in the basement for the officers' enjoyment and which now served as a dungeon for us. We were there without shoes and belts; everything had been taken away from us.

There we lost track of time, because the lights were left on and some of us slept that night while others did not. The custodians didn't tell us anything, and there was a general feeling of confusion among us. It seemed to me that everything had happened very quickly, without giving me time to gauge the situation clearly. Besides, the group had grown and there were now 92 of us arrested. We talked among ourselves, exchanged opinions, but they were all speculation, since, for sure, nobody knew all the details of the situation, much less the intentions of Fidel Castro and his people.

We spent a day-and-a-half or two in the cinema. At one moment, which we assumed to be at night, all the lights suddenly came on. It was Raul Castro arriving with a large military entourage. Raul, it was obvious, was freshly bathed and groomed, as his uniform was very clean; I thought that maybe he was trying to impress us in some way.

When he saw Caiñas Milanés, he greeted him very politely, and also Arturito, whom he asked how they were treating "the gentlemen." Someone answered him: "They haven't given us any food; we haven't eaten for three days. We can only drink the water from the bathroom sink, it's the only thing we've put in our mouths."

Raul asked who was in charge of "taking care of the gentlemen" and a "rebel" who was there, jumped up, squared up in front of him and greeted him... Raul told him with a firm voice: "Bring them food and make sure the gentlemen lack nothing," after which he left.

After the polite visit, we spent another day-and-a-half without being given anything to eat, not a thing. Evidently, the purpose of Raúl Castro's presence there had been to humiliate us even more, to make fun of us. However, there were among us some deluded people who said: "Wait until Raul finds out that his orders weren't obeyed." It's clear to me that Raul, on leaving our presence, had given a counter-order that they shouldn't give us anything, for it's very doubtful that they would've otherwise disobeyed his previous order.

Two days later they made us get on buses, and they took us to the fortress of La Cabaña, with its gloomy prison, and in cell 13 they put us all 92 men. Cell 14 was for those condemned to death, who were taken in the night to be executed by firing squad. That painful circumstance was what we had next door, what we heard every night.

Loneliness occupies a good part of a prisoner's life. When in the solitude of our nights in La Cabaña we listened to the voices and noises that indicated that the guards were taking one of the condemned to their death, many dark thoughts crossed my mind. I inevitably wondered whether I had made a wise decision in conspiring against a government as bloodthirsty and at the same time as popular as Fidel Castro's, and I remembered the words of some friends who, when talking about the situation in the country, were convinced that it was best to keep a low profile, avoid going out into the streets. They would say it was better "not to get involved in anything, because anyone can be shot here."

Perhaps they were right to be cautious. However, I did not berate myself, nor did I feel sorry for having made the decisions that had led me to that precarious situation as a political prisoner. Precisely because "anyone can be shot here," I felt that was the most powerful reason to try to change things in Cuba.

We were waiting to be tried. The trials were very quick, purely a matter of formality, because they shot the accused immediately afterwards. There was no appeal possible. In our case, I don't know why, but the trial was delayed, and we were kept there, in an anguished wait. Although I must say, in all honesty, that in our group, almost everyone showed great fortitude.

Once a week we were given a family visit. My wife Irma visited week after week. My parents and my brother were in Washington, all suffering because of my situation.

Very early one morning, after midnight, Commander Efigenio Ameijeiras, who had been appointed chief of the National Revolutionary Police, arrived with a unit of soldiers or policemen, it was the same thing. They ordered us to undress and go outside; they were conducting a search.

I remember it was a very cold night, but as naked as we entered the world, so did we have to go outside, supervised by some of the guards. During searches, the guards would rummage through everything, looking for weapons, a radio receiver, etc. They almost never found any of that, but they took advantage of these searches to steal any tubes of toothpaste we might have and other personal items, which family brought us. They took everything, while outside, naked and standing in a line, they mistreated us and made fun of us.

While the search was in progress, I felt the barrel of a machine gun smack against my back. I asked, "What is it? Who is it?" and someone answered me in a whisper: "Tony Lamas."

Tony Lamas, my childhood friend, my playmate in Ampliación de Almendares, was there, as part of the police unit that carried out the search. It was unbelievable.

"What are you doing here?" he asked me. "How long have you been here?" Hastily and in a low voice, I explained: "I fell prisoner in William Morgan's house… the Menoyo conspiracy." Tony's look conveyed assurance as he said, "Tomorrow I'm coming to get you," and left my side.

I was in the same cell with Renaldo Blanco Navarro and Enrique Ovares. I told them what happened, and they both said to me: "Forget it, Manolo. These people don't throw in the towel." That's to say, they don't yield.

However, their words didn't discourage me. I had great confidence in Tony, and I wasn't wrong.

Tony was in Ameijeiras' unit and had the rank of police captain. He had fought in the Sierra Maestra under the orders of Commander Victor Bordón Machado, who had been appointed as Che

Guevara's second in command at La Cabaña. It happened that, in those days when the search took place, the macabre Argentinean was not in Cuba. He was presiding over a delegation of the new regime in the United Arab Republic, which was a newly created country at that time, artificially formed by Egypt and Syria, an alliance that would be dissolved in the early 1970s.

The fact was that, for that reason and to my good fortune, Bordón Machado had been left in charge of La Cabaña. Tony Lamas – I learned this after everything happened – went to see Mario Rojas, who was the judge in our case, and obtained from him a release certificate in my name. He took it to Bordón Machado and the next morning, they ordered José Manuel Reboso to go to the office and to take his belongings with him. The belongings were only a small coffee mug.

When I arrived at the office, Tony was there. He signed a document they gave him and took me out of there in a patrol car, accompanied by two others. Inside the squad car I took off my prisoner's shirt, a shirt that had a big letter P on the back, and I stayed in my t-shirt. Tony asked me where I wanted to go.

I didn't think it wise to go home. I asked Tony to drop me off at my friend Willy Vals's house, and there he left me. As we said goodbye, he advised me: "Try to leave Cuba, because it's bad here."

I have no words to describe the gratitude I have since felt for Tony Lamas, who endangered his life to help me get out of that terrible situation in which I found myself. Shortly after, Tony would be arrested for his anti-Castro activities and would serve 22 years in prison as a *plantado*, a prisoner who refused to submit to his jailers' orders.

I knocked on the door of Willy Vals's house, thinking that was the end of the fright, at least for the moment. When Willy opened the door, he was very surprised to see me there. But I was even more surprised to find out that his relatives, who lived there with him, were still sympathizers of the revolution.

Chapter 6
Say Goodbye to the Palm Trees...

> *In a society where there is nothing worth dying for, there is nothing worth living for either.*
> Benedict XVI

Willy received me in his house in a friendly manner, and his relatives were not hostile nor discourteous to me, quite the contrary; but, after learning the reason for my presence there, they tried to convince me of something that seemed too risky to me.

They offered to put me in contact with a revolutionary commander, a friend of theirs, because, they believed, this commander would help me resolve my problem. I tried to be even-tempered and calm, thanked them for their offer, and told them, as an excuse, that it wasn't necessary, since I was confident that I could resolve my situation in a few days, due to other contacts I already had.

After a while, they didn't insist any more. I thanked them and called another friend, Manuel Balbis, who told me to go to his house.

I did so; and I have always been grateful to Willy and his family for the protection they gave me and their interest in helping me, and for all those who helped me in that predicament.

Balbis's house was close to the Mexican Embassy in La Habana, and this immediately reminded me that, before leaving La Cabaña, Enrique Ovares had recommended that I try to seek asylum in that embassy, since he knew the ambassador, Gilberto Bosque.

I told my first cousin Laura, and she immediately contacted the owner of the famous *Fin de Siglo* store, who was a close friend of ours. Laura tells her that I'm in hiding and that I need to take refuge in the Mexican Embassy. This friend had many contacts in the diplomatic world, and, like other brave Cubans of that time, she was constantly taking risks trying to help persecuted people who, like me now, were in danger of death or imprisonment if they were captured by Castro's police.

She made the necessary arrangements and in just a few days, a week or so, she informed us that the ambassador was waiting for me. She warned me, when I arrived at the embassy, to tell the guards that I was going there to get my passport stamped, as I had to travel to Mexico. I could say that I needed asylum only to the Mexican official who would be attending me.

I followed her instructions to the letter and had no setbacks. When I arrived, I met Hugo Sueiro, who was also there seeking asylum. Hugo, whom I didn't know, later told me that he was part of the group of military officers who were conspiring in the same network as me and that, on the day that my companions and I had been arrested, he had also been summoned to William Morgan's house. He passed by there and realized that something unusual was going on, so he walked on. Some men stopped him, but he told them that he was a student and, being, as he was, so young, they believed him and let him go.

So, we both got asylum at the same time. They gave us a room to share. Now, we had to wait for the revolutionary government's Ministry of Foreign Affairs to give us the corresponding safe-conduct papers.

Conditions at the Mexican Embassy were not the best. We lacked nothing of what was strictly necessary, but we were confined to a room, without access to newspapers, radio or television, without knowing any news, all of which made our days endless and at the same time made us uneasy due to the lack of information.

We stayed like that for the first two or three days of our stay, until, by pure chance, I was able to recognize Ambassador Bosque's daughter, who was in the hallway leading to our room, apparently playing with her little dog. I opened the door, greeted her and asked her to tell her father that I was a friend of Enrique Ovares, who sent his regards.

That was enough for our situation to improve considerably. They began bringing us newspapers every day, they often asked us if we needed anything, and they responded quickly when we asked for something.

Although we trusted in the protection that, according to the inter-American political asylum treaties, the Mexican Embassy was offering us, we had reasons to be concerned, since there was talk of irregular situations in some other embassies and of tensions that were arising between La Habana and some Latin American embassies due to the large number of asylum seekers in some of the diplomatic headquarters.

Some of those tensions were blamed on inexperienced officials who were part of the staff of the new *revolutionary* Ministry of Foreign Affairs, since not all of them were educated and experienced people like the Minister of Foreign Affairs, Dr. Raul Roa Garcia. The latter had the credentials of a man of the radical left, but he was supposed to be anti-communism, since he had written a book titled "En pie," in which he strongly condemned the Soviet Union for having brutally crushed the Hungarian revolution in 1956.

However, to the disappointment of many, Roa remained Fidel Castro's faithful servant until his death in 1982, many years after Castro himself admitted that he had lied to the Cubans when he assured them that the revolution was not Marxist in nature.

The fact is that Hugo and I had no major difficulties at the Mexican Embassy, nor in the procedures to leave Cuba. We had no contact with other asylum seekers, nor did we know if there were any, and in two weeks, more or less, Ambassador Bosque obtained our safe-conducts.

On the day we were scheduled to leave Cuba, a Foreign Ministry official named Calzadilla arrived at the embassy, wearing a ponytail in imitation of Raul Castro and who could well have been a security agent. He came to check our luggage, which he did.

The ambassador himself took us to the airport in his car, with Calzadilla also traveling with us. I remember perfectly well that when we were on the road to Rancho Boyeros, near the airport, Calzadilla turned in his seat to look at me and said: "Do you see those palm trees?"

There were royal palms lining the road, and I replied, "Yes, Lieutenant, I see them. They're very beautiful."

"Well, take a good look at them," he said, "because this is the last time you are going to see them." I remained silent, holding in the discomfort his acidic words caused.

We arrived at José Martí International Airport. The car drove up to the Mexicana de Aviación plane that was on the runway. Hugo and I thanked Ambassador Bosque, said goodbye to him and climbed the stairs. Before entering the aircraft, we turned to look back.

I had asked my relatives in Cuba not to see me off. I wanted by all means possible to avoid any incident that would put them in a conflictive situation. My wife, my newborn son Alejandro, my elderly grandparents – I didn't want to see them during such a tough moment because I thought it would be too emotional for all of them.

We entered the plane, which was waiting only for us. They closed the hatch and the powerful four-engine plane slowly, very slowly, began to rise. It seemed to me as if it was trying to delay our departure from Cuba as long as possible.

It was a regular commercial flight, full to capacity, and at least some of its passengers knew that Hugo and I were traveling to Mexico as political asylum seekers.

In the middle of the flight a beautiful passenger traveling in first class came to us and introduced herself. She was the famous actress Ninón Sevilla, considered one of the best, if not the best, Cuban *rumberas* (rumba dancer) in the film industry at that time. She had found fame and fortune in Mexico and told us that she knew the circumstances under which we were leaving Cuba. She herself was very badly impressed by what she had seen on the island. With great straightforwardness she gave us her telephone number and told us to call her if we needed anything in Mexico.

No one was expecting me in the Aztec capital, nor Hugo either. We decided to stay at the Regis Hotel, where some other Cubans who were in Mexico lived or visited. There was a small group that would gather at the hotel. Its most notable member was Santiago Rey Pernas, who had been Cuba's Minister of the Interior until Batista fled.

Sometimes I participated in the group, almost always as a listener. It was a great pleasure, and one learned a lot about Cuba and its history listening to "Santiaguito" Rey. He was a man of vast knowledge, a great conversationalist and formidable in any debate. I also believe that he tried to be fair and to stick to the truth, at least what he understood to be true. He didn't hide Batista's mistakes, nor did he excuse the faults of the Cuban political class, both the opposition and the government, and he didn't speak to win applause, but, he said, to spread the truth about Cuba, about whose short-term future he was not at all optimistic.

Also among those who frequently attended the group was a Cuban who would achieve great recognition a few years later: Felipe Rivero. Felipe was a member of the prominent family that owned the *Diario de la Marina*, the longest-running Cuban newspaper. He was very intelligent and extremely knowledgeable not only about universal history, but also about the major current affairs of the moment; he was also very eloquent.

In 1961, he would land in Cuba as part of the Bay of Pigs Invasion. There he was imprisoned, along with the rest of the survivors of Brigade 2506. As prisoner in Cuba, he pretended to have been indoctrinated by his captors. He did it so convincingly that he was included in a small group of *brigadistas* supposedly repentant of having fought against the revolutionary government and, on a memorable occasion in which those members were presented on television, he starred in an unforgettable live encounter with those who were interrogating him before an audience of millions of Cubans.

The televised interrogation was conducted by the old communist agent Carlos Rafael Rodriguez. At one point, Felipe stood up in front of the cameras and verbally lambasted Castro and his revolution, destroying Carlos Rafael's arguments and making a fool of him before all the Cuban people who were watching the televised appearance. This earned Felipe the admiration of the many Cubans who, by then, opposed the new dictatorship, and I'm sure it also earned him the quiet respect of many of his adversaries.

My stay in Mexico was quite short, lasting about a month. Then it was time for me to come to the United States, only this time the circumstances were totally different. If before I had arrived at the university in Atlanta as a happy young Cuban man, who envisioned a future full of hopes, now I was on my way to Miami, as an exile full of uncertainties.

It was the end of October 1959.

Chapter 7
Rendezvous with Duty: Brigade 2506

If life gives you lemons, make lemonade.
Dale Carnegie

When I arrived in Miami, the first thing I did was tell my wife Irma that she could start the paperwork to come with our child and join me, which she was able to do promptly and without any problems. Seeing them arrive and reuniting with them was a great joy for me.

Here in Miami, just arrived, we lived in General Martin Diaz Tamayo's house. His wife, Rosaura, was related to my wife. Diaz Tamayo (1904-1995) was a military man with a brilliant record, who had overcome his humble origins and gained his colleagues' respect. He had been at Batista's side since 1933 and had fought with vigor against Castro and his guerrillas in the eastern region of Cuba. Under the auspices of the United States Central Intelligence Agency (CIA), well into 1958, he had been one of the leaders of a military plot to overthrow Batista and replace him with a transitional government that would have prevented Fidel Castro, whom Díaz Tamayo himself had identified as a communist years earlier, from coming to power. This is reported by the general himself in his memoirs, where he also recognizes that it was already too late when an attempt was made to replace Batista's government.

We stayed in his house for a short time, until we moved to one of the apartments Anselmo Alliegro owned in Little Havana. The exact address was 547 SW 6th Street, Apartment 3. There we tried to settle in as best we could. I started working with the engineering and architectural firm H. J. Ross, whose offices were on Biscayne Boulevard and 17th Street, very close to Los Violines night club. This was an enjoyable place where many artists who had been successful in Cuba worked as waiters-singers, and here they faced exile working hard, with great dignity.

We Cubans who were in Miami at that time, those who some have called the exile pioneers, met almost every night, today at the home of one, tomorrow at the home of another. We needed to talk about Cuba, to exchange news about what was happening there. Rumors also abounded about the Americans' supposed plans regarding Cuba.

Those were times when the political divisions and quarrels of previous eras were very much in evidence, especially among former military men, Batista supporters on the one hand and on the other, those who sympathized with Carlos Prío, the president of the Partido Auténtico who had been overthrown by the March 10 coup. To this was added a growing group of what we called "repentant *fidelistas*," who didn't inspire confidence in the others.

I had no problems with anyone, because I didn't discuss the old issues of Cuban politics and, as I was still young, I wasn't seen as an active member of any of the different groups. In all those groups there were some who were very radical, extremists, and those are the ones who've always made Cuban unity very difficult.

I used to meet with a group of ex-military men, in which Manolito Blanco Navarro, brother of my great friend Renaldo, who was imprisoned in Cuba, also participated. In 1960, in one of those meetings, I learned about a group of Cubans who had been recruited by the CIA and were training in Useppa, a small island on the west coast of the Florida peninsula, near the city of Fort Myers. This was a clear indication that the Americans were up to something regarding Cuba.

Subsequently, there began a broader recruitment for a military force of Cuban exiles. They opened an office on 27th Avenue in

Miami – I don't remember the exact location – where they sought to form a group called "Operation 40." This was to be an intelligence group, which was said to be destined to be "the future CIA of Cuba."

In Miami, the details of the military actions for which the men being were being recruited were not known. But as for Operation 40, it was assumed that, as the democratic forces took over towns and cities in Cuba, those assigned to that operation would be in charge of analyzing the documents left behind by Castro's forces, interrogating the prisoners, etc.

For a short period of time, the trainers gave us some classes here in Miami, in Homestead, if I remember correctly. It was basically intelligence techniques, how to conduct interrogations, and so on.

One day, with very little notice, we were told the date we were to report to the office on 27th Avenue, ready to be taken to the camps. This was at the end of February 1961. Earlier, in 1960, they had begun to open the training camps.

Irma didn't object to me doing what I considered my duty. When I left, she decided to return to the Diaz Tamayo house, where we were always welcome. In general, the families of all of us who went to the camps accepted the situation very well. They understood that we felt a commitment to Cuba's destiny, that we had to fight to rescue it from communism and, although they were worried and saddened by the dangers to which we would be exposed, they accepted our decision with fortitude.

I also said goodbye to my bosses and colleagues at the architectural firm and explained to them the reasons for my departure, which they understood and respectfully accepted.

On the appointed day, I arrived at the recruiting office, where other Cubans were already waiting. Some more were arriving and when the group was complete, which was about 62 men, we got on buses that took us to the Opa-locka airport. There we were directed to board a plane that, with its windows covered, was waiting for us. We didn't know where we were going, but we knew our final destination.

The flight was smooth and uneventful, and about three hours later, the aircraft descended gently and came to rest on the ground. As we descended on a rustic runway, there was nothing in the landscape to indicate precisely where we were, but we could tell that we were in the middle of what appeared to be an intricate jungle of lush vegetation and in a very mountainous country.

It was so mountainous that that place was about 7,000 feet high, on the slopes of a volcano. Later we would learn that we were at the Helvetia farm, an abandoned coffee plantation in the municipality of El Palmar, bordering the departments of Ratalhuleu and Quetzaltenango, in Guatemala. Roberto Alejos, brother of the then-ambassador in Washington, Carlos Alejos, owned the farm. They were members of one of Guatemala's most prominent political families and had provided that site to the CIA for our training.

There we were received by American instructors, who welcomed us with few words. When we were already at the base, the first Cuban I saw was Mirto Collazo, a big, burly, curly-haired man from Artemisa with an easy smile. We were all happy to meet him and, later, other Cubans who had preceded us.

We were taken to tents that had with dirt floors and would serve as our living quarters while we were there. Each tent housed four or six men. Living conditions were extremely harsh there. There were no toilets nor showers. We bathed every two or three weeks, when we went down to a river that was 3,000 feet above sea level. We had to relieve ourselves on the ground, sitting on a board that had several holes, one next to the other, with no privacy whatsoever. The food was the same every day: Spam with rice. To drink, we were given Kool-Aid, and the rice was cooked with Kool-Aid left over from the day before. So, if we got strawberry Kool-Aid today, the rice was red the next day; if it was lemon Kool-Aid, we knew we would have yellow rice the next day – not the yellow rice we know, but rather, one much less appetizing.

We got up every day at half past five or six in the morning and then we had to run and march. There were terrible, torrential downpours, with gigantic drops, bigger than I'd ever seen; they fell on us every day. I remember that, in Cuba, when it rained and I got wet, I would get a cold. Not there; I didn't catch a single cold during my time there, even though the downpours happened almost every day.

In the camp we had two doctors and, apparently, the only medicine they had on hand was the popular cough suppressant Coricidin, red pills they gave you for whatever ailment you had. If you had a cough, they gave you Coricidin; if you broke a bone, they gave you Coricidin; whatever you had, they gave you Coricidin, there was nothing else.

There were radio receivers there, but they were controlled by headquarters. We had no radios, no other way of learning the news. We didn't have any kind of recreation, and training was seven days a week. We did have mail, and from time to time we received letters from family.

I don't know if those extreme living conditions were part of the training, if they were designed to toughen us up and make us resistant to the worst scenarios we might encounter in the fulfillment of our mission. However, that doesn't appear to have been the purpose, according to journalists and Kennedy administration officials who, independently of each other, seemed to have concluded that it was simply a poor job of site selection and suitability for the purpose of training men for a secret mission.

For example, an Associated Press investigation published in April 2000 cites an internal assessment of the Bay of Pigs operation performed in February 1962 by then-Central Intelligence Agency Inspector General Lyman B. Kirkpatrick, which, among other things, states:

"A worse training site could hardly have been chosen than the one in Guatemala. But conditions there actually got worse. In September the training camp was plagued by torrential rains, shortages of food, plus trouble with alligators... The use of Guatemala for a training base was, in terms of security, unfortunate. The base was not easily hidden and not well explained."

I didn't have a very bad time, in spite of those major deficiencies, simply because I've always tried to have a positive attitude towards life. I've always thought that everything happens for the best. When something bad happens to you, it's for a reason; something worse could have happened to you. I adapted to the camp, just as I had previously adapted to the hellish conditions in La Cabaña prison, which were the worst I had ever experienced.

The cells at La Cabaña were old stables from Spanish colonial times. There we had one toilet and one shower for 92 men. The water there was very cold, icy cold, but in spite of that, I showered every day. This was strange to some of my fellow prisoners, but I told them that this was what we had, and I adapted to survive.

I remember telling them, "Look, this is the way it is. If they sentence us to death, well, it's the family who suffers; we aren't going to suffer anything. If they give us 30 years, well, it's better than the firing squad, if they give us 20, it's better than 30, and if they give us 10, we'll try to have a party here, in the cell, to celebrate."

They laughed and shook their heads, but, in the end, most of them said that I was right. I remembered what I had gone through at La Cabaña, and the hardships of camp seemed minimal in comparison.

In the camp we all got along well. Three of us from the Operation 40 group were always together: Pepín Medina, Rafael Arce and me. We were called the three turkeys of Operation 40, because we did all the work together.

This doesn't mean that there were no problems, or that everything was in perfect harmony. We are men, not angels, and the Holy Scriptures say that even angels have had problems among themselves.

The truth was that time was passing and there was some discontent in the camp. Some paratrooper members of the Brigade had left for Mexico, crossed the border and deserted. Others had been arrested and were imprisoned in El Petén, in northern Guatemala.

I never really knew why those Brigade members were imprisoned. The only thing that was said was that in January 1961, they had been insubordinate, because they didn't agree with the way things were going. These facts and the rumors about the desertions made me think that the invasion had to be imminent, given the possibility that the Brigade would disintegrate if it didn't act quickly.

I estimate that there were about 1,100 – 1,200 of us in the camp. Some had arrived before my group and others arrived later. For example, we arrived in February; in March people began to arrive en masse, and some arrived even in the first days of April, with almost no time for training, but the Brigade had to be reinforced. That's how it was. It seemed to me that there were only a few of us, but we all thought that there would be other camps, which we didn't know about for security reasons.

I think it's important to point out that, despite the harsh conditions of the camp, the existing problems and the uncertainty we had about various aspects of the mission for which we were preparing, which we accepted as necessary secrets, morale was very high there. We were all imbued with a great patriotic spirit and never doubted that victory would be on our side.

I believe that I am one of the few, perhaps the only one among the members of the Brigade, who was part of it *after* having been imprisoned in the jails of Castro's Cuba, which happened as a result of my participation in the first conspiracy against Fidel Castro, in August 1959, as I have already shared.

I experienced the terror of the regime in cell 13 of La Cabaña prison, next to cell 14, which was for those already condemned to death. At the head of that fortress and prison was the gruesome Che Guevara. The privations and humiliations I suffered there for two months and 21 days didn't discourage, but rather stimulated, me so that, as soon as the opportunity presented itself, I enlisted in Brigade 2506. In this way, I fulfilled the commitment I made to the brave prisoners of cell 14, the commitment to return at the first opportunity that presented itself to me.

I've always believed that he who wants to, can, and in reviewing this part of my life, I was able to prove that this is so.

What's certain is that the order came: we had to move from where we were. The moment of truth had arrived. From Retahuelu, Guatemala, they put us on airplanes, without telling us where we were going, and took us to Puerto Cabezas in Nicaragua. We were happy and excited, because, at last, we were going to Cuba. We were finally going to liberate it from communism.

Chapter 8
Playa Girón: The Sad Reality

Never give in, never, never, never, never.
Winston Churchill

When we arrived at Puerto Cabezas, the first thing we saw were the Brigade's aircraft, the B-26s, painted in the same colors as Castro's Air Force. On the other side of the dock, five merchant ships were waiting for us. They were the *Houston*, the *Atlantic*, the *Rio Escondido*, the *Caribe* and the *Lake Charles*. Two other ships, the Landing Craft Infantry (LCI), were waiting elsewhere. One of them was the *Blagar*, which was where the Brigade leadership went, and the other was the *Barbara J*, which would join after the landing.

The ships would leave from different points and travel different routes until they would meet at a point near Cuba, which would make it more difficult for them to be detected and identified as part of the same mission. I and the other members of Operation 40 were to go on one of the merchant ships, the *Lake Charles*, which also carried the Brigade's medical team, as well as gasoline and pumps for the planes.

Our ship left Puerto Cabezas two days after the others. Some allege that the fuel hadn't arrived on time, that the ship that had come from Panama to give us the fuel had not wanted to approach ours because the sea was too rough, and its crew feared the possibility of an accident due to the dangerous cargo we were carrying. Others claim that the delay was planned in advance, since both the medical team and we of Operation 40 were to act after the Brigade had taken the first villages; the medics to attend to the wounded that would be in those villages and us to carry out the intelligence tasks.

We were scheduled to land two days after D-Day.

We finally set sail, eager and willing, anticipating the excitement of reaching a piece of Cuban land liberated by our comrades. I felt a world of illusions in my heart. I thought of my friends waiting in the 13th and 14th cells of La Cabaña, and I could not help but feel, at least to a modest extent, part of an epic story.

A small strip of land could already be glimpsed on the horizon. We were very close to Cayo Guano del Este, 24 nautical miles south of Playa Girón... We were only minutes away from setting foot on Cuban soil. Then, crushingly, the counter-order came.

From an aircraft carrier we were ordered to turn back, not to continue advancing. According to what we were told, all was lost.

Lightning striking the deck of the *Lake Charles* would not have had a more devastating effect: the Brigade, which had landed two days before, was out of ammunition. The ships carrying ammunition, the *Houston* and the *Rio Escondido*, had been sunk. We would later learn that several of our planes had been shot down and their pilots, as well as many other *brigadistas*, had been killed. Those killed were our friends, our comrades in arms and in dreams.

On the *Lake Charles*, we were devastated. What a few minutes before had been the joy and excitement of a journey whose success we had no doubts about, now turned into a harsh reality that was the opposite of what we had anticipated and meant the heroic and, for the moment, useless, sacrifice of a bunch of young Cubans, good men who hadn't hesitated and had taken that enormous risk only for the love of Cuba.

Some time later we would learn that 10 of our men, from Operation 40, had been assigned to the flagship, the *Blagar*, and had landed in Cuba, together with the rest of the Brigade. Four of them had fallen in action and four were wounded, so ours was the Brigade group that, proportionally, had the most casualties.

We would also learn that Castro had taken our arrival as an excuse to get rid of esteemed men who had been imprisoned before. In the early morning of April 18, Virgilio Campanería and Alberto Tapia Ruano, among others, were executed in La Cabaña. On the 19th, seven Cubans and two Americans, Angus McNair and Howard F. Anderson, were executed in Pinar del Río. The following day, April 20, Humberto Sorí Marín, Rogelio Hernández Corzo (Francisco), Rafael Díaz-Hanscom, Eufemio Fernández and Manuel Lorenzo Puig Miyar were executed in La Cabaña.

Now, still unable to absorb all that had happened, we were ordered to go to the island of Vieques, Puerto Rico, but that changed after almost a full day of sailing; we were to return to Puerto Cabezas, Nicaragua.

We returned to our point of departure, where Major Manolo Villafaña, head of the Brigade Air Force, met us. Upon arrival I could see, on the dock, my dear friend Julito Gonzalez Rebull, whose face reflected a deep sadness: he had lost almost all his comrades, the pilots.

That sadness was shared by all those involved in the failed liberation attempt. With it we went ashore, with it we spent our sleepless hours. Add to this how we were kept almost completely in the dark, with no knowledge of what had really happened in Playa Girón or why we had been abandoned. No one with sufficient authority or rank, civilian or military, ever gave us an explanation.

And not only us. To learn, some time later, that the members of the Cuban Revolutionary Council, our civilian leadership, all prestigious Cubans and some of whom had their sons among the members of the Brigade, had been locked up in the Opa-locka barracks, practically imprisoned and incommunicado during the Bay of Pigs operation – departure, landing, outcome, etc. – was very hard to accept and impossible to understand.

We were only told to get ready to be taken back to Miami, each one to their home. It was all over.

In the years since then, the Bay of Pigs mission has been analyzed by a great number of experts and so-called experts. Journalists, academics, historians, military, intelligence officers, politicians, observers, combatants and some of its main protagonists, as well as the occasional dilettante, have written books and university essays, have participated in symposiums and talks, radio programs and historical reports; they have given lectures, have engaged in political debates and, apparently, have dissected everything that can be dissected and have uncovered every secret that could be uncovered, in relation to these historical facts that, for many, are simply that: pages of the book of our times. For others, such as the one who is writing this, they are experiences experienced in the flesh, wounds that have not yet healed, because they still hurt, they still burn.

For me, one of the main factors in the history of the conception, planning, development and end of the Playa Girón tragedy, or "the Bay of Pigs fiasco," depending on who narrates it, was the unfortunate fact that the plan was conceived in the final days of an administration in the White House, that of General Dwight D. Eisenhower, a Republican, and was executed in the early days of the next administration, that of Democrat John F. Kennedy.

The officials of both administrations who were in charge of the development and execution of the plans don't seem to have had a realistic assessment of the situation in Cuba at that time. It seems that a good part of them didn't understand the phenomenon of the Cuban revolution very well. It seems that many of them applied old stereotypes about Latin American governments in their appraisals, which didn't have much to do with the *sui generis* nature of the Cuban situation.

The original plan designed by the Pentagon and the CIA in Eisenhower's time contemplated a landing of no less than 3,000 men along the coast of Trinidad, some 160 kilometers east of Playa Girón. Trinidad was chosen because of its proximity to the Escambray mountain range, where the *brigadistas* were supposed to head after the initial clashes at the landing point, if the Castro armed forces were able to mobilize quickly enough to repel the invasion on the coast as soon as it occurred.

There, in the mountains, the *brigadistas* would begin a guerrilla war similar to the one carried out by the Second Front of the Escambray against the Batista regime just two-and-a-half years earlier. In order to maintain the guerrilla action, a nearby airport was needed, where airplanes could land with the necessary supplies: weapons, food, logistic elements, etc.

That area near Trinidad lacked this vital element, an adequate airport. The runway of the nearest airport lacked 300 meters needed for the B-26s to land on. This, plus the absence of the minimum of 3,000 men required by the Pentagon, made the officials of the new Kennedy administration change the original plan and choose Playa Girón as the landing site, since there was an airport nearby that could be used in the support missions to the internal insurgent force that the Brigade would become.

In addition, the entire territory was surrounded by the Zapata Swamp, which it was estimated would prevent the regime forces from surrounding the core of the Brigade. There was only one road, the one that connected to the Central Australia (Australia sugar mill), and it was assumed that, once the paratroopers took that road and Battalions 2 and 5 disembarked at Playa Roja, they would be able to contain anything coming along that road, as, in fact, they did.

However, there were other geographical and accessibility elements, above all, that made the idea of landing at Playa Girón questionable. There are other details, many in fact, that call into question the decisions made by both the Eisenhower team and their successors, the Kennedy team.

One of the details that's been most discussed and is generally pointed out as the main cause of the operation's failure is the cancellation of the air cover that the U.S. government was supposed to provide for the landing. President Kennedy decided, at the last minute, not to provide such coverage to the Brigade, because to do so would've meant exposing to the world the United States' direct participation in a military action against a small neighboring country to which Congress had not declared war. But the truth is that the withdrawal of that vital element left the skies of the Zapata Swamp open to Castro's aviation force and, therefore, put those who disembarked at its mercy.

Without detracting one iota from the importance of this unfortunate decision, it should be remembered at the same time that this was only one in a series of errors that sealed the project's fate, something we'll see in greater detail a little later on.

In addition to the bulk of the Brigade that was training in Guatemala, there was another group, 150 men or so, under the command of Major Higinio (Nino) Diaz, that was training in Louisiana, and which was to land at a point near Baracoa, Cuba's first and easternmost city. The objective of this was to make Castro's forces believe that the invasion was coming from the east and not from Trinidad. Before landing, Nino Diaz sent one of his men ashore on an exploratory mission and when he returned on board, he reported a large military presence in the area, capable of successfully repelling the landing of that small force, which caused the mission to be aborted and its members to return without having disembarked.

It was at the beginning of January 1961 when Kennedy was briefed and he learned that there was a group of Cubans training, but, unfortunately, they were not the 40,000 men expected by the most optimistic, not even the 3,000 that were calculated to be the minimum necessary to actually carry out the plan conceived by members of Eisenhower's team. It was only 1,100 or 1,200 men expected to land in a Cuba where 90% of the population supported the government in place at the time, who were supporters of a Fidel Castro who had not yet unmasked himself and who had the support not only of the Cuban people, but also of almost the entire world. It was invading a nation where the people supported their government, a government that had in its arsenal squadrons of new Russian tanks and a mobilization capacity, between soldiers and militiamen, of one million men.

Eleven hundred soldiers against that massiveness of popular support and military capacity? Kennedy thought that this was illogical and tried to prevent those plans, conceived as they were at the time, from being implemented. Where were the others, the Cubans who remained "patrolling the streets of Miami," and never went to a recruiting office to join the Brigade?

A decision had to be made and there was no time to delay. Either the go-ahead was given, and the 1,100 men were sent to Cuba, or they were returned to Miami and the operation was cancelled.

The Revolutionary Council was very emphatic that the plans should go ahead, that the Brigade should land in Cuba. The Brigade really wanted to disembark in Cuba, to go into Cuba, where we hoped that many Cubans would join us. Castro thwarted this possibility when he proceeded, swiftly, with the preventive imprisonment of thousands of opponents throughout the country, just minutes after the landing took place.

Anyone could ask, why the Brigade's insistent determination to carry out the operation anyway? It's a question whose answer is difficult to understand for anyone who hasn't lived through the historical circumstances that fed the illusions of victory to us, the enemies of the Castro dictatorship. Perhaps it was naivety, and that certainly contributed to our lack of information regarding many aspects of what was happening. We didn't have, therefore, a complete vision of the plans to be executed, of the correlation of forces between us and our adversaries, nor of the Cuban people's real attitude at that time. We were also unaware of the exact number of our forces and the total proportions of the operation.

We trusted our allies, the Americans, whose relationship with Cubans in their struggles for independence had been mostly positive. The mere fact of seeing American personnel training us at Ratalhueleu, at the Trax Base, knowing that they were giving us B-26 planes, knowing that it was the U.S. government that had gotten Guatemala to lend its territory for training, and that Nicaragua allowed our planes to take off from its airport to fly to Cuba on a war mission, in addition to allowing the Brigade to leave Puerto Cabezas for Cuba, all this increased our confidence in Washington's support.

Moreover, in our thoughts was the incontrovertible truth that, up to then, wherever the Americans had gone, they had triumphed. We had a joyful confidence in our fighting ability, in our determination to liberate Cuba and in the support of the United States.

The decision was a very difficult choice for Kennedy, an inexperienced president, who had taken office less than three months before. But the Revolutionary Council wanted the landing, the Brigade itself wanted the landing... Kennedy gave in, and the rest is history, this sad story that the people of Cuba still live and suffer.

A detail that shouldn't be overlooked is that the men who were in charge of the operation had been inherited by Kennedy from the Eisenhower administration. That is to say that these important officials, each with decision-making power in his area of command, had to carry out a plan very different from the one they themselves had originally conceived.

Charles Cabell was ultimately responsible for the operation in his capacity as Deputy Director of the CIA. Among his subordinates, those who, like himself, came from the Eisenhower administration, were Richard Bissell, Deputy Director for Plans, and Jake Esterline, Chief of the Cuban Task Force. Likewise, those ultimately responsible, the senior officials, came from the Eisenhower administration: Allen Dulles, Director of the CIA; General Lyman Lemnitzer, Chairman of the Joint Chiefs of Staff; Admiral Arleigh Burke, Chief of Naval Operations; and McGeorge Bundy, U.S. National Security Advisor.

Almost every reason argued against going ahead with the operation, was confirmed by the facts. There were, in addition, unforeseeable but equally important details, like the sinking of the *Rio Escondido* and the *Houston*, the ships that carried the ammunition. The Brigade, in three days, ran out of ammunition, after which 1,202 members of the Brigade were taken prisoner.

At the end of the day, I believe that a fundamental aspect in how the events that led to that disaster unfolded was the tremendous lack of experience in the Kennedy administration at that time. He was a very new president, having taken office in January, and three months later this happened. Conclusion: they were not prepared.

The purpose of this book isn't to describe and analyze everything that's been argued and debated by the different sources that've dealt with this subject for so many years. Here, regarding this matter, I'm only offering my thoughts about the facts, as one more of the participants and as one of those affected by their outcome.

However, so that we can all have a clear and realistic understanding of the reason for the failure of that heroic adventure that could have changed Cuba's destiny for the better and avoided, by the way, the rivers of blood that Castro's interference has caused to flow in Latin America and other parts of the world, I will share with you, in the following addendum, some of the most relevant and revealing points of the report I've referred to before, which was produced in February 1962 by Lyman B. Kirkpatrick, who was at the time the CIA's Inspector General.

This report, which was kept secret for more than 35 years, was finally declassified at the end of the last millennium and was published by *El Nuevo Herald* on March 1, 1998, and from which I have taken the information included in the addendum. The report was more than a hundred pages, so it's not possible to reproduce it here in its entirety. However, I believe that the annotations that I'll share with you are sufficient to understand the fundamental reasons for the fatal outcome of the Bay of Pigs operation.

Now, neither that fatal outcome, nor the assignment of guilt in it, nor the mistakes made, nor the pain of our wounds, can tarnish or dwarf the heroism shown by the members of Brigade 2506, nor their courage and real commitment to the cause of Cuba's freedom. Beyond the fact that I myself am one of its members, I stand before all my colleagues from the Brigade with true gratitude and true admiration, and I thank God for having allowed me to be part of that beautiful effort. To our martyrs, those who gave their lives in the patriotic endeavor of the Bay of Pigs Invasion, I offer my respect, my admiration and my gratitude as a Cuban. May God give them eternal rest. And to the noble ideal that impelled their sacrifice, I give my promise of fidelity until the end of my days.

Adendum N° 1

> *It is worse than folly... not to recognize the truth, for in it lies the tinder for tomorrow.*
> Pearl S. Buck

As presented to its readers by the newspaper *El Nuevo Herald*, on March 1, 1998, the report by the CIA Inspector General in the early 60's, Lyman B. Kirkpatrick, on the Bay of Pigs operation, is a thorough and frank assessment of the many details that make up an amphibious military operation, details that escape most laypersons' perception, but which become clearer as they are analyzed by the expert.

I will try to show here some of those details, those that seem to me the most important and that can better answer the questions still asked by those who, in one way or another, were affected by the historical events that took place in the Zapata peninsula, on the southern coast of Cuba, between April 17 and 19, 1961.

It should be noted that, in the preparation of this report, about 125 CIA employees at all levels were interviewed, and a large number of documents were studied.

The U.S. government adopted the blueprint for what would be the plan to overthrow the Castro regime on March 17, 1960, when President Eisenhower approved a CIA document entitled "A Program of Covert Action Against the Castro Regime." The budget to cover this activity was estimated at $4,400,000.

A condition of impossible fulfillment and counterproductive effects

Right from the beginning of the extensive document, in the introduction with which the newspaper presented it, a condition is established for the execution of the plan of action, one that can't be forgotten if one wants to understand well the reason for some decisions that were made when the plan was conceived and developed, decisions that notably influenced the final result: "the hand of the U.S. Government would not appear," says the report.

I think it's easy to understand that trying to hide the U.S. government's leading role in an operation that directly involved, among combatants and assistance personnel before, during and after the events, about 2,000 people, and where they provided air, sea and land military equipment, as well as the participation of more than a thousand men, all of whom resided in this country until a few days before the action without being U.S. citizens, not even residents, was, from the outset, an impossible mission. Moreover, the burden of having to act in support of this fiction contributed, in no small measure, to its failure.

I will now copy some of the report's paragraphs, selected by me in no specific order, with the sole purpose of exposing some of the errors and mistakes that contributed to the unfortunate end of that project for the liberation of Cuba and which, in my opinion, demonstrate that this was not only due to a presidential decision, but to a series of misunderstandings and false assessments of the Cuban reality at that time.

Indispensable requirements beyond the control of the planners and executors of the plan

For example, regarding conditions that needed to exist in Cuba for the operation to be successful, conditions that were beyond the control of the U.S. intelligence agencies, it was said, among other things:

"On 22 June (1960), the Deputy Director of the Central Intelligence Agency briefed the National Security Council on the project... This briefing contained an expression of doubt that a purely clandestine effort would be able to cope with Castro's increasing military capability, pointing out that implementation of the paramilitary phase of operations would be contingent upon the existence of dissident forces who were willing to resist and that such groups had not as yet emerged in strength."

"In August WR/4 Branch prepared papers for use in briefing the President and the Joint Chiefs of Staff, respectively... The briefing paper for the Joint Chiefs made the point that 'obviously the successful implementation of any large-scale paramilitary operations is dependent upon widespread guerrilla resistance throughout the area'."

Here are some observations that seem pertinent to me. In the preceding paragraphs and in others that appear in the report, the need for support from the internal opposition in Cuba in the form of guerrilla activity in the landing zone, as well as from disaffected Cubans who would join the expeditionary force to fight the regime's forces, is emphasized. The latter was estimated at around 30,000 men, an extremely disproportionate number that would be very difficult to achieve, given the isolation and the conditions of the terrain where the landing would take place.

On the other hand, the CIA itself decided not to inform the members of the underground of the day and time of the landing, in order to prevent the information from falling into the hands of Castro's counterintelligence and to avoid losing the element of surprise. How, then, could those who were waiting in Cuba "on the day of the invasion" join the Brigade without being informed? In addition, the Agency grossly underestimated the dictatorship's ability to imprison thousands of opponents as soon as the Invasion occurred, which contributed enormously to its success.

The political front
The report states, in different sections:

"After a series of' meetings in New York and Miami a nominally unified Frente Revolucionario Democratico (FRD), composed of several Cuban factions, was agreed upon on 11 May 1960."

"Although Cuban leaders had formed a "front" at Agency urging, it was an uneasy one. They were by no means in agreement, either among themselves or with Agency case officers, on politics or on operations."

"Power struggles developed early in the life of the FRD. The Cuban leaders wanted something to say about the course of paramilitary operations. As early as May 1960 one of the more prominent leaders was urging-an invasion on a fairly large scale from a third country."

"While the project moved forward, acquiring boats, planes and bases, training men, negotiating with foreign governments, seeking policy clarification, training an FRD security service, publishing magazines and newspapers, putting out radio broadcasts, and attempting to move arms, men and propaganda into Cuba by sea or air, the FRD, in whose name most of this

activity was being carried on, was making little progress toward unity."

"Members would resign in a huff and have to be wheedled back. Each faction wanted supplies to be sent only to its own followers in Cuba, while groups inside were reluctant to receive

infiltrees sent in the name of the FRD."

"Tentative plans for a provisional government were first discussed with FRD leaders in December, and this set off a flurry of intrigue and bickering which delayed the recruiting process and did nothing to advance the cause of unity. In mid-January Miami Base reported that 'the over-all problem is simply to maintain the Frente (FRD) as an operational facade until military action intervenes and a provisional government can be established.'

Until the question of how and by whom such a government was to be selected could be answered, the base reported, 'we are at political dead center'."

"This dead center remained until very near the target date and was only resolved by an ultimatum to the FRD Executive Committee directing its members to agree on the chairman for a Revolutionary Council or risk the loss of all further support."

"As the project grew, the Agency reduced the exiled leaders to the status of puppets, thereby losing the advantages of their active participation."

In all of the above, two attitudes on the part of the Cuban leadership, meaning, the FRD officials, who would later become part of the Revolutionary Council, stand out. The first is laudable: "The Cuban leaders wanted something to say about the course of paramilitary operations." That's to say, the Cubans nominally in charge of the operation weren't content to play a purely decorative role and leave everything in the hands of the U.S. government, something I believe was consistent with their duty as Cubans and with the public responsibility they were assuming.

The second thing is different; it's the presence among those leaders of an evil that seems to accompany us Cubans since we became a nation: the lack of unity, excessive egoism and ambitions of power that always work against any freedom project or any other important project that brings some prestige or power to those who participate in it. No matter how much some say this part of human nature and not exclusive to Cubans, it's still shameful and counterproductive and, sad to say, has greatly delayed Cuba's liberation from the Castro-communist regime.

One detail that's important to keep in mind is the fact that the FRD did not have a single military officer among its directors.

Exile response to the creation of the Brigade
"In the first three months of 1961 the problems faced by the project were many and complex... the brigade trainee quota was still only half fulfilled and a call went to the training camps for special recruiting teams to be sent to Miami."

"By 28 January 1961 the strike force strength was 644, on 3 February it was 685, by 10 March it had risen to 826, by 22 March to 973. On 6 April 1961 [11 days before landing] brigade strength was reported at 1,390."

"The invasion brigade comprised 1,511 men, all of them on the invasion ships excepting one airborne infantry company of 177 men."

Here we return to an equally shameful subject, which I've already mentioned in these pages: the insufficient response of those first Cuban exiles to the call to join in an armed force and go fight in Cuba as liberators. The initial project estimated the necessary force between 3,000 and 5,000 men. In the end, we were less than 1,500.

I don't highlight these facts of undeniable negative connotations for us anti-Castro Cubans to put anyone in the pillory. Those who didn't show up to fight for Cuba's freedom are part of my people, and I don't care to establish divisions between those of us who went to Playa Girón and those who stayed in Miami.

I do so because I'm convinced that if Cubans, as a nation, don't face the truths of our history and don't admit our mistakes, it'll be impossible for us to achieve the moral stature and capability necessary to one day build a new and stronger Republic of Cuba.

And, in the particular case of what happened on April 17, 1961, so that, when speaking and assigning blame, we don't fall into the ridiculous, the unjust or the unproductive.

Operational and organizational failures

"Late September 1960 saw the almost simultaneous occurrence of the first maritime operation and the first air drop over Cuba. The former was successful. The latter, the first of a series of failures, resulted in the capture and execution of a paramilitary agent on whom the project had set great store."

"The Agency became so wrapped up in the military operation that it failed to appraise the chances of success realistically… The Agency failed to build up and supply a resistance organization under rather favorable conditions. Air and boat operations showed up poorly… The Agency failed to collect adequate information on the strengths of the Castro regime and the extent of the opposition to it; and it failed to evaluate the available information correctly."

"… the project lacked a single, high-level full-time commander possessing stated broad powers and abilities sufficient for the carrying out of this large, enormously difficult mission."

"The upshot of this complex and bizarre organizational situation was that in this tremendously difficult task the Agency failed to marshal its forces properly and to apply them effectively."

Here we've seen a small sample of errors committed due to lack of care and coordination. I don't believe it was due to bad faith on the part of different people. It just clearly shows, in my opinion, that it's very difficult to attribute responsibility for the defeat to one person, one decision or one single cause. The issue, as we see, was much more complicated.

Between two administrations

"President Eisenhower had given a general go-ahead signal on 29 November and had reaffirmed it on 3 January 1961, but the impending change in administration was slowing matters down."

"... during the months immediately preceding the inauguration on 20 January 1961, the Agency was recruiting and training Cuban troops and otherwise proceeding with a changed plan not yet definitely formulated or reduced to writing, with no assurance that the invasion, which was now the essence of the plan, would ultimately be authorized by the new Administration. The Agency was driving forward without knowing precisely where it was going."

This last paragraph, above all, shows the great clumsiness of having chosen to carry out the liberation project at a time of presidential transition, when the officials of the outgoing administration, those who conceived the plan, did not feel committed to its execution, and the officials of the incoming administration inherited a project for which it's unlikely that they felt fully responsible for, as they didn't create it.

Communication and discipline problems

"Meanwhile trainees who had been in the camp for several months had had no contact with the political front and were wondering what sort of a Cuban future they were expected to fight for. Disturbances broke out, and the project leaders persuaded three FRD figures to visit the camp and mollify the men." [In February 1961, Manuel Artime, Tony Varona and Dr. Antonio Maceo visited Trax Base. In March of the same year, Dr. Miró Cardona, as president of the Revolutionary Council, visited Trax Base. Previously, Colonel Martin Elena had been there.]

"The Cubans conferring in New York disagreed on various aspects of a post-Castro platform. The Guatemala camp vas having counterintelligence problems."

This is a small sample of the communication and discipline problems that plagued the project. On the one hand, there was a lot of disconnection between the Cuban leadership and the Brigade members preparing to fight in Cuba. On the other hand, there was no lack of Cuban rebels among the troops. There were even desertions and rebellions that had to be contained by imprisoning some of the rebels in a jail in El Petén, Guatemala.

As if that were not enough, the secrecy that was supposed to surround the project quickly evaporated. In Miami and, therefore, in Cuba, the project was known about; there were whispers of inside information and discussions about the date the invasion would occur. There were even newspapers in Miami that published photos of the camps. In spite of all this, the project went ahead without any changes being made.

Aerial coverage

"The air attacks continued throughout the day. The 11 B-26s of the Cuban exile force which were available for close support and interdiction were no match for the T-33 jets. However,

at least four of Castro's other aircraft were shot down by machine gun fire from maritime craft, assisted by friendly air support."

"Late on 16 April, the eve of D-Day, the air strikes designed to knock out the rest of Castro's air force on the following morning were called off. The message reached the field too late to halt the landing operation, as the decision to cancel the air strike was made after the landing force had been committed."

"Jet cover from the Navy aircraft carrier "Essex" had been expected to protect the 19 April sorties, but a misunderstanding over timing hampered its effectiveness."

"In spite of this air action, however, and in spite of a reported 1,800 casualties suffered by the Castro forces, the brigade's ability to resist depended in the last resort on resupply of ammunition, which had now become impossible."

As we can see, and without ignoring the negative aspect of suspending air cover in the combat zone, it's clear in this report that this important mistake was one more in a succession of errors that, by themselves, condemned the actions taken to failure. Note how the report points out the superiority of Castro's T-33 jets when facing the Brigade's B-26 aircraft.

What should have been done, but was not

"It should be especially noted that the project's paramilitary chief bad strongly recommended that the operation be abandoned if policy should not allow adequate tactical air support."

"On 17 February the Agency presented a paper (Annex B) to the President... the paper escribed the growing strength of the Castro regime under Bloc support and observed: 'Therefore, after some date probably no more than six months away it will become militarily infeasible to overthrow the Castro regime except by the commitment to combat of a sizeable organized military force. The option of action by the Cuban opposition will no longer be open'."

"The Special Group had, however, not yet agreed on a substitute plan and strong doubt was expressed whether anything less than overt U.S. forces would suffice to obtain Castro's downfall."

"The Agency committed at least four extremely serious mistakes in planning:

> Failure to subject the project, especially in its latter frenzied stages, to a cold and objective appraisal by the best operating talent available, particularly by those not involved in the operation, such as the Chief of Operations and the chiefs of the Senior Staffs. Had this been done, the two following mistakes {band c, below) might have been avoided.

> Failure to advise the President, at an appropriate time, that success had become dubious and to recommend that the operation be therefore cancelled and that the problem of unseating Castro be restudied.

Failure to recognize that the project had become overt and that the military effort had become too large to be handled by the Agency alone."

"Timely and objective scrutiny of the operation in the months before the invasion... would have demonstrated to Agency officials that the clandestine paramilitary operations had almost totally failed, that there was no controlled and responsive underground movement ready to rally to the invasion force, and that Castro's ability both to fight back and to roll up the internal opposition must be very considerably upgraded... It would also have raised the question of why the United States should contemplate pitting 1,500 soldiers, however well trained and armed, against an enemy vastly superior in number and armament on a terrain which offered nothing but vague hope of significant local support."

"At some point in this degenerative cycle they should have gone to the President and said frankly: 'Here are the facts. The operation should be halted. We request further instructions'."

I believe the examples I've reiterated in this section speak for themselves: from the very beginning, the operation was doomed to failure. And this became even more evident as the mistakes that were made as the plan progressed towards its consummation were added to it. It's not by coincidence that the Inspector General of the CIA, the agency in charge of bringing the project to a successful conclusion, repeatedly pointed out that the operation should have been cancelled.

The summary of the evaluation is also illuminating.

Summary of the assessment

The report states, in its final part:

"1. In evaluating the Agency's performance it is essential to avoid grasping immediately, as many persons have done, at the explanation that the President's order cancelling the D-Day air strikes was the chief cause of failure.

2. Discussion of that one decision would merely raise this underlying question: If the project had been better conceived, better organized, better staffed and better managed, would that precise issue ever have bad to be presented for Presidential decision at all? And would it have been presented under the same ill-prepared, inadequately briefed circumstances?

3. Furthermore, it is essential to keep in mind the possibility that the invasion was doomed in advance, that an initially successful landing by 1,500 men would eventually have been crushed by Castro's combined military resources strengthened by Soviet Bloc-supplied military materiel.

4. The fundamental cause of the disaster was the Agency's failure to give the project, notwithstanding its importance and its immense potentiality for damage to the United States, the top-flight handling which it required – appropriate organization, staffing throughout by highly qualified personnel, and full-time direction and control of the highest quality.

5. Insufficiencies in these vital areas resulted in pressures and distortions, which in turn produced numerous serious operational mistakes and omissions, and in lack of awareness of developing dangers, in failure to take action to counter them, and in grave mistakes of judgment. There was failure at high levels to concentrate informed, unwavering scrutiny on the project and to apply experienced, unbiased judgment to the menacing situations that developed."

I would like to reiterate that the excerpts from the "Inspector General's Survey of the Cuban Operation" that I've reproduced in this addendum have been grouped according to the subject they deal with, without a specific order and taking care not to take them out of context. Everything that appears in quotes is taken directly from that report. Anything in brackets are clarifications on my part for the reader's better understanding.

To summarize, regarding the Cuban problem and the participation of the United States in that problem, we can't ignore the evil's origin: Fidel Castro came to power, among other factors, thanks to the Eisenhower administration's ineptness in forcing Batista to leave Cuba without having a reliable democratic succession ready and, even worse, counting on the pressure exerted by some of its diplomats and other officials who demanded that Castro be the successor.

On the other hand, Eisenhower, being as he was an experienced and capable military man, doesn't seem to have paid much attention to the plan he himself approved to overthrow Castro. His officials involved in the project don't seem to have made a realistic assessment of the situation in Cuba, especially in terms of the resources and support available to the regime, nor do they seem to have taken seriously the series of mistakes and bungling that, from its inception, undermined the project.

Thus, what his administration created in its aftermath, perhaps in the indifference of its departure, was inherited by the Kennedy administration during its inexperienced beginnings.

No one can deny the negative effect President Kennedy's decision to suspend air cover during the landing had on the final outcome. However, we must consider the views documented here by the Inspector General as to the superiority of Castro's jets and Sea Furies, the multitude of errors that plagued the project, the false assessment of the ability of Cubans on the island to join the expeditionary force, and the views repeatedly expressed that Castro's advantage in numbers and weapons would eventually prevail in any event. Hence, the report reflects the conviction of more than one of the Agency's own officers who proposed cancelling the operation.

Conclusion

I would simply like to emphasize some of the details that seem to me to be decisive in the final outcome of the Bay of Pigs operation:

The Eisenhower administration's determination to conceal the hand of the United States in the events of the Bay of Pigs, from its conception to its implementation, hindered the proper development of the plan for something that, in any case, was impossible to accomplish for the reasons that have already been pointed out.

Maintaining the team of mission managers appointed by the Eisenhower administration, especially after major changes were made to the original plan, was not the new administration's best decision. Kennedy should've had not only capable people there, but also his closest confidants, who would've been able to make him see, in all honesty, the inappropriateness of the operation.

Secretary Dean Rusk, a prominent member of the new President's team, warned that it was not the right time to invade Cuba. Why did he do it?

He did so because he couldn't make heads nor tails of the plan that Kennedy inherited. There weren't the 40,000 men that had been talked about at the beginning to make up the expeditionary force. There weren't the 3,000 that Eisenhower's team said were the minimum required – there were only 1,200, of whom only half were ready for combat. The other half were not properly trained.

As for the plan to land at Trinidad, scrapped because the runway at the nearest airport was 300 meters too short for the B-26s to land and take off from, it's been said that the runway could have been extended after the landing. I ask myself: who would extend the runway in the middle of a battle? Extending the runway could take weeks, but some Miami "experts" say they can do it under enemy fire in three hours!

What was the supposed advantage of disembarking at Trinidad? Well, to make it easier for the Brigade to reach the Escambray mountains, but, was there anyone in the Brigade who knew that hillside? How many would have arrived alive... a thousand, maybe? What would happen if Fidel Castro sent 25,000 soldiers there, under the command of Che Guevara, who *did* know the Escambray? Would the peasants in the area have helped us or would they have sided with Che, whom they already knew and had supported before? Would any of us have survived against thousands of soldiers backed by an entire people?

Actually, beyond we Cubans' responsibility, there are two major culprits in the United States: President Eisenhower, for allowing himself to be influenced by Fidel Castro's sympathizers in the State Department by preventing Dr. Rivero Agüero, a decent and honest Cuban, from taking office as President of Cuba in January 1959, and imposing communism on our homeland; and President Kennedy, for following the previous administration's advice and allowing the mission, causing the deaths of more than one hundred heroic *brigadistas* who perished trying to liberate Cuba.

Perhaps someone may think that a long and detailed digression such as this one has no place in a biography. To those who think so, I must repeat that the Bay of Pigs operation had such an impact on my life, as a member of Brigade 2506, and on the lives of all Cubans, those in Cuba and those in exile, that without a proper understanding of that historical episode, many aspects of our existence could not be understood.

Also, I'm encouraged by the hope that, by exposing these facts, I'm helping many of my compatriots to better understand our own history, to accept the responsibilities that correspond to us and to correct our mistakes, believing that Cuba's liberation is still a duty that we have pending.

Chapter 9
Robert F. Kennedy – The Rescue of the Brigade Members

When there are many men without decorum, there are always others who have in themselves the decorum of many men.

José Martí

We were on our way back to Miami, under the worst circumstances imaginable. During the flight back, I was trying to process in my mind everything that had happened – how, in the course of a few hours, everything had changed, and all this now galvanized by the news we'd received on our return to Puerto Cabezas.

There we learned, among other information and rumors, that seven of our B-26 planes had been shot down with their crews on board. There were many dead; in fact, the Brigade lost more than 120 men in the invasion. We also learned that we had inflicted heavy casualties on Castro's forces.

Other sources, some of them the Americans, stated that we had caused around 2,000 casualties to the dictatorship's army. As a matter of fact, it was known that Hugo Sueiro and his comrades of Battalion 2 had caused many casualties to Osmani Cienfuegos' battalion. I was thinking, with sadness, of the certain fact that the Brigade had run out of ammunition, that they had fought courageously until the last bullet, and in the end, they had ended up in Castro's hands.

With these thoughts in my mind, we arrived at Homestead Air Force Base for a bittersweet reunion with those waiting for us there. Base officials greeted us cordially, albeit unceremoniously, and no one spoke to us or explained what had happened and why. To me, it was clear that there was an unmistakable hastiness about us, as if they wanted to turn the page quickly. They provided transportation and we were each taken, individually, to our homes.

The reunion with my wife and my son Alex was the only pleasant thing in those dark days. It was also a complete surprise for them, as they hadn't been notified beforehand. I also found on my return an exile community that was talking about the bravery of the Brigade and was beginning to talk about Kennedy's treason, that the Americans didn't disembark, that their pilots didn't fight. We *brigadistas* were described as heroes, in such a way that many of those who didn't join the Brigade now changed their arguments: if before they said that they hadn't shown up for recruitment because they thought it wasn't necessary, that, since the Americans were with us, the fight was already won; now they alleged that they hadn't shown up because they knew that it was going to be a failure, that the Americans "*nos iban a embarcar*" (were going to desert us).

While having most people's respect and admiration was very comforting, the opportunism shown by others, the more verbose ones, was somewhat discouraging. However, I think I said before that it's not in my nature to be easily crushed by circumstances; therefore, I gathered my spiritual strength and said to myself: life has to go on.

I spent a few days in Miami and then moved to Washington D.C., where my parents and brother were. Once there, I immediately started working with the architect Ronald Senseman, a well-known and highly respected name in the field. I worked with him for a few months, until I made an exploratory trip to Miami, trying to see if it was possible to work in what we already called the capital of the Cuban exile community.

I returned with Irma and Alex to Miami and started working with H. J. Ross construction company. After a few months there, I decided to get a general contractor's license. Once I got the license, I started with small building jobs. I built the Flagler Medical Center for Tony Perez and a few other jobs.

Some time later, I became fully involved in the efforts being made at that time to form a group of the Bay of Pigs participants, which would be called the Bay of Pigs Veterans Association. There was some discussion as to whether we should call it the Veterans Association or the Combatants Association, but, in the end, we would all call it simply, Brigade 2506, its name to this day. Working for myself gave me the freedom to manage my time and endeavors, which I could distribute between work and these activities.

I dedicated myself to trying to see what could be done for the *brigadistas* imprisoned in Cuba, a project in which I was part of a fairly large group. The United States began to reintegrate the members of the Brigade who were in Miami and elsewhere. For example, the officers who led the frogmen, Grayston Lynch, etc., formed two groups to infiltrate Cuba, one under the command of Vera, who was the second-in-command of the paratroopers, and the other led by Roberto Pérez San Román. These groups began their work and for them, for the rest of the *brigadistas* and for the exile community, they were like proof that we were still fighting, that all was not lost.

In fact, there's one, of the many things that happened during Playa Girón, that is, for me, a clear example of most of the *brigadistas'* will to fight. Vera, the second-in-command of the paratroopers, had been at the scene of the fighting in a very unusual way. The plane that dropped him over Playa Girón didn't do it right, and Vera fell in the middle of the Zapata Swamp. When, with great effort, he managed to get out of there, the Brigade had practically run out of ammunition and there was nothing that could be done. He managed to get to La Habana, took refuge in an embassy, returned to Miami and immediately rejoined the fight, leading one of those two infiltration groups. This, to me, is admirable.

With Roberto Pérez San Román, Chief of the Heavy Gun Battalion of the Brigade in Miami in 1961.

Around the end of April 1961, Dr. Carlos Jones, an eminent lawyer from Cardenas, came to see me. His son Jorge, whom we called Yoyi, an exceptional young man with a promising future ahead of him, was one of the four members of Operation 40 killed in combat. Hugging his father under those circumstances was very emotional for me.

To my surprise, Dr. Jones asked me to accompany him to visit Robert F. Kennedy, the President's brother and then U.S. Attorney General. In Cuba, Jones had been George Skakel's lawyer. Skakel was Ethel's, RFK's wife, father. Bobby, as everyone called the Attorney General, and Ethel had visited the "Ciudad Bandera," as Cardenas is known, on occasion, and there they formed a friendship with the Cuban lawyer.

Of course, I immediately accepted Dr. Jones' invitation, and we both went to Washington. Bobby Kennedy received us cordially and within a minute I grasped his modesty, his intelligence and his sincerity, all virtues that were transparent in his straightforward conversation.

The Attorney General was also impressive for his vast knowledge of politics and history, despite his youth. At the age of 35, he was the youngest person to serve in a presidential cabinet in the United States since the days of Alexander Hamilton. Those who knew him, whether allies or political adversaries, knew well that he didn't occupy his high position because he was the president's brother, but because of his great ability to perform his job.

Bobby had an insatiable thirst for information about everything that happened before, during and after the failed Bay of Pigs operation. He insistently asked about the smallest details about the preparation and execution of the plan and didn't hide his admiration for the Brigade's bravery on Cuban soil, nor his concerns about the fate of the *brigadistas* imprisoned on the island, concerns that I shared in a special way.

People who knew him, authors of books about him, and politicians who dealt with him in those times, have said that Bobby Kennedy felt the failure of the Bay of Pigs as something very personal, as a debt he owed to the Cuban people and as something for which Fidel Castro had to pay and would have to be made to pay. I also came away with that impression after meeting with him.

I thanked Dr. Jones for the extraordinary opportunity that his invitation had given me and back in Miami, I continued with both the work of the construction company and the activities of the Brigade.

I continued then, with great interest, in my self-imposed task of seeing if it was possible to do something for the Brigade comrades who had been captured in Cuba and were imprisoned there. In the meantime, RFK decided to form a committee to study what mistakes were made and by whom in the Bay of Pigs operation. He did this after his brother the president had assumed full responsibility for what happened during a speech before the American Society of Newspaper Editors, at a dinner held at the Statler Hilton Hotel in the District of Columbia, three days after the Brigade landed.

Of what follows, I've already given a foretaste elsewhere in this book, but it's necessary to tell it again now. It was a time when the Bay of Pigs issue was being intensely debated in every political and journalistic forum in the country, and so it was that I was invited to participate in a TV show that aired in the New England states. I was being interviewed by a panel of four journalists, and one of them asked me who, in my opinion, was responsible for the Bay of Pigs fiasco.

I replied that the president could no longer be accused, because he himself had acknowledged his responsibility in the matter. A person can be accused when he denies his guilt, but once he's acknowledged his guilt, then he should no longer be (accused).

And I added something that perhaps they didn't expect: "In my opinion," I told them, "a good part of that responsibility falls on the more than 40,000 Cubans of military age who stayed 'patrolling the streets of Miami' and did not go to the camps."

I must say here that I still maintain that belief. And although it embarrasses me as a Cuban, I still believe that all my compatriots who read this can use it as a foundation for a serious introspection which, I reiterate, we need to make as a people, to heal our national conscience, to recognize our mistakes with due humility, and, above all, to correct them and not relapse into them, remembering that, sadly, shamefully, Cuba is still waiting for us.

As a result of that television program, Bobby called me and invited me to breakfast at his home in McLean, Virginia. There, he told me that he was going to form a committee to rescue the *brigadistas* imprisoned in Cuba, which I was very happy about, because I saw in that effort a great possibility that the prisoners could be released.

Then-retired General Maxwell Taylor was called upon to chair the committee. Other well-known international figures, such as Admiral Arleigh Burke, head of the U.S. Navy, and CIA Director Allen Dulles, also served on the committee.

On March 29, 1962, the rigged trial of the *brigadistas* began in Cuba, and my friends and I, Cubans in general and, most especially, the Revolutionary Council members, were tense and expectant, awaiting the worst fate for those who had landed in Cuba seeking its freedom and had ended up losing their own. Their lives were in the hands of a cruel executioner, Fidel Castro.

Something that disturbed us all was knowing that the lives of our fellow prisoners in Cuba depended on the whims and political expediencies of Fidel Castro, since Cuba was, and unfortunately still is, a country without laws and institutions. We couldn't forget that on September 8, 1961, 14 *brigadistas* had been convicted under accusations of having committed torture and murder in Batista's time – that is, before the Bay of Pigs operation. Five of those 14 were shot by firing squad, and the remaining nine were sentenced to 30 years in prison. Among those executed were Ramón Calviño, Emilio Soler Puig and Jorge King Yun.

On April 6, 1962, the sentences to be imposed on the *brigadistas* were to be handed down. The day before, Bobby met with me in Washington, and I told him that there was a meeting that night with Dr. Miró Cardona and other members of the Revolutionary Council at the Manger Annapolis Hotel. Bobby asked me for the room number where we were going to meet; I gave it to him and, in passing, I told him that there was a large number of *brigadistas* who were willing to go to Cuba in peace and shoulder the same sentence imposed on the rest of the Brigade, if necessary. I told him that this was one of the topics we were going to discuss with Miró Cardona that night. I remember that I was accompanied on that occasion by Dr. Arturo Pérez Heredia, who was the medical chief of the third battalion of the Brigade, and Felipe de Diego, one of my colleagues in Operation 40.

Indeed, that evening we met at the Manger Annapolis Hotel. Among others, Dr. Miró Cardona, Dr. Tony Varona and Dr. Ernesto Freyre were present. Nestor Carbonell, the prestigious lawyer and great patriot, also a member of Operation 40 who had been with us all the time on the *Lake Charles*, ready to disembark at Playa Girón, was also there.

In the middle of the meeting, the phone rang. If I remember correctly, it was precisely Nestor Carbonell who answered the call. It was Bobby, and he asked to speak to me. He said that I could inform those gathered there that, the following day, at the trial, there would be no death penalty, there would be no firing squad. They would all be sentenced to 30 years.

I informed everyone at the meeting, and we all breathed a great sigh of relief. In the midst of that meeting that had been called under the black cloud of adversity that enveloped us, it was joyful to know that there would be no firing squad, that the three Brigade leaders, Artime, San Román and Oliva, would not lose their lives.

Bobby had told me that he wanted to see me the next day at three o'clock in the afternoon in his office at the Justice Department. I asked Dr. Miró Cardona to accompany us, as I felt that having the Revolutionary Council meet with RFK was opportune, especially regarding the prisoners. Dr. Miró Cardona delegated to Tony Varona and Tony, in turn, said that he preferred Dr. Ernesto Freyre to go instead, since he was more in contact with the prisoners' relatives.

It should be remembered that in May 1961, Fidel Castro had proposed to exchanging the Brigade prisoners for 500 large tractors. Shortly afterwards, he set the price at $28 million.

Freyre accompanied me, and that was a meeting for the ages. It was at that meeting that Bobby told Freyre that he could offer Fidel Castro $26 million in food and medicine as ransom in exchange for the release and return of the Brigade prisoners to the United States. It was right then and there that the liberation of the 2506th Assault Brigade really began.

The next day, Freyre traveled to La Habana to present the offer to Fidel Castro. There, his first contact would be Berta Barreto, the widow of Cuban diplomat and writer Guy Pérez Cisneros, whose son, Pablo, was a *brigadista*.

Pérez Cisneros was a member of the Cuban delegation of and played a prominent role in the United Nations General Assembly that adopted the Universal Declaration of Human Rights in 1948. He was also in Colombia as part of the Cuban delegation for the signing of the OAS Charter, also in 1948, when the violent riot known as "el bogotazo" occurred. Fidel Castro, who, as I mentioned earlier, had participated in those events, managed to return to Cuba thanks to the protection provided to him and the other Cubans involved in the revolt by the Cuban ambassador in Bogota, Carlos Tabernilla, and to Ambassador Perez Cisneros's help.

Fidel Castro was never known for being a grateful person, but it should be noted that four years after "el bogotazo," Francisco Tabernilla Dolz, the ambassador's brother, became Chief of Staff of the Cuban Army following the March 10 coup. When Castro's revolution triumphed, Ambassador Tabernilla's widow was the only member of his family who was not dispossessed of her house, nor was she harassed by the new regime. In that same order of things, Conchita Fernandez, Fidel's devoted secretary, who knew about those events, maintained a good relationship with Mrs. Barreto, the ambassador's widow.

Conchita had previously been secretary to Eduardo Chibás, the leader of the Partido del Pueblo Cubano (Ortodoxo) (the Cuban People's Party or Orthodox Party), a party in which Fidel Castro himself had been a militant. This proved to be providential in establishing the line of communication with Castro that was necessary at that time. Conchita, through Celia Sanchez, Fidel's lover and confidant, informed him of Ernesto Freyre's offer as president of the Committee of Relatives of the Prisoners of the Brigade.

The next day, Celia called Mrs. Barreto and put her on the phone directly with Fidel Castro. The Maximum Leader had previously ignored Freyre's presence in La Habana and had refused to even listen to his ransom offer. But, on this occasion, he announced that he was ready to meet with the Committee of Relatives at Berta Barreto's house and asked that Erneido Oliva, second-in-command of the Brigade and a prisoner in Cuba at the time, be present. Freyre and the other members of the Committee, Alvaro Sanchez, Enrique Llaca and Virginia Betancourt, flew to La Habana and went directly to Berta Barreto's house, where, after a while, Fidel arrived.

As is well known, that offer rose to more than $60 million. Afterwards, Kennedy appointed attorney James Donovan to be in charge of the negotiations with Castro and his men. On December 21, 1962, Fidel Castro and James B. Donovan signed the agreement for the exchange of 1,113 prisoners for $53 million in food and medicine and that is how, in the end, the Brigade members were freed.

Earlier, on April 14, 1962, 56 *brigadistas* wounded in combat and four others, a total of 60, were released and transported to the United States. Castro himself offered this as a gesture of good will, apparently pleased and interested in the ransom offered. Among those released was Enrique Ruiz Williams, who had been designated by the remaining Brigade members to represent them and assist in raising funds for the ransom, which Bobby agreed to.

Robert Kennedy's high regard for the members of the Brigade was demonstrated on other occasions. I would like to highlight one of them, because it shows the human side of that man who, in my opinion, was called to a higher destiny which, due to his early death, could not be fulfilled.

Among the *brigadistas* who returned from Cuba after the rescue negotiations was Gustavo Villoldo. Upon his return, Gustavo began to work with the CIA, in one of the infiltration groups. On one occasion his wife comes to see me and tells me that he's away from Miami with the CIA and that Alejandro, his youngest son, is suffering from Tetralogy of Fallot, a dangerous congenital heart disease, and that he needs to be operated on.

At the children's hospital in Miami, which was then called Variety Children's Hospital, they asked her for $5,000 for the operation, a sum which, in those days, was a fortune for most Cuban exiles. She didn't have those resources, nor did she have any way to get in touch with Villoldo, given the nature of the work he was doing.

I call Washington, talk to Bobby. He asks me for all the details of the case, asks how to get in touch with her, and the next day an Air Force major from the Homestead base goes to see her, accompanies her to Washington, and there they operate on the child at Walter Reed Hospital, all completely free of charge.

Bobby and Ethel, his wife, visited them in the hospital showing genuine interest in their welfare. The boy recovered satisfactorily, but he had wires inserted in his heart, which were to be removed after two years.

When the time came for that second operation to remove the wires, RFK was no longer the U.S. Attorney General. His brother, the president, had been assassinated, and he was then one of the two senators from New York. When I called him, his secretary, Angela Novell, told me that the senator was in the Bahamas and that she will give him my message as soon as he calls.

That same afternoon he was calling me. I explain the situation to him:

"Do you remember the Villoldo kid?"

"Of course..."

I explain that he's ready for the second operation, that it's necessary to operate now, and that the economic situation is the same. He asks me for the details, which I provide. One or two days later, a civilian, sent by the senator's office, went to see Mrs. Villoldo and gave her the tickets for the trip to Washington. When she arrived, they were already waiting for her at the airport. From there she was taken to Walter Reed, to the same hospital, with the same doctor, and the second operation was a complete success. Just like the first time, the Villoldos didn't have to pay a penny.

This wasn't the only occasion on which Bobby Kennedy showed me his great humanity and, in particular, his appreciation for Brigade 2506. When a group of *brigadistas* imprisoned in Cuba came to the United States, sent by Castro in order to get the tractors and other items that he himself was asking for as ransom, and who, moreover, came with the obligation to return to prison once their mission was over, I called Bobby, told him what was happening and confided to him my fears that they would have to return to Cuba empty-handed.

He said to me, "Come here, to Washington." I went, and he sent me to Maryland, to a specific place where I was given ownership of seven tractors. I gave them to Ulises Carbó, the prominent journalist, also a *brigadista*, who was part of that group that was to return to Cuba. That donation was an important contribution to the desired purpose, that is, to enhance the ransom demanded by the cynical executioner who had in his hands the lives of so many patriots. Bobby always responded positively and willingly to any endeavor or need that the Brigade had, and this was demonstrated many times, but especially in those efforts to bring the *brigadistas* back to the United States. He was the primary driver in obtaining the ransom Castro demanded, which amounted to more than $60 million.

Despite the friendship that was spontaneously established between Bobby Kennedy and me, he never confided his own impressions of the Bay of Pigs tragedy. He was, above all, someone who, due to the high position he held in the U.S. government, respected very much his oath of fidelity to the confidentiality inherent to all governmental administration, especially when they involved military actions. However, as I said earlier, he had an abiding interest in knowing everything about our ill-fated mission, to which he felt personally attached.

I believe that the assassination of Robert Kennedy on June 6, 1968, deprived the United States of a leader who was truly passionate about democracy and justice. When he was assassinated in Los Angeles, he was already well on his way to the presidency, and I'm sure he would have been a great president. Let no one doubt this: the Cuban cause also lost, with his death, a friend who was personally committed to the liberation of the Cuban people.

Something that has caught my attention is that no Board of Directors of Brigade 2506, including those of which I was Secretary (1968-1969) under the presidency of Alfredo González Durán, has had the initiative to pay a posthumous tribute to Robert F. Kennedy, the person who did more than any other to get the *brigadistas* out of Fidel Castro's prisons and bring them back to the United States. A photo of Bobby Kennedy should be in the Brigade's museum, as a debt of gratitude to his memory, for all he did for us.

Brigade 2506 Board of Directors (1967-1968) when I was elected Secretary.

Chapter 10
One Make Mistakes in Life... Death of the Kennedys

> *Always forgive your enemies;*
> *nothing annoys them so much.*
> Oscar Wilde

The *brigadistas* who were imprisoned in Cuba returned to Miami on December 23, 1962, just in time to reunite with their families for a jubilant Christmas Eve, ecstatic for their freedom after the trauma of their defeat. But at the same time, their joy was tinged with pain for their harsh experiences and for the loss of their fallen companions in the attempt to liberate Cuba.

Earlier, Fidel Castro had received the ransom demanded, collected by the committee that the attorney Donovan headed, thanks to the generosity of various institutions in this country and the contributions of thousands of Cuban exiles, who overcame their own economic limitations to help the heroes to whom they felt indebted. At the last minute, $4 million were missing to complete the $53 million ransom. RFK appointed General Lucius Clay to raise funds, and he quickly raised $3 million, while the Archbishop of Boston, Cardinal Richard Cushing, a great friend of the Kennedy family, put up the remaining million.

Along with the joy I felt for my companions' return, I received an additional reason to be happy: with them came my great friend Renaldo Blanco Navarro, who had been arrested with me and the others indicted because of Eloy Gutierrez Menoyo and William Morgan's betrayal. Renaldo had been sentenced to 20 years by Castro's courts, and the last thing I expected was that he would be released along with the *brigadistas*. Happy as I was when I learned of his release and return to Miami, I was also very curious to know how that miracle had occurred.

It turned out that, once the *brigadistas* had been ordered to return to Miami, Fidel Castro went to see the Brigade's leadership off at the San Antonio de los Baños base. Taking advantage of that circumstance, some of the *brigadistas*, among them Hugo Sueiro, asked the dictator, who masqueraded as magnanimous on that occasion, to release Renaldo Blanco Navarro and allow him to return to Miami with the Brigade. They presented their reasoning in a very skillful way, trying to convince Castro that this gesture would be of mutual convenience.

Manolo, Renaldo's brother, had also been a member of the Brigade, but he had landed in Cuba before April 17, on an infiltration mission. In Cuba he was arrested and imprisoned awaiting trial, but when the invasion occurred, he was summarily executed. Nelson, the youngest of the three brothers, was also a member of the Brigade, one of those captured at Playa Girón and was at that time waiting to be returned to Miami with the other prisoners.

"You are forcing Nelson, the youngest of the Blanco Navarro family, to continue fighting your government, because his remaining brother is imprisoned here."

On the one hand, this rationale sounded convincing; on the other hand, it's known that Fidel Castro respected Hugo Sueiro as an enemy, since, though he was still very young, he was the one who had caused the most casualties to Castro's troops in Playa Roja, and everyone considered him a great military man.

Fidel didn't commit himself to anything at that moment. He said that he would see if something could be done and left, but the truth is that Renaldo was quickly taken out of the Isla de Pinos prison, transferred to the San Antonio de los Baños base, taken to where the *brigadistas* were waiting for the plane and came to Miami with them.

Six days after the Brigade's return, on December 29, President John F. Kennedy and Jacqueline, his wife and First Lady, came to

Miami to welcome them back. The emotional meeting took place at the Orange Bowl stadium, which was filled with Cubans who wanted to witness that historic occasion. I wasn't there; I was away from Miami that day, but more than one friend told me the story of what happened... The Brigade parade amid thunderous applause, the solemnity of the moment when the Brigade flag was handed to the president by one of the Brigade leaders, Erneido Oliva, and, above all, the president's promise to return that flag "in a free Havana," a promise he could not keep because, less than a year later, he would be assassinated in Dallas, Texas.

All of this Cuban ebullience in Miami, all of this patriotic revival, which was based on the hope that the United States would continue to move forward with efforts to liberate Cuba, was occurring barely two months after the (Cuban) Missile Crisis. We Cuban exiles didn't even suspect that in the talks held at that time between Washington and Moscow to avoid a nuclear conflict that seemed imminent, the United States had committed to ceasing all activities aimed at regime change in Cuba and even more, to not allowing Cuban exiles to carry out hostile actions against the Castro dictatorship from U.S. territory. It was what we would later come to know as the Kennedy-Khrushchev Pact which, for all practical purposes, made the U.S. government the guardian and protector of the Castro regime.

Years later, the Board of Directors of the Bay of Pigs Veterans Association demanded that the White House return that flag, since Kennedy's promise to return it "in a free Havana" had not been kept. The flag was returned to the Brigade and, unbeknownst to us at the time, that was perhaps a symbol of the new status quo between La Habana, Washington and Miami.

After the event at the Orange Bowl, the year 1962 ended with the illusion of Cuba's freedom once again burning in Cuban hearts. But even so, the realities of our daily life prevailed.

A good number of *brigadistas* enlisted in the U.S. Army, in response to an offer made by Kennedy. I wasn't really attracted to the idea of a military career. I stayed in Miami, ready to continue working with my construction company, with which I was doing quite well, and to continue with my activities in the Brigade.

These activities sometimes took me to New York and New Jersey, where many *brigadistas* lived, and with them we would carry out patriotic acts and actions in favor of Cuba's freedom.

It was during one of those trips to New York, in a conversation with friends and colleagues who lived in that "Babel of Steel," that someone commented on the increasing frequency with which former *fidelistas* were arriving in exile. These were Cubans who had believed Fidel Castro's promises and had been strong supporters of the revolution in its early days, but to whom the facts were now showing the "Maximum Leader" and his regime's true tyrannical and communist nature.

Some of these former *fidelistas* had committed abuses or had been violent to those who didn't sympathize with the revolution, and because of this they tried to keep a low profile once they themselves became what they once despised, "exiled worms."

"Well, there you have it," commented one of the participants in the discussion. "One of those who arrived recently is Lieutenant Calzadilla, who screwed with so many people when they were leaving Cuba. Here he is, in New York, working as an elevator operator in a hotel."

When I heard that, I felt my soul stirring inside my body and I asked the person who had spoken to take me to that hotel: I wanted to see Lieutenant Calzadilla.

We arrived at the hotel lobby; I think it was in Manhattan. An elevator descended, its doors opened, and the people who occupied it came out, all except the elevator operator, who simply looked out to see if anyone was going to the upper floors. It was Calzadilla, the former official of Fidel Castro's Ministry of Foreign Affairs.

I had asked my friends who were with me to stay in the lobby; I wanted to be alone with Castro's former official who had become an elevator operator in a New York hotel. Luckily, no one else entered the elevator; it was just him and me. He closed the inner door of the elevator, moved the lever, and we started to go up. He hadn't recognized me. He asked me which floor I was going to. I stared at him:

"Calzadilla," I said, "don't you remember me?"

"No, the truth is that I don't recognize you," he answered.

"When we were going from the Mexican embassy to the airport," I told him, "you told me to take a good look at the palm trees, because I would never see them again. What are you doing here?"

Calzadilla lowered his gaze and with a firm voice, but speaking softly, said: "Well, one makes mistakes in life..."

I told him to leave me in the lobby and said no more, because my intention wasn't to humiliate him, but to make him see his mistake by having to swallow those words he had said to me in Cuba. He didn't raise his head again until I got out of the elevator.

This must have occurred in early or mid-1963. The following year there would be presidential elections in the United States and the political atmosphere was already heating up with aspirations, not only for the presidency, but for many other electoral positions as well. There in New York, as in the whole country, the newspapers reported the possible candidates' statements and movements, and in the Sunday opinion programs the topic was becoming more and more frequent. And that topic, logically, was discussed among Cuban exiles, too.

In New York and New Jersey, as well as in Miami, Cubans were interested in the upcoming presidential race based on our interest in Cuba's freedom. We speculated and discussed which candidate would be more favorable to our cause: John F. Kennedy, who was running for reelection, or Eisenhower's former vice-president, Richard Nixon, who was once again considered by many to be the Republican nominee.

I followed the electoral battle with great interest. When I arrived as an exile in Miami in 1959, I had found a similar situation, because the following year, 1960, would also be a presidential election year. Kennedy, the current president, was in full campaign mode, fulfilling the promise he'd made four years earlier, when he was denied the vice presidency with the then-candidate of his party, Adlai Stevenson. And Richard Nixon, for his part, had already bagged the Republican nomination, so that what was expected in 1964 was in fact a rematch between Kennedy and Nixon.

I took my first steps into U.S. politics by campaigning for Kennedy in 1960. I joined the *Viva Kennedy* teams that were formed at that time to support the young senator from Massachusetts who, in addition to his brilliant intellect, had an admirable record as a combatant in the U.S. Navy in World War II, where his personal courage had won him a Purple Heart, no less.

Undoubtedly, the political bug that had bitten me when I ran for president of the Pan American Club at Georgia Tech in my undergraduate years had stayed very much alive in my heart.

Looking back now, I realize that my modest participation in the 1960 Democratic campaign in some ways also served as motivation for my later decision to enlist in the fight for Cuba, to go to the camps and be part of Brigade 2506. Kennedy had made Cuba one of his presidential campaign's main issues, as well as the islands of Quemoy and Matsu, which were threatened by Mao Tse-tung's communist China. In both cases, he bluntly accused the Republicans of being weak in the face of the communist enemy and promised that this would change if he were elected president.

Of course, that was music to my ears. Moreover, by the time JFK's reelection campaign began, my friendship with his brother Bobby had grown stronger. I can say that Bobby Kennedy was very genuine and sincere in his interest in Cuba, in his admiration for Brigade 2506, and in his determination not to let Fidel Castro get the last laugh in our confrontation with his dictatorship.

And as for the president's mistakes in relation to Playa Girón, I realized that those mistakes had been the product of inexperience and bad advice, not bad faith. He had to deal with a flawed war effort, conceived and prepared without his participation and launched at the wrong time. To believe otherwise is to believe that a U.S. president knowingly sought military defeat, which is simply inconceivable.

Wrong decisions? Yes, more than one. Bad faith? I don't think so.

So, it's clear that my friendship with Bobby and my participation in JFK's first presidential campaign were important factors in my closeness to and subsequent integration into the Democratic Party as soon as I became a U.S. citizen. But those were not my only reasons. I followed from the outside the ups and downs of local politics in Miami, and I could see the way the local congressmen, Claude Pepper and Dante Fascell, both Democrats, conducted their relations with the Cuban community in Miami at a time when most of us were not American citizens and therefore could not vote for them. They were helpful and tried to pass laws favorable to "those at the bottom," among whom were then most of the Cuban families.

Of course, those were other times, and it was another kind of politics, very different from what we see today. Claude Pepper has been, in my opinion, the politician who, with his laws, most influenced the lives of millions of men and women in this country for the better. He participated in the creation of Social Security and also in the adoption of Medicare. Imagine how we would live today in the United States without these two institutions. During his time as a congressman, there was no initiative benefitting our community that didn't have his support. Dante Fascell had a political trajectory very similar to Pepper's. This, in spite of the fact that at the time, there were Cuban candidates running against them, such as Evelio Estrella and Evaristo Marina. I believe they ran for the sake of running, since it was known that winning against Pepper or Fascell wasn't possible.

So the fact that I channeled my political vocation into the Democratic Party has a lot to do with my friendship with Robert Kennedy and my closeness to Pepper and Fascell. This was also influenced by the fact that the political philosophy then prevailing among the Democrats was very similar to the one that had given shape in Cuba to the 1940 Constitution and had promoted the adoption of the social laws of the governments that emerged from it: Batista in 1940, Grau in 1944 and Prío in 1944.

So much so that, for example, the great Republican president, Ronald Reagan, was a Democrat at the beginning of his political career, and he had previously been a union leader for Hollywood actors.

Of course, at the local level, the Democratic Party made many mistakes in dealing with issues of concern to our community and in promoting Hispanic candidates. The Republicans have been more adept in that regard, and this has resulted in what we've seen over the years, the great exodus of Cuban voters to the Republican Party.

Needless to say, in the course of Cubans' and their descendants' participation in U.S. politics, this wasn't as clear before as it is now. But looking at everything objectively, I don't seem to be very wrong in these assessments.

Returning now to where our story left off, after the events at Playa Girón, while I was active in business and in the patriotic activities of the Brigade, it was in the 1960s that two great tragedies shook this country, abruptly changed the political panorama and, to a great extent, affected Cuba's destiny.

On November 22, 1963, a sniper with distinct Castro-Marxist sympathies named Lee Harvey Oswald assassinated President Kennedy in Dallas, Texas. Then Vice President Lyndon B. Johnson becomes President, and the assassination creates a climate of vulnerability the likes of which hadn't been experienced before in the United States. The assassination has been investigated ad nauseam by the relevant agencies, and the conclusion has been that Oswald acted alone and on his own, despite his ties to the Castro regime and the Soviet Union. However, this conclusion has failed to convince large sectors of the population who believe in the existence of some internal or external assassination plot.

Then, on June 6, 1968, Robert F. Kennedy, then Senator from New York and candidate for the presidential nomination for the Democratic Party, died in Los Angeles, California, victim of an assassination perpetrated by a Christian Palestinian Jordanian refugee named Sirhan Bishara Sirhan. This other political assassination has also been investigated to the point of exhaustion, and investigators concluded that, like Oswald, Sirhan acted on his own, motivated in his case by his hatred of Israel and the support that Senator Kennedy gave that country.

Everything that can be argued about the deaths of these two brothers, important as they are in U.S. history, remains in the realm of speculation. To say that both were in Fidel Castro's sights, among other potential assassins, is neither uncertain nor far-fetched. Proving that Castro had something to do with these crimes is another matter.

However, this reality isn't enough to satisfy all the doubts that exist around these two political assassinations. Certainly, it's striking that Oswald could have fired two shots into President Kennedy's head while he was aboard a moving automobile and Oswald was shooting with an Italian Carcano rifle that cost him $14.00 – in other words, it wasn't a high-powered weapon.

It's also striking that Lee Harvey Oswald had been an active propagandist for Fidel Castro in New Orleans and that, prior to the assassination, he had visited the Cuban embassy in Mexico.

On the other hand, Castro knew that the Kennedys had contemplated the possibility of physically eliminating him. The president never forgot and never recovered from the failure of the Bay of Pigs Invasion, and it's not doubtful that he would have wanted to make the Cuban dictator pay. And the same can be said of his brother Bobby, the attorney general, the senator from New York, the presidential aspirant: anti-Castro always.

Having known Robert Kennedy, I can affirm that his death deprived the cause of Cuban freedom of a true ally, more committed than any other American politician to ending the Castro dictatorship. Had he become president of this country, it is, in my opinion, very likely that by now the history of Cuba would be different and much better.

The Kennedys' deaths affected me very much, above all and for obvious reasons, that of Robert, my friend Bobby. And the moving tributes that the people paid the two Kennedys convinced me of the beauty and satisfaction of dedicating oneself to public service, something that interested me more and more every day.

Chapter 11
New Directions – Florida Politicians

*Do not take life too seriously.
You will never get out of it alive.*
Elbert Hubbard

Between being in Miami, being active in the Brigade, and frequenting places where Miami Cubans usually gathered in the 60s, it was very difficult not to cross paths on some occasions with local leaders and to get to know some of the most prominent politicians at that level. Some of them tried to get closer to our community, some because they sincerely shared our ideals of justice, freedom and democracy, and others out of pure political calculation, foreseeing that, in a relatively short time, many of those Cubans would acquire American citizenship and, with it, the right to vote.

It was in this civic activity that I met Steve Clark, one of the most seasoned politicians I have ever known and, above all, a loyal friend and a great human being. Clark, like his Cuban friends, was not a Miamian by birth; he was a transplant. He was born in Kansas in 1923, and his family moved to Miami when he was a teenager. In 1963, he successfully ran for city commissioner and four years later, in 1967, he was elected mayor of his adopted hometown. In 1970, he became mayor of Metro-Dade, which was what we called then what is now Miami-Dade County. He lost that position in 1972 to Jack Orr, then regained it in 1974 and held it until 1993. He then returned to his original mayorship, the City of Miami, in a close election against a very popular political figure, Commissioner Miriam Alonso. He served as mayor of Miami until his death in 1996.

In addition to a passion for politics and many similarities in the way we saw things, we were united by the fact that, like me, Clark had been in the construction business for many years with his three brothers. It wasn't difficult for me to form a strong and lasting friendship with him.

I also met Dave Kennedy, an astute politician, a good friend and someone who had the virtue of knowing his own limitations. Dave, who wasn't related to the Kennedys of Massachusetts, knew, however, that his last name did him no harm in the world of politics, quite the contrary. He was a native of Baltimore, Maryland, where he was born in 1934, but, like almost all of us who have cavorted on Miami's sands, it didn't take him long to feel as much a South Floridian as any native. In 1961, when the flow of Cubans to Miami was growing rapidly, Kennedy was elected city commissioner, and in 1970 he became mayor. He was a visionary who promoted environmental protection when few were talking about it and, thanks to his initiative, Bicentennial Park was created between Biscayne Boulevard and the bay. It was inaugurated precisely in 1976 during the celebration of the 200th anniversary of the Declaration of Independence of the United States. A man of centrist philosophy, in the 1968 elections he was vice president of the "Democrats for Nixon" group, since his party's candidate, Hubert Humphrey, was too far to the left for his taste.

In 1973, Dave Kennedy, then mayor of Miami, was formally accused of participating in a bribery conspiracy and was suspended as mayor by then governor Reubin Askew. However, four or five months later, he was reinstated when the charges against him were dismissed by a Sarasota County judge. Although his name was cleared and he had a good chance of being reelected, Kennedy, however, decided not to run. No longer an elected official, he became a political force in his own right, someone whose support candidates in our area jockeyed for.

Clark was liked by everyone who met him. He was very pleasant, and always, from the beginning of our presence in these parts, was sympathetic to Hispanics, especially Cubans, although, in reality, he didn't give much importance to appointing Hispanics to prominent positions in both the City of Miami and Dade County. Dave Kennedy was better than Steve Clark in that regard. Steve was a very nice, friendly person, always willing to do a favor for anyone who needed it. My relationship with him was always very good. We traveled together for many years, and I enjoyed his friendship very much.

Dave Kennedy, for anyone who didn't know him well, was more serious than Steve. Steve joked a lot and was always laughing. Dave Kennedy appeared to be more serious than Steve Clark, but, in private, he wasn't. He was friendly, a womanizer... but he only showed that part of himself when he got close to someone. Kennedy had bigger political ambitions than Clark, legitimate ambitions that he could never fulfill, but, with them in mind, he gave greater importance to appointing Hispanics to key positions. And so he did appoint Hispanics, Cubans above all, to positions on the different city boards, and among those Cubans was me, which I'll tell you about later.

But it wasn't only me. Kennedy appointed many other Cuban Americans to different boards. He was looking for the most qualified, but his appointments were also influenced, as I said, by his plans for his own political future. He, apparently, was thinking of one day running for governor.

As I write this, I have fond memories of my experiences with Mayor Clark, with whom I traveled several times on official missions. On one occasion, in the early 1970s, we traveled to San Diego, California, where the U.S. Conference of Mayors was being held. Maurice Ferré was then the mayor of Miami, but he was unable to attend the conference due to complications with his schedule and, as I was the vice mayor, he appointed me to represent our city there. Clark was going as mayor of the County, and we were accompanied by Chuck Hall, then-mayor of the City of Miami Beach.

There were three days of mayoral meetings, and one of the nights we decided to go to Tijuana. Other mayors joined us, and, in the end, we were four or five mayors in a limousine. We crossed the border without problems, the traffic was light, and we were in Tijuana, drinking, until about two or three in the morning, when we decided to return.... But, to our surprise, at that time of the morning, the line of cars going to the United States, to California, was more than a mile long. They were probably people who lived in Mexico but worked in the United States and had to be at their jobs first thing in the morning.

We had conference activities in the morning and needed to get some sleep and a shower to be in good condition, so we decided to go through a special lane reserved for the highway patrol. When we were near the checkpoint before entering California, a patrolman made us stop. The officer was well over six-and-a-half feet tall and stood in the middle of the road and there, in the semi-darkness of the early morning, he looked even taller. I thought to myself, "with what we've had to drink, let's see how we get around this situation, because it could end very unfavorably for us."

Chuck Hall, who, along with Clark, was one of those who had had the most to drink, said, "Let me handle this situation," and without giving us time to do anything, he got out of the car and started up to the officer with great determination and asked him, "Do you know who I am?"

And that patrolman, in the middle of the road between Mexico and the United States, in the middle of the night, answered him very softly: "Yes, I know, you are Chuck Hall, the mayor of Miami Beach."

We all gasped at the unexpected response. It turned out that the patrolman had been stationed in Dade County, had patrolled Miami Beach for some time, and had recognized the mayor. Sure enough, he let us go, escorted us to the checkpoint, and we passed through without difficulty.

On another occasion, Steve Clark and I were invited to Mexico. The plan was to visit Cancun, since a tourism development plan was to be launched for this beautiful resort on the Yucatan Peninsula. Miguel Alemán Valdés, who had been president of the country from 1946 to 1952 and since 1961 had been in charge of the Commission for National Tourism, was putting all his efforts and influence into this project.

Alemán himself was our guide in the then-rustic spot; he took us all over the place and explained his development plans. I remember that he put great emphasis on stressing that the same mistakes he said had been made in Acapulco, where, he said, "there's not even housing for hotel employees," were not going to be made there.

We went to Tulum and Chitchen Itza, but when we got there, Clark was attacked by "Moctezuma's revenge," the stomach ailment that afflicts many first-time tourists in Mexico. Steve spent the next two or three days unable to leave the hotel, as he had to go to the bathroom constantly. I filled in for him at all the public events we had during those days.

The farewell event on the last day of that visit was in Merida, Yucatan. The Mexican government had hired the National Folkloric Ensemble and a famous mariachi band. Steve said he felt completely well and insisted on giving the farewell speech himself.

And so, he did. I served as his translator, and he began by saying that he had enjoyed Mexico very much, because he had been "in Tulum, in Cancun and in the bathroom." Of course, it was not easy for me to translate that in front of the Mexican officials, but, fortunately, most of the people present there understood very well what I was saying and laughed a lot. And such were Steve Clark's witticisms, which we didn't always get away with.

Like the time we were invited to Spain and while in Jerez de la Frontera, were taken to the Domecq family winery, where we were offered a tasting of their best wines. Steve asked them if they didn't have a bourbon, or a rum... That hit our hosts like a bucket of ice water, asking for a rum in the heart of the region known to produce the best Spanish wines! I didn't know where to hide myself, although inwardly I laughed at that monumental blunder, made in ignorance and frankness, but with no bad intentions.

Those trips of ours irritated our political adversaries and the *Miami Herald* most of all, despite the fact that, most of the time, the trips were invitations we received – that's to say, no official funds were used for them. Only if the trip was due a specific interest of the city's, if it was official business, was taxpayers' money used. I was always very scrupulous in separating the official from the private, because I believed that this was the way it should be and because I wanted to avoid problems.

That, however, didn't placate the *Miami Herald*'s animosity. With Clark, there came a time when he wouldn't give interviews to the *Herald*, which accused him of giving preferential treatment to his brother in government construction contracts. Clark was a friend to his friends and if he could favor them, he did so without seeking any compensation for himself.

Dave Kennedy was treated very well by the *Herald* at first, because the newspaper was interested in favoring the county government, and Kennedy had already given some important business, such as the port and the airport, to the county. But, when Kennedy was singled out for those corruption charges, they turned their backs on him and criticized him heavily, before he was exonerated in the subsequent trial.

Now, of all those politicians with whom I had close dealings, the most admirable of all was Governor Reubin Askew.

Florida Governor Reubin Askew (1970-1978)

Askew was a truly virtuous man and at the same time, humble. He was very religious, but he wasn't self-righteous, and in spite of his high political position he communicated very well with everyone. This was because he was a man of humble extraction and understood very well the day-to-day difficulties faced by families who depend on a poor salary.

He was born in Oklahoma in 1928, the youngest of six children. His parents divorced when he was very young and his father was largely absent from his life, due to what Askew himself described as "a serious drinking problem," which probably had a lot to do with his own rejection of alcohol. Askew was a teetotaler and didn't smoke. As a child, he worked as a shoeshine boy and sold his mother's candy door-to-door to earn a little extra to help them survive, since what she earned from sewing and waitressing was barely enough to feed the family.

When he was nine years old, his mother decided to move to Pensacola, in the Florida panhandle. With much sacrifice he was able to enroll in Florida State University and years later completed his studies at the University of Florida (UF) Law School.

Askew also served the country as a paratrooper during the Korean War and as an intelligence officer. When I met him as a senator from Florida, he enjoyed a solid reputation, especially for his honesty, and was considered one of the best senators in the state by friends and foes alike.

I remember that when former New York Mayor John Lindsey was toying with the idea of becoming president, he was in Tallahassee as part of tour exploring his chances. Knowing that Askew's only sport was tennis, he brought him a racquet as a gift and handed it to him in the middle of a press conference. Askew, in front of everyone, said, "Mayor, I'm sorry, but I have to ask you the price, because if it's worth more than $25, I have to report the gift." This he said very naturally, without any affectation, for everyone there knew that any gift valued at more than $25 that he received, he would donate it to the capitol, so that it would remain state property.

Many were pointing to him as future president. I was at the 1976 Democratic Party Convention, which was held at Madison Square Gardens in New York, and I remember very well that prominent national figures tried to convince Askew to run for the presidential nomination, but he refused on the grounds that a presidential campaign would require raising a lot of money, and he rejected that process. That ended with the nomination of Jimmy Carter, former governor of Georgia, as the Democratic nominee. Askew was one of the few Florida governors to be reelected. He finished his term in 1979, and his political career ended there.

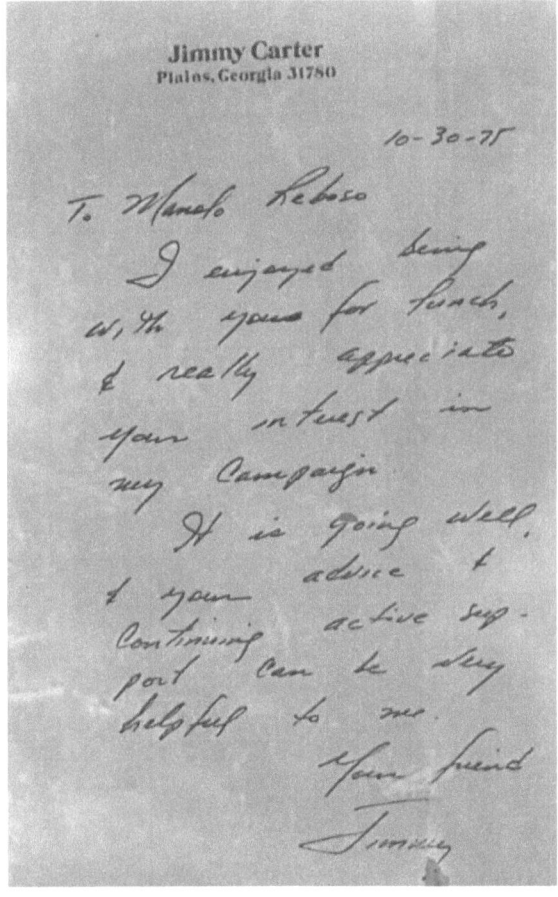

Personal letter from former Georgia Gov. Jimmy Carter, October 1975.

Steve Clark, David Kenney and Reubin Askew were the three politicians who had the most significant influence on my decision to enter the beautiful and rewarding world of public service. Not only did they help me take my first steps as an elected official, but they were also examples for me to follow because of each one's performance, which weren't free from mistakes, because they were human and all humans make mistakes. But I never saw in them vile intentions or selfish attitudes, and I witnessed many occasions in which they had to sacrifice their personal interests for the benefit of the community.

Other politicians I should mention are Dante Fascell and Claude Pepper, whom I have already referred to above, and Bob Graham, former governor of Florida and former U.S. senator.

Graham is a man of great personality and a tremendous human being. He is one of the state politicians who helped the Cubans a lot and valued them very much, as was Pepe Villalobos's case. I know how much Villalobos influenced Graham to appoint Cuban Americans to different state boards and to enact laws that helped Cuban exiles. It's a pity that Graham didn't become president of the United States, because he is a very honest man who dedicated himself to politics only as a means to improve the lives of others.

Although I wasn't as close to Graham, Pepper and Fascell as I was to Askew, Clark and Kennedy, those three were also good friends whom I remember with gratitude, and men whose time in politics inspired me.

Let me now return to the 1970s....

Chapter 12
The First Cuban in State Government

> *Men are four:*
> *He who knows not, and knows not he knows not. He is a fool; shun him.*
> *He who knows not, and knows he knows not. He is simple; teach him.*
> *He who knows, and knows not he knows. He is asleep; wake him.*
> *He who knows, and knows he knows. He is wise; follow him.*
>
> Popular wisdom

In 1970, City of Miami Mayor Dave Kennedy appointed me as a member of the city's Planning and Zoning Board. It was the first time that a Cuban had been appointed to this important urban body, and I was honored to be chosen to join this auxiliary government group, which until then had been a white stronghold despite the growing ethnic diversification Miami was already experiencing then.

I would say that this appointment marked my entry into the world of local politics, to which I had been paying more attention and interest every day, precisely because of my friendship with Steve Clark and Mayor Kennedy himself. In a short time, I was able to learn the workings of the Board, and I took a liking to that position. It allowed me to observe how the city was run, gave me a seat where the commissioners sat, and broadened my political contacts. It was at that time that Dave Kennedy introduced me to Reubin Askew, then a state senator from the Pensacola area.

Precisely in that year, 1970, the political environment in Florida was in a vibrant phase. Claude Kirk was governor, the first Republican in that office since Reconstruction. In November of that year there would be an election, and Kirk was running for reelection. His reelection campaign was based almost exclusively on his opposition to racial desegregation, part of his reactionary attempts to keep Florida as a bastion of the old South.

Askew, a Democrat at heart rather than a partisan one, decided to take him on. But it wasn't easy. Three other Democratic politicians, state Attorney General Earl Faircloth, state Senate President Jack Mathews, and then Dade County Mayor Chuck Hall, were vying for the party's nomination to challenge Kirk in the November election, and some polls and analysts indicated that Askew had the least support, because, although everyone admired him for his personal qualities, his own decency was seen as something that didn't help him much against an aggressive and unethical candidate like Claude Kirk.

Dave Kennedy was Askew's campaign manager here in the southern part of the state, and after talking with Askew himself on two or three occasions, he asked me to take charge of his Hispanic campaign. I accepted the assignment with great enthusiasm, was appointed Hispanic Chairman in the state and gave myself body and soul to that mission.

This direct participation in an electoral campaign was for me like school, not only of electoral politics, but also of various aspects of the Americans' way of thinking, of their way of seeing things. I came to understand that many of the mistakes that have traditionally been made by the governors and diplomats in Washington in outlining their policies for Latin America have more to do with their stereotypes and their misinformation about the peoples of the continent than with any presumption of superiority or arrogance towards them.

Some of the people with major responsibilities in the Askew campaign, for example, were very much struck by the fact that, before visiting certain cities in the state, where we were supposed to have events and meetings with voters and some of the people of influence in that particular area, I would try to find out where the Hispanics were from, where they worked, and what percentage of them were registered to vote.

One of those staff members once asked me, I think it was when a campaign visit to the Orlando area was being coordinated, why I was sweating those details so much when what was customary in almost every campaign was to repeat the same speech, with slight variations, in the different cities that were visited. I tried to explain to him that it wasn't the same to speak to Cubans as to Mexicans or Puerto Ricans, since they were people who, although they had many similarities, also had great cultural and historical differences.

The man, a young businessman, told me that it couldn't be that different, that it was the same to talk to gringos (so he told me) from Miami as to those from Jacksonville, and that there couldn't be much difference in that aspect with Hispanics.

I tried to explain to him that "Hispanics," as the American mainstream perceives them, that uniform mass of more or less dark-skinned people who speak Spanish, don't really exist. The man was very surprised by what I was saying, and I had to give him as an example the differences between a typical Argentinean and a typical Guatemalan so that he would understand a little.

I also explained to him that, although we all speak Spanish, each people has its own idioms and its own accents and that, in many matters of national and international politics, what is of great interest to Colombians, for example, is of little importance to Dominicans.

I don't know if that American came out of that conversation with me more confused than when we started talking, but I hope that wasn't the case. What is truly sad and worrisome is that I've encountered these misperceptions about Hispanics in the United States on different occasions and in different circumstances throughout my political career.

At the time this wasn't a big problem for me, because I had full freedom of action in running Askew's Hispanic campaign, but it's something that still worries me, because I believe that misperceptions of that nature make relations between U.S. Hispanics and their governments very difficult, as well as Washington's relations with Latin American peoples and governments.

It took a lot of hard work, but Reubin Askew won the Democratic nomination for the Florida governorship in an intra-party runoff against Earl Faircloth. Now it was time to do everything possible to defeat the Republican incumbent and return reason and justice to Tallahassee.

For my part, I was very enthusiastic. I believed in what I was doing in trying to convince Hispanic voters to elect Askew and even though it was my first purely political experience in the United States, and the work was intense, it was actually easy for me.

It was easy for me because I had to defend a good, religious, honest and open-minded man against a recalcitrant racist whose views about Hispanics were no different from what he expressed and implied about African Americans, which was neither good nor fair.

In his attacks against Askew, Kirk called him "a mama's boy who doesn't have the courage to stand up to legislators...a very sweet guy chosen by liberals...to serve as their front man," lies that it's sad to see are still used today by politicians who try to cover up their lack of rationale by disparaging their opponents.

I traveled with Askew to different parts of the state for campaign events and meetings, speaking in Spanish to Hispanics in Tampa, Jacksonville, etc., and pointing out the stark differences, especially in each candidate's human qualities.

Askew won the governorship by a margin of 14 percentage points over Claude Kirk and needless to say, there was rejoicing among all of us who had helped in his campaign. For me personally, his victory gave me great satisfaction and led me to the conviction that politics properly understood, public service, was my true vocation, since I had enjoyed every minute of that campaign.

Additionally, that electoral effort greatly strengthened my conviction in democratic ideals and the power of truth. On occasions like that I couldn't help but hear an inner voice telling me, "this is what I want for Cuba."

Reubin Askew's victory was in November 1970. He took office in January 1971 and immediately began restructuring the state government.

All the governors back then had - I don't know if this still exists - what they called a patronage committee made up of people they trusted throughout the state. Whenever there was a vacancy in government, that committee would send the governor a list of three names from which he could select the right person to fill the position.

Askew didn't like the name "patronage committee" and changed it to "advisory committee." He also reduced the number of members from 50 to 25. He appointed me as a member of that committee, thus becoming the first Cuban in the history of Florida to occupy such a position.

It so happened that, almost immediately after Askew's inauguration, there was a vacancy on the Dade County School Board. I recommended Alfredo González Durán to fill that vacancy. There were two other people who had been recommended, but I, seeing the dilemma this put the governor in, went ahead and spoke personally with him. I made him see the importance of, for the first time, a Hispanic having a seat on the school board in a county with a substantial number of Hispanic students, and it didn't take much effort to convince him. Askew appointed Alfredo.

Unfortunately, when Alfredo's interim seat went up for election, he lost the position. Remember that the Hispanic vote in South Florida was not yet a strong enough bloc to decide races.

At the same time, Askew began to replace officials in different positions and, in May 1971, without my expecting it, he asked me to oversee the International Bureau in the Florida Department of Commerce, the state agency in charge of trade and tourism with Latin America. I accepted the offer, although I wasn't quite sure what the position entailed. However, it seemed to me that the fact that a Cuban-American exile was nominated for such a position was an opportunity that shouldn't be missed. This was something really important to me.

I spent a week in Tallahassee, trying to familiarize myself with everything related to my new position. I was given a place in the Port of Miami to set up my office and there I began this new phase of my life.

The place was very small, and its location wasn't suitable for the plans I had in mind. I had two employees whom I had never met before, and the reality is that I wasn't very optimistic about what could be achieved in those conditions.

I was determined to do a good job, not only for my personal prestige, but also because I knew that, inevitably, my performance in the position would be used as an example and measure of Hispanics' capacity to occupy important positions at the state level, since I was the first Cuban to occupy a position representing the state government before governments and companies of other countries.

As it was, I left for Tallahassee shortly after taking charge of the Bureau, but already better steeped in the workings and possibilities of that position. I spoke with Askew and told him that I considered that the best place from which to run the Bureau was Coral Gables, since most of the companies involved in trade with our southern neighbors were based there and many of the consulates of the countries of the region were also there.

Askew immediately understood the logic of what I was asking and told me to proceed, to find a location and to increase the payroll to 10 employees. I found a location at 301 Almeria Ave. and rented the entire third floor of that building across from the Mercedes Benz dealership in Coral Gables and hired the 10 employees.

One of them was Otto Reich, who a few years later would be the U.S. ambassador to Venezuela and would also be assistant secretary of state for Latin America. Otto was there with me for a year or so, and some time later he went to the City of Miami and from there to Washington, where he got a position in the Council of the Americas.

The first thing I did as head of the International Bureau was to establish contacts with the diplomats, that is, with the consuls who were stationed in Miami, most of whom, as I said before, lived and had their offices in Coral Gables. I organized a luncheon with the consuls that was a tremendous success and from that moment on, the trips to Latin America began, trips in which I always included some commerce and banking professionals who were looking to make their own contacts in different parts of the continent, both for tourism and trade.

For example, I always tried to include in those trips people like Luis Sabines, the president of the Latin American Chamber of Commerce, CAMACOL, and businessman Manolo Arqués. I also brought business owners who were just starting out here but were already important in their own right, to establish links with those countries and start bringing merchandise from them. One of my main objectives was to attract capital and Latin American investors, here, a task that turned out to be very prolific and opportune for our state.

In the meantime, I was still on the lookout for positions that were opening up where it was possible to appoint Hispanics well prepared for them, and I was fortunate that Askew understood the need for his government officials to be truly representative of the communities they served.

And not only that: wherever there was an opportunity to help our community's progress, Reubin Askew responded favorably to the requests made to him. For example, I brought to him, in Tallahassee, the leaders of the Federación de Profesionales Cubanos del Exilio (Federation of Cuban Professionals in Exile), presided over by an excellent person, Dr. Cristobal González Mayo. The organization included doctors, lawyers, pharmacists, architects, veterinarians like Gonzalez Mayo himself, etc., who had come together to fight for reforms that would allow them to legally practice their professions in the state of Florida.

On this occasion, they advocated that they be allowed to take the exams for the revalidation of their degrees in Spanish, which was strongly resisted by the different professional boards in the state, none of which included a Hispanic.

It's only fair to mention that another prominent Cuban professional, Dr. Rafael Peñalver, Sr., was working very hard on this issue. Well, the governor agreed, in spite of the fact that some people told him that this would not favor him electorally, because those who opposed it were voters from different parts of the state and Cubans, in their great majority, couldn't vote because they were not yet American citizens. Those who advised him in this way were forgetting that Reubin Askew was a man who, when deciding something, looked for where justice was and not where the votes were.

When Askew served his two terms as governor, voters elected Bob Graham to succeed him, solidifying what some observers of politics have called "the golden age" of our state's status. With Askew, civil rights were established in Florida, and the aspirations of some to make this part of the nation a fortress for the worst of the old spirit of the Confederacy collapsed. And with Graham, the state opened itself to modernity within a framework of decency and civility through which we celebrated the exercise of politics.

As for Hispanics, the policy of inclusion begun by Askew was consolidated by Graham. These are two names without which the history of Hispanics', particularly Cubans', integration into Florida's political process cannot be written.

Chapter 13
From Florida to Latin America

*Success is easy to obtain,
what is difficult is to deserve it*
Albert Camus

I was very fortunate in Governor Askew's decision to appoint me as Chief of the Department of Commerce's International Bureau, because, among other factors, I was being given a blank slate to work with, where there was much to be done. I soon realized that I would have no time to be bored in my new position.

As Chief of the International Bureau of Florida's Department of Commerce.

When I took over the Bureau, the State of Florida conducted its international affairs through various departments, agencies, etc. independent of each other, and without much coordination among them. There was no well-defined policy to follow, no procedural protocols. Moreover, some areas of immediate or potential importance were not being adequately addressed, due to a severe lack of leadership in that area.

The importance of international affairs to Florida, a state surrounded by the sea on three sides, with 14 deep-water ports and five international airports bringing business and tourism from around the world, obvious as all that is, was not being given the attention it deserved.

Despite this state's growing role in the international arena, there had been no official policy or even a defined approach to international affairs. This had logically led to duplication of efforts in many cases and an inevitable weakening of the state's presence in the region. For example, the development of international tourism, a fundamental factor for the state economy, had been relegated to a neglected sector within the Department of Commerce's Tourism Division. The development of international trade, which is and has been a major factor in both the nation's and state's economies, had been diluted within the Office of the International Coordinator, within the Bureau of International Development, within the Department of Commerce's Economic Development Division.

Other important issues, such as coordination with different international agencies and organizations; coordination of our part of disaster relief activities, activities originating here in Florida; relations with the consular corps; the development of an important visitors program, as a complement to the federal government office in our area, had received little or no attention from the state.

Therefore, I made it a top priority for the International Bureau to focus on several activities, such as: tourism and cultural affairs; contact with consuls, as well as with universities and international public and private organizations; international finance, trade and commerce; everything related to transportation to and from the ports and airports; and publicity and media relations.

The International Bureau was responsible for several other matters, to which I proposed giving a more visible dynamic, all in order to make them work more effectively. This could only be achieved by promoting and supporting closer and better-coordinated relations between the state and the private sector in everything related to international trade and commerce, including foreign investment facilities and increasing the promotion of international tourism to Florida.

However, in order for this to be done as effectively as possible, it was necessary that all levels of government be well informed so that our projects would find sufficient support and interest. One of our priority tasks would therefore be to advise the governor, the legislature and the agencies related to our areas of interest in order to establish a well-defined state policy aimed at stimulating, together with the federal Department of Commerce, everything related to international trade. In all of this, it was also necessary to support all non-profit organizations dedicated to increasing trade.

It was also necessary to actively help international missions and exhibitions that also sought to boost trade between Florida and other parts of the world. And equally important, we had to make ourselves known, to make our state, its beauty and its business opportunities known, on a personal level, face to face, with Central and South American government officials, politicians and private enterprises. These, because of their geographic proximity and prior knowledge, would be the focus of our efforts for the level of exchange we wanted to establish.

As can be easily seen, I had no small task ahead of me as the new head of the Florida Department of Commerce's International Bureau. I concentrated on my work, determined to do a good job, not only out of professional pride, but also because I didn't forget that I was the first Hispanic, the first Cuban, to head an important sector of state government and that what I did would have an impact on the judgments that could be made about our community.

So, I rolled up my sleeves, and with an excellent team that I put together, we developed a work plan that produced the fruitful benefits that we had hoped to obtain.

We carried out promotional trips to Colombia and Venezuela and once there, we held seminars for local businessmen interested in doing business here. We also took trade missions to Central America, where we did very well.

I particularly remember a trade mission to Manaus, Brazil, in which we were accompanied by 23 businessmen from our state and achieved sales of more than $600,000.

I also remember a trade mission to Mexico, Guatemala, Colombia and Venezuela that was very successful and which the manufacturers who accompanied us liked very much.

I also remember a trade mission to the Dominican Republic and Haiti that generated more than $3 million in sales in its first year. And something truly spectacular was the COTAL (Confederation of Latin American Tourism Organizations) conference held in Panama in May 1972, which brought together around 3,000 travel agents from all over the continent, from Mexico to Argentina and Chile, and became an incomparable source of contacts for the best performance of our activities.

Another activity that proved to be very successful was the familiarization tours to Florida, to which we invited, among others, travel agents from all over the continent, with whom we toured the main tourist attractions in our state.

In all these activities we tried to involve large companies already established in trade to and from Florida. We sought, above all, the participation of airlines such as Braniff and Avianca, which were well known and covered, between them, almost the entire continent. Likewise, we didn't undertake any mission if we weren't accompanied by a good number of merchants and businessmen from the state, since they were our most efficient promoters.

I believe that the Bureau was able to establish action strategies and a workflow that proved to be effective over time.

This is easily demonstrated by mentioning a few of the many countries I visited in the course of my duties. With Governor Askew, I traveled on a trade mission to Colombia and Venezuela. With Vice Governor Tom Adams, I traveled twice to Colombia. I traveled with different trade missions throughout the southeast of Mexico, visiting on different occasions the states of Yucatan, Campeche, Tabasco, Guerrero, Quintana Roo, as well as Mexico City, the capital of our great neighbor to the south. I believe I've already mentioned the visit that, together with Steve Clark, and at the invitation of former Mexican President Miguel Alemán, we visited Guerrero to see what was then the Cancun development project.

The Dominican Republic was another country with which we strengthened our relationship and increased our trade. On two occasions we were in Santo Domingo at the invitation of the mayor, Guarionex Lluberes, and on both visits, we were received by the then president of the country, Dr. Joaquín Balaguer.

Bicentennial Friendship trip in 1975 to Venezuela and Colombia with Governor Askew.

They say that the only thing that's permanent in life is change and, as I've already said, when I was appointed interim commissioner of the City of Miami in July 1972, I was forced to resign from the International Bureau.

However, the person I recommended to replace me in that position and who was immediately appointed by Governor Askew, my dear friend Julito González Rebull, now deceased, did an excellent job of continuity and cemented the work I had begun into one of the strongest foundations for Florida's commercial and tourism industry's growth.

Let's remember what this beautiful state was in those days and see what it is today. It seems to me that the enrichment, in every sense, of what Florida can offer today to visitors and businessmen from all over the world would not have been possible without the intense work of those days.

Chapter 14
The First Cuban Commissioner

> *The pessimist sees difficulty in every opportunity.*
> *The optimist sees opportunity in every difficulty.*
> Winston Churchill

The successful election campaign that led to Reubin Askew becoming governor of Florida, and the fact that I had helped in that victory, which in the beginning many saw as impossible, greatly increased my interest in local issues, local politics and electoral matters. How were polls conducted? What was the strategy for getting campaign donations? What were the positions from which once could help solve community problems?

I had made good friends with people directly involved in the Clark, (Dave) Kennedy and Askew campaigns. I asked questions and tried to learn, and that interest of mine didn't go unnoticed by activists and officials, some of whom asked me to consider the possibility that, when the time came, I might run for elected office in the city or county.

But the truth is that I was very happy with my work in the Florida Department of Commerce's International Bureau. I had been able to bring different groups of businessmen from our area closer to their colleagues in various countries of the neighboring continent. I had excellent relationships with the consuls stationed in Greater Miami and, through them, with their respective governments. Trade between South Florida and Mexico, Central America, the Caribbean and South America had increased to everyone's benefit. And the governor was very satisfied with my work; even the press was praising us.

Besides, I proved something that I had always believed and practiced: the person who's interested in serving others doesn't need to have an official position to do so. For example, 1971 was the 10th anniversary of the Bay of Pigs Invasion and many Cubans, especially the *brigadistas*, thought that this occasion should not go unnoticed. Thus, the board of the Bay of Pigs Veterans Association agreed to build a monument to honor the memory of the fallen at Playa Girón, and so it was that the beautiful marble-covered column was erected where the Cuban Memorial Boulevard begins (SW 8th Street and 13th Avenue, Miami).

Miami - Little Havana: Cuban Memorial Plaza - Bay of Pigs Monument

The Bay of Pigs Monument, also known as the 2506th Brigade Memorial or Giron Monument, designed by Manolo Reboso and sculpted by Tony Lopez, was dedicated along Cuban Memorial Boulevard at the intersection of SW 13th Avenue and SW 8th Street in April 1972. The monument pays tribute to the efforts of 2506th Brigade, which made an unsuccessful effort in April 1961 to overthrow Fidel Castro's regime in Cuba. Reboso was a veteran of the Bay of Pigs invasion.

The memorial consists of a 12-foot-tall hexagonal column covered with gray marble tile and topped with an urn containing a perpetual flame. On the front of the column is a plaque depicting the 2506th Brigade's coat of arms, a Cuban flag wrapped around a cross. On each side of the column are commemorative inscription plaques. At the foot of the column is a small hexagonal base that rests on a larger hexagonal base which is ringed with a iron chain. The chain is threaded around six artillery shells mounted one at each corner of the larger hexagonal base.

I designed the hexagonal column, and the great Cuban sculptor, the late Tony Lopez, put all his artistic skills into the piece. At the top of the column is an eternal flame that burns in memory of the operation's martyrs. On the front, in bronze, is the Brigade's shield, and on each of the sides of the hexagon there are commemorative plaques. At the base, around the column, the hulls of six artillery rockets are linked by a chain that surrounds the whole monument.

I felt a great satisfaction in participating not only in the project, but also, through my construction company, in laying the monument's foundation. Carlos M. Couto was the master builder. Commissioner Rose Gordon secured Florida Power and Light's support for the torch's installation and maintenance.

The monument was unveiled on April 17, 1971. The unveiling and the lighting of the torch was very solemn, with a large audience, with Mayor Kennedy and Senator Lawton Chiles in attendance. President Nixon joined in the tribute by sending a message. That experience also served as an incentive for me: if as a simple citizen I could help in works that benefitted the community, how much more could I do if I could count on the resources of local power?

So it happened that in mid-1972, Irving Christie was appointed judge and had to resign from his post as City of Miami commissioner. He does so, and Mayor Kennedy tells me that he is going to propose that I be appointed to replace him. I see it as a great opportunity. Through my many contacts in the community, I was very aware that Hispanics, and Cubans specifically, were affected by the problems, but we were not part of the solutions. That one of us, me in this case, could be where the decisions were made, was tantamount to having a voice and a vote in the search for solutions.

The great responsibility that came with being the first Cuban-American commissioner in Miami didn't escape me. I knew I'd have many eyes scrutinizing my work and not all of them were well-intentioned. But that responsibility didn't intimidate me, because, without smugness or false modesty, I was confident in myself, and I thought that if I was doing well in the International Bureau, why shouldn't I do well in the Miami Commission as well?

Now, even though Mayor Dave Kennedy had my back, the commissioners had to vote, and not all of them supported me in the first place. The Miami commissioners at that time were, in addition to the outgoing Irving Christie, Reverend Theodore Gibson, a patriarchal figure in the African-American community; Mrs. Rose Gordon, a successful real estate entrepreneur; and funeral director Joseph Lionel Plummer, Jr., who was referred to throughout Miami as "J.L."

Well, J.L. wanted to nominate my friend Alfredo Durán for the seat being vacated by Irving Christie. Alfredo, I shared earlier, had been appointed by Governor Askew, at my urging, to fill a vacancy on the School Board, but, when that position went up for election, Alfredo lost and could not continue there. Alfredo and I are like brothers, and he—I don't know if in deference to me — showed no interest in being a commissioner. I was interested, and Mayor Kennedy was the one who suggested me for the position. Reverend Gibson endorsed me from the first moment and Rose Gordon joined us later.

The idea of Alfredo being commissioner never really took shape because of his own refusal to be considered, but there was a group that proposed Demetrio Pérez Jr., and I don't remember if there was another name in the mix. The fact was that Plummer apparently felt pressured and didn't want to have to decide, and he escaped that situation by going to the hospital to avoid having to vote, a maneuver he used more than once when the Commission had some tricky issue on its hands.

So it was that on July 6, 1972, I was appointed to fill Irving Christie's term, which would expire in November 1973. This gave me a little more than a year to familiarize myself with all aspects of my new position and, in practice, to see if I really liked the position and if it was worth serving in it.

Being sworn into office in July 1972 as the first Cuban-American commissioner of the City of Miami.

I realized that the first thing I had to do to perform well as a Miami commissioner was to learn: to learn what I could do based on the position's responsibilities; to learn how to do it in the best possible way; and to learn what the limitations were, what I shouldn't do.

In that initial learning period, the help I received from then city manager Melvin Reese, who spontaneously and generously became something like my city government coach, was vital. I vividly remember his wise advice, the first of which was: "You will never regret anything you didn't say. Try to speak little and do your homework. Always come ready to vote, analyze all the points and the less you talk, the better, especially now, at the beginning."

So that's what I did. I followed his advice and was very much guided by him. Whenever I had a question, I called Melvin Reese.

Dave Kennedy was also very helpful to me, even though we disagreed on two or three issues. Kennedy was of the philosophy that it was best to relieve the city government of many of its obligations. The city had already ceded the port and airport to the county, and among Kennedy's plans was to give the city parks to the county, for which he already had the three Commission votes he needed, including Irving Christie's. But when Christie resigned and I took his place, that plan fell through for the mayor, for I was not in favor of that idea. Nothing more was given to the county and Kennedy willingly accepted it.

As soon as I became a member of the Miami Commission, I made it my business to go around the different neighborhoods to learn about their needs. At the same time, I made a great effort to meet and establish contacts with those people who I saw as having the greatest interest in their respective communities and who had some influence on their neighbors.

There was a common problem throughout the city at that time, and that was the lack of representation that we Cubans, Hispanics in general and African Americans had in the organizations that held power in Miami. White people controlled all aspects of life in South Florida, and, in general terms, they were very reluctant to share any portion of their power with us, as many saw us as intruders who came to displace them.

For example, the shortage of affordable housing for low-income residents, as were almost all those arriving from Cuba, was very difficult to solve or even alleviate, and one of the main causes of the problem was that many landlords didn't want to rent their houses or apartments to Cubans, because, generally, they were large families and, in addition, many times, two families agreed to live in the same house and share the expenses.

I never missed an opportunity to suggest qualified Cubans whenever a vacancy arose in any city agency, but I tried to do it very discreetly so as not to alarm the white establishment. I tried to be very cordial with them and this I did sincerely, trying to stop them from seeing us as invaders who came to seize their territory.

The Cubans who were here since the early days of Castro's tyranny in Cuba and those who subsequently arrived – what today we call the historical exile – had a very unique problem: almost all of us were convinced that our stay in the United States was temporary and that, soon, we could return to a free Cuba to resume our normal lives there. This way of thinking was, in my opinion, praiseworthy, because it clearly showed the Cubans' love for their homeland. But as I said before, it was, at the same time, a very unique problem, because it obstructed to a great extent our integration into the place where we lived.

A large number of exiles were not interested in becoming U.S. citizens, nor did they want to put down roots here, or even buy a house, much less interfere in local affairs, because "what for, if we will be back in Cuba by Christmas Eve?"

Contrary to what sociologists prophesied every time they did a study on Cubans in Miami, this way of thinking was maintained for many years, I would say until the late 70's or early 80's, when various factors – the needs of daily life, children's access to universities, the requirements for well-paying jobs and the evident need for political participation, precisely because of Cuba's situation – made it very clear to everyone that one could be a good Cuban and a good American citizen at the same time, without any contradiction.

But that came later. The truth is that when I joined the Miami Commission, it wasn't easy to advance our priorities, because the Cuban vote was not yet a major electoral force. The small gains that were achieved then for our people's benefit were due more to the influence of a few wealthy Cubans who contributed to some local politicians' campaign funds and made their weight felt in favor of one or another proposal beneficial to our people.

In addition to all of the above, don't forget that, even though I was appointed on an interim basis, I was the first Cuban in the Miami Commission, and this provoked a very severe scrutiny of my performance, especially by agencies and persons who had traditionally dominated, and still dominated, the political scene.

I didn't resign from my position with the Florida Department of Commerce's International Bureau immediately after being installed as a commissioner. I simply felt that I could hold both positions since I saw no conflict of interest and, in fact, none of the other commissioners had had to leave their respective jobs upon being elected, since employment with the City of Miami was considered a part-time job, with a ridiculous salary of $5,000 per year.

But the fact was that the editorial writers of the *Miami Herald* wasted no time in giving that situation a scandalous tinge and asked that I resign from one of the two positions since, according to them, no one should be employed by both the state and the city at the same time.

I realized that, beyond the legal aspect of their argument, the *Herald*'s hysteria could create a negative image for me among those thousands of people who only read the headlines. As soon as I could, I went to Tallahassee and resigned to the governor, who had very generous words for me. At the same time, as I mentioned earlier, I asked him to appoint Julito González Rebull to the position I was leaving, and he did so. I was sure that Julito would continue the good work in that department, and I wasn't mistaken.

The year 1973 began, which was to be a year of important changes in my life, both personally and politically. Previously, my marriage to Irma had ended in divorce and in February of the new year I married my then-girlfriend, Nora Díaz. With her I would have three more children: Noreen, Melissa and Manolo (Manny).

Continuing this story, in 1973 I was already at ease in everything that had to do with local government. I thought, at the beginning of the year, that I should start preparing for what would be my first election, since my seat would be up for election in November of that year. I no idea that a series of events would unfold that would substantially change Miami's political landscape and mark what could perhaps be called the beginning of Hispanic political power in South Florida.

On the night of April 6, 1973, Miami Mayor Dave Kennedy was arrested at a truck stop, along with Circuit Judges Murray Goodman and Jack Turner, the Reverend Temperance Wright, who was a leader in the African American community, Mrs. Mina Davidson, and Frank Martin, a colorful character who controlled the operations of the NW 12th Avenue produce marketplace in Miami, to such an extent that he was known as "the mayor of the market" and who, at the same time, enjoyed great influence in Miami political circles.

All were formally charged with conspiracy to commit bribery. Kennedy was a friend of Mrs. Davidson and, according to the indictment, the objective was, through Frank Martin's influence, to get Judge Turner to reduce the sentence handed down against her son in a drug case. On the other hand, "the mayor of the market" and Reverend Wright were accused of trying to convince Judge Goodman to also reduce a sentence handed down, in this case, against a man convicted of sex crimes. It was reported that since 1971, the Miami and Dade County police departments had been investigating, and, according to the prosecutor's office, that all of those involved had been recorded in their conversations regarding the case in question.

It was as if a high-powered bomb exploded in the middle of Miami, and it had a very unfavorable repercussion for the city in the national press. Beyond all political considerations, I felt tremendously bad and incredibly shocked by the news, because Dave Kennedy was my friend. I knew he was an honest man, a decent politician and a good human being, to whom I am grateful for all the help he gave me in my early days in local politics. I found the accusations made against him hard to believe.

But, acting in accordance with state law, as soon as Kennedy was formally indicted, Governor Askew suspended him as Mayor of Miami pending due process. It was now up to the commissioners, me among them, to appoint an interim mayor until Dave Kennedy's situation was fully settled.

The task ahead of us was not an easy one.

Chapter 15
The New Mayor

> *It takes two years to learn to speak and sixty to learn to keep quiet.*
> Ernest Hemingway

When Governor Askew removed Mayor Kennedy after he was formally accused of criminal misconduct, in April 1973, he left us commissioners with the thorny task of appointing an interim mayor, in accordance with state law.

The task wasn't an appealing one for we commissioners, since it was a time when, precisely because of the scandal of the accusations against the mayor, we had to appoint someone in the midst of an atmosphere of great popular dislike for politics and politicians, as we know the ease with which most people judge an entire human group, politicians in this case, when a prominent member of that group's reputation is seriously questioned. Under these conditions, the responsibility of appointing a replacement was doubly heavy.

On the other hand, elections were only seven months away, and this forced those of us who aspired to an elected office to be extra careful in the selection, to avoid the risk of giving our adversaries any ammunition. And if that wasn't enough, there was also that factor, so typical of human nature, that when you use your power to elevate someone to a prominent position in the community, you please one person, the nominee, but displease three or four others, those who wanted to be appointed but for whom you didn't vote.

However, we had to do it; it was our job. I, faithful to my habit of not worrying over what's inevitable, immediately started to shuffle names around in order to make the best possible selection.

While it might've been tempting for me or any of the other commissioners to become the interim mayor, considering that it might become a springboard for holding the position permanently, we all knew that this was out of the question because of the internal alliances and voting patterns among us. Plummer and Rose Gordon always voted in agreement and almost always against my and Reverend Gibson's proposals. Like them, he and I always voted the same way. In the absence of a fifth tie-breaking vote, it would've been a waste of time and energy to nominate one of the four of us, so that wasn't even attempted. We all agreed that we would not have agreed on this!

There was, of course, the vice mayor, which was Reverend Gibson, but according to our bylaws, he could replace the mayor only in a ceremonial way, as long as an interim mayor was not appointed. So we had to be very careful.

The first people to come to my house to discuss the matter were activist Eliseo Riera Gómez and my good friend, former Mayor Steve Clark.

Clark had lost the election for county mayor to businessman Jack Orr and was asking me to nominate him for interim mayor of Miami. It was very difficult to refuse, given the ties of friendship and gratitude that bound me to Clark. But I knew that his nomination wasn't feasible, since he had been badly beaten in the still-recent campaign against Orr, so I didn't commit to supporting him. Instead, I tried to make him see that it would be wiser to wait for some time before launching a new political campaign.

For his part, Dave Kennedy was asking me to keep in mind Athalie Range, a prominent African American businesswoman and community leader and a former commissioner. Kennedy was telling me that, if I nominated Ms. Range, it would guarantee me the Black vote in future elections, and certainly her opinion was worthy of my attention. So, as soon as the search for an interim mayor began, we already had two strong contenders, Steve Clark and Athalie Range.

And then along came Fusté.

Tomás García Fusté was at the height of his popularity and had great influence on the Hispanic public, the Cuban public in particular, in Miami and throughout the county. In Cuba, he had been a sought-after model for advertising agencies, and his face appeared in newspapers and magazines, in television commercials and on billboards. He advertised a particular brand of cigarettes, and his presence and likability generated a lot of sales for them.

He had left Cuba among the first exiles after Fidel Castro's rise to power and, unlike most of his compatriots, his horizons broadened considerably in Miami. He ventured into the region's Hispanic radio, first with entertainment programs and, shortly after, in journalistic spaces, through which he became a popular political analyst specializing in the Cuban case.

Little by little, he moved up in administrative positions in radio and over time became the principal personality in several radio stations in which he worked, such as W.F.A.B., known as "La Fabulosa," with which he was at that time; W.Q.B.A., "La Cubanísima"; W.C.M.Q., etc. Likewise, his influence in the U.S. political arena grew exponentially.

Fusté is an example of astonishing durability, since, even today, he hosts a very popular television program. In addition to all of the above, he's an excellent human being, close to his people and a loyal friend.

Well, he comes to see me and tells me that, as Hispanics, we should think of one of our own for mayor of Miami; that the time is right; that I can increase my political clout by making the cause of a Hispanic as the exile capital's new mayor my own; and that the man for that position is Maurice Ferré.

I didn't know Ferré. I only knew that he was Puerto Rican, that he came from a very wealthy family and that he had held some political position in Tallahassee. I would later learn that that position was that of a member of the state House of Representatives and that his taste for politics came from his family, since his uncle, Luis Ferré, had been governor of Puerto Rico. I would also come to know that he had a very solid education; that he was a graduate of the School of Architecture at the University of Miami; that he was active in the Democratic Party; that he was "well connected" in political circles as well as in the business world; and that his gentlemanliness was impressive.

From the first moment I liked Fusté's idea that we should put a Hispanic in the Miami mayor's office, but I was not yet decided, nor was I sure that Ferré was the man for the job.

Suspended Mayor Kennedy comes to see me again to insist in favor of Athalie Range, and I took the opportunity to ask him about Ferré:

"Ferré has lost two elections in a row," Kennedy told me. "He previously lost the mayoral election to Steve Clark, before Steve's loss to Jack Orr, and he lost when he wanted to be a state senator. If you nominate him for mayor, you're closing yourself off, because there isn't going to be more than one Hispanic on the Commission, and that'll be a symbolic thing, a 'token Hispanic.' He's a millionaire, and you're not, so he has a chance to win in November, and you don't."

I thought long and hard about Dave Kennedy's words, because, as a political calculation, they didn't seem too far off the mark.

Those were very intense days in which the political whispering was constant. There were many who came to see me or sent me messages in favor of *Fulano* or *Mengano* as interim mayor, but I tried to meet only with people I trusted, because the more names I heard, the more displeased those people would be if I didn't favor them.

Fusté came to see me again and convinced me that I should go for a Hispanic. I didn't think it was the right time to propose Steve, nor was I particularly attracted to the idea of supporting Athalie Range. So, I met with Ferré.

He made a very good impression on me, and I said, "Look, I agree with Fusté, I'll choose you." He smiled broadly and thanked me.

When I told Dave Kennedy my decision, he said, "I don't think you should nominate Ferré, because if you do, you're going to lose the white vote and the Black vote. So, vote for him if you want to, but don't nominate him yourself; let someone else nominate him and then you'll go unnoticed."

I thought Dave's advice was very wise and explained it to Ferré: "I'm voting for you, but I won't be the one to put your name forward."

Ferré told me that was fine, that all he needed was my vote, since he already had someone to nominate him for mayor. And that's what we agreed on.

When the day came for the Commission to meet, our rules required that the appointment of the mayor be the only business we handle. When I arrived at City Hall, there was a huge crowd, many media photographers and television cameras, more people outside in the rotunda than inside. I entered without difficulty, dodging the questions that some journalists threw at me.

The previous week Rose Gordon had said that she was going to nominate Sidney Aronovitz, an attorney who had previously served as a commissioner and would later become a federal judge. Aronovitz was a great jurist, so much so that the federal courthouse in Key West is now named after him. So we already knew how Rose was going to vote.

We had to see how the other commissioners would vote. Ferré had told me that he had the necessary votes, so I calculated that Plummer's, Rev. Gibson's and mine were assured.

I should clarify that, at that time, there was no Sunshine Law, which prohibits private meetings and discussions among the commissioners. Our commission offices were on the second floor, above the commission chamber, whose sessions could be viewed through wide glass windows so built for that purpose.

Before going down to the floor, I see Plummer and ask him if he's going to vote for Ferré and he answers me: "No, I'm not going to vote for him. Ferré is a spoiled brat. I'm not Ferré's friend, but Aronovitz's, who's my neighbor, and my vote is for him."

Hearing him say this, I said to myself, "Well, that's a tie, two to two," but I was wrong again. I then approached Gibson and asked him: "Father, are you going to vote for Ferré?" And he says, "No, no, I'm going to vote for Aronovitz; he's my vice president at HUD and my personal friend. Ferré is not my friend."

With that I was convinced that Sidney Aronovitz was already the new mayor of Miami. We then went down to the floor, I saw Fusté and gave him the update: "Hey," I told him, "Ferré doesn't have a single vote. Aronovitz is the mayor – he already has the three votes."

Fusté was kind-of perplexed; this was not what he expected.

"Look, Tomas," I said. "We're going to do the following, to stay on good terms with him. Although I told him I wasn't going to nominate him, I'm going to do it. When he loses three to one, I'll change my vote so that Aronovitz's appointment is unanimous, and that way we will look good, and I fulfilled my part." Fusté agreed.

When the session began, Rev. Gibson, who was the vice mayor, declared the nominating process open. Rose Gordon began to read Aronovitz's complete resume. I didn't have Ferré's resume, not even notes on some of his resume, because I wasn't supposed to nominate him, but mentally I was prepared to nominate him anyway.

Rose Gordon finished reading Aronovitz's hefty resume and then Gibson asked, "Are there any other nominations?" I replied, "Yes, father, at this time I would like to nominate Mr. Maurice Ferré for mayor of Miami."

That was it. If a vote had been taken at that time, Sidney Aronovitz would have become mayor of Miami. But then, Rose Gordon, I don't know if it was because she wanted to show off to the crowd or for some other reason, takes the microphone and addressing me specifically, says:

"Manolo, you should be ashamed of yourself for nominating a person who is not qualified to be mayor of Miami. Mr. Ferré is polluting the Miami River, he owes the IRS sixty million dollars in back taxes..."

This was a brutal attack against Ferré, based, moreover, on a misrepresentation of the facts, since, in reality, it was not Ferré personally, but Maule Industries, that was accused of these things. Her attack was, additionally, offensive to me and served no real purpose, since her candidate had already secured the mayoralty.

As the saying goes, he who speaks much, errs much. Rose Gordon had said a key phrase when referring to Maurice Ferré: "A person who is not qualified to be mayor of Miami." Without intending to, Rose was giving me the pretext I needed to buy time and try to breathe new life into Ferré's candidacy.

I turn to the city attorney, Alan Rothstein, and say, "Mr. City Attorney, I want to invoke the five-day rule." Miami commissioners have the power to stop any meeting for five days just by invoking that rule.

There was a muffled expression of collective astonishment in the chamber; no one expected the vote to be postponed. I continued with great composure: "Mr. City Attorney, I want you to come in five days and report whether or not the person I am nominating is qualified to be mayor of Miami."

Rose Gordon, who knew she had the three votes her candidate needed and who surely also knew that to delay a vote when you have the upper hand is to take an unnecessary risk, quickly tried to correct her mistake. She turned to me and exclaimed: "Manolo, I take back what I said, I take back what I said!" But I didn't give in. "No, Rose," I told her, "that is part of the record and I invoke the five-day rule."

I managed to stop the session; there would be no vote that day. As we were leaving City Hall, I asked Fusté to locate Ferré wherever he was and for the two of them to come to my house. Once the three of us were there, I asked Ferré: "Where were your votes? They were all with Aronovitz."

Ferré confided to me that Monsignor Coleman Carroll, Archbishop of Miami, had promised him Plummer's vote, because he was the undertaker who buried all the priests who died in Miami, and that Tanny Dean had assured him that he had Reverend Gibson's vote.

"Well, neither of them were with you. They both confessed to me that they were voting for Aronovitz."

I then urged Ferré to go quickly to speak to the Archbishop again and secure Plummer's vote. I would take care of Gibson.

Without wasting any time, Ferré urged Carroll to secure J.L.'s vote, and it wasn't difficult for me to convince Gibson that we should go with the minority candidate. As it was, those interminable five days passed, and the interrupted Commission session resumed.

Rose Gordon nominated Aronovitz, and I nominated Ferré. Aronovitz got Rose Gordon's vote only. Ferré got the three votes he needed. Perhaps if Rose had shut up in time the first time, giving way immediately to the vote, the outcome would've been different.

And so it was that Maurice Ferré became the first Hispanic mayor of the City of Miami.

Chapter 16
The First Cuban Elected in Miami

Rectifying is for the wise.
Popular wisdom

The appointment of Maurice Ferré as interim mayor of Miami brought a short period of relative calm to the city's political circles, although no one lost sight of the fact that November elections were approaching.

That relative calm contrasted sharply with the acute crisis that suddenly and quickly erupted in Ferré's inner circle, those of us who had endorsed and achieved his mayoral appointment. A crisis that, in order to grasp it in all its magnitude, you had to live and understand Hispanic Miami, the Cuban Miami, of those times.

Cuban radio in Miami was a bastion of influence and power in our community that all politicians wanted as an ally. As an enemy, it was a hard nut to crack; it was capable of raising and destroying ambitions. The main radio stations whose programming was full of news and opinion programs with listener participation all had a main personality, professional journalist or not, who served as director, editorialist and host of their most-listened-to programs.

This radio personality generally had a huge following who endorsed the opinions he expressed and passionately defended them. As a general rule, the radio stations that occupied the first places in audience measurements constantly maintained bitter arguments among themselves, trying to gain followers, because, aside from the different political sympathies and the different opinions regarding Cuban problems, the larger the audience, the better the advertising sales and, therefore, the richer the profits for the radio company.

In those days of Ferré's appointment as interim mayor, two radio stations battled for primacy: WFAB, popularly known as "La Fabulosa," and WQBA, "La Cubanísima," which competed fiercely for first place among listeners. Tomás García Fusté, my friend, was the director and main personality of "La Fabulosa," while "La Cubanísima" had my friend Emilio Milián, a very capable, courageous and eloquent journalist, in the same position.

Miami City Commission when Ferré is named interim mayor

Ferré, the newly inaugurated mayor, was then more American than Latino and apparently was not very aware of radio's power in our community and the importance of people like Fusté and Milián. The fact was that as soon as Ferré's appointment as interim mayor was announced, Emilio Milián invited him to be interviewed on his program on "La Cubanísima," which Ferré gladly accepted, without stopping to think that that news scoop, his first statements as mayor, belonged to Milián's arch-rival, Tomás García Fusté, who had been the first to suggest him for the position. It was the least he could do out of gratitude, and because Fusté merited that scoop.

When Fusté found out about Ferré's appearance in "La Cubanísima" he was furious. He called Ferré a traitor and ungrateful and without saying it explicitly, he clearly showed his willingness to make him fail as mayor.

I felt like heaven and earth were crashing down when I heard about the situation, but I wasted no time and ran to try to settle the dispute before it reached the airwaves and spilled out to the public.

Not only was Fusté rightly offended, but he was also a good friend of mine. Frequently, he and Luis Sabines, the president of CAMACOL, would have lunch with me, and together we would discuss different issues, and I would pay attention to their opinions. He might've thought that I should've prevented Ferré's interview with Milián from taking place, which would've been the case if I had known about it before it aired, even though I also counted Milián among my friends. Anyway, I immediately tried to locate Ferré, met with him privately and made him see that not having given his first interview as mayor to Fusté had been a monumental blunder, since, in fairness, he had earned the right to the breaking news.

Fortunately, Ferré recognized his big mistake and quickly went to meet Fusté, who didn't even want to see him. The mayor gave the journalist a thousand platitudes, expressed his gratitude to him and swore to him that it had all been an error of judgment, a slighting on his part, with no hint of malice.

Fusté accepted Ferré's apology, and everything ended amicably in a lunch between the two of them, Luis Sabines and me. I took a deep breath; things didn't escalate any further.

Once that incident, which could have been fatal for our own advancement, was over, we had to go back to our routines, but we had to do it already thinking about the November elections.

But, before going into that part of the story, and just to emphasize how important the local media, especially radio, was, I must point out a fact that shows my sincere conviction on this topic. In 1976, while convalescing after a fall, I learned that the radio station WOCN, known as Ocean Radio and whose studios were located in one of the famous towers of the Four Ambassadors Hotel, was for sale. I quickly became excited about the idea of buying the station. I first called my friend, Judge Carlos Benito Fernández, and we managed to put together a group of investors, including Ramón López and Abdón Grau. Ed Wynton, the owner of the radio station, was interested in our offer and even visited me at my home to discuss the matter. My enthusiasm grew when Armando Pérez Roura, a true expert in everything concerning radio broadcasting who had a good sense for listeners' feelings, joined us.

We bought it, and it went very well. Ocean Radio quickly established itself as a favorite of the Miami public and although that venture didn't last long, it was an enriching experience for me.

I should also add here that for some time I was the host of television programs that on both channel 23, Univision, and channel 51, Telemundo. Joaquín Blaya, the Chilean who held the highest executive position there, led me to Univision, and I entered Telemundo through Carlos Barba, the former Cuban television star who became a certified businessman and was vice president of programming and promotion of that network. Both were excellent friends of mine, and I've always been a great believer in the importance of this medium.

Returning now to the November 1973 elections, an uncertain factor regarding the candidates was growing, and we all wished for it to be clarified as soon as possible, since some of the alliances depended on this factor. And depending on what happened, those alliances should be either reasserted or put into hibernation. That uncertain factor was called David Kennedy.

The suspended mayor's future depended on a court ruling. Needless to say, if the court found him guilty of the crimes he was accused of, that was the end of his political career. Otherwise, if Kennedy was acquitted, the question would open up as to what direction he would take with his future.

Beyond all political calculations, I wished with all my heart that Dave would be exonerated and that the accusations against him would be proven false. He was my friend, and I owed him a debt of gratitude for the help he had given me so that I could also participate in local politics. Plus, in the midst of all this, his family's happiness was also at stake. Political considerations would come later, as I saw it. What was important now was that justice be done and that his good name be restored.

Personally, there was something that wouldn't change substantially for me but would have to be readjusted according to how the case against Kennedy would end.

Once Maurice Ferré was appointed as interim mayor, he and I had met for a serious conversation of what our accomplishments and our futures in our respective positions as mayor and as commissioner might be.

It was clear that we envisioned that, at the conclusion of our interim terms, Ferré would run for mayor, and I would do the same for commissioner. There was, however, a great difference in the possibilities of reaching our goals. I had a clear path to start my campaign, but Ferré would be on hold until Dave Kennedy's situation was settled.

If Kennedy was acquitted, as I expected, he could run for reelection as mayor with every right to do so, and I felt obliged to support him unreservedly. Ferré would then have to decide what to do.

That settled, Ferré and I made a pact. If Kennedy was convicted or if, being acquitted, he decided not to run for reelection, I would support Ferré in his run for mayor and in his subsequent reelection campaign; that is, for eight years. After that time, I would run for mayor, and Ferré, as former mayor, would support me. It was understood that, by then, Ferré would run for U.S. senator or Florida governor. We sealed that pact with a handshake.

Ferré had been appointed interim mayor in April. Months passed and there was no end in sight to the case against Kennedy, Martin, the "mayor of the market," and the others involved in the high-profile case. Finally, on August 15, 1973, Sarasota District Court Judge Lynn Silvertooth ruled: Kennedy and all of the others involved were exonerated. The magistrate dismissed all charges against them.

That same day, Kennedy told the press that he would seek authorization from Governor Reubin Askew to resume his duties as mayor of Miami, and two days later he was reinstated, thus concluding Maurice Ferré's interim administration. A few days later, Dave Kennedy announced that, his innocence proven and his name cleared, he had decided not to seek reelection and to retire from active politics. He believed he had served the community well for many years and had enjoyed it, but now wanted to devote more time to his family. After the announcement, Kennedy was applauded at length.

Kennedy renounced all personal ambitions for public office and freed himself from the great pressure that electoral campaigns put on candidates. It's also possible, I suppose, that he was somewhat disappointed, because it's in situations such as the one he experienced, facing serious and unjust accusations, that one learns who are real friends and who are not. And although the judge's ruling did him justice, what one suffers is not forgotten.

However, he didn't give up politics as such, because through his knowledge, his sharpness and his contacts, he continued to be a great political force, whose support was sought by almost all those who pursued elected positions in our area. He and I always maintained the best of relations.

With the question of whether or not he would seek reelection out of the way, and with less than three months to go before the November election, I knew I had to pick up the pace to make my desire to be popularly elected as a commissioner a reality. Likewise, Maurice Ferré, now certain that Dave Kennedy wouldn't run, had to get a jump start and maintain a high level of momentum so that his mayoral campaign could be successful.

Judge Carlos Benito Fernández, a good friend, great jurist and leader of local Hispanics since before we Cubans began to arrive as exiles and whom I've mentioned before, was my campaign manager. He made me see a detail that I hadn't noticed. He said to me:

"Everyone knows you as Manolo, but the law obliges you to put your real name on the ballot. If you appear there as José Manuel Reboso, American voters are going to get confused, and some Hispanics as well. I think it's better if you legally change your name to Manolo."

I had obtained U.S. citizenship a couple of years earlier and had kept my name as it was. At first, I saw Carlos Benito's reasons, which were very valid, but it was a little hard for me to let go of the name my parents had given me, even though I never used it. After thinking about it for a while, I realized that my parents had also been the first ones to call me Manolo, and I didn't have to think about it anymore. We filed the petition and in a few days, I was officially Manolo Reboso, aspiring Miami commissioner.

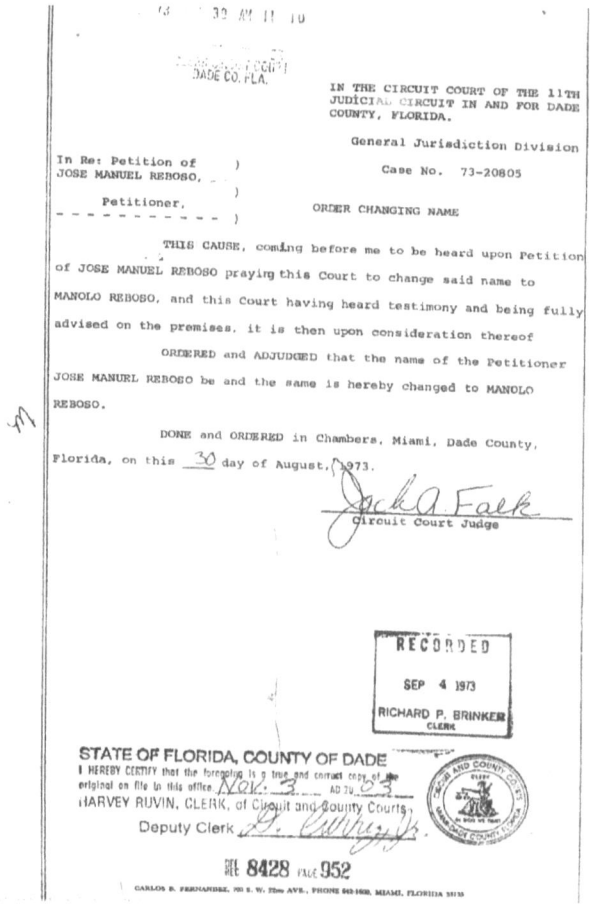

Petition for change of name from José Manuel to Manolo in 1973.

I must now make an aside in this narration to pay tribute to the memory of that great friend and mentor, Carlos Benito Fernández. He had emigrated from Cuba to Miami years before the beginning of the massive exile provoked by the Castro dictatorship. He was a lawyer by profession and had been appointed municipal judge, a position he held for several years. He helped, abundantly and unselfishly, the Cubans who arrived from the 60s onwards and from then on, we maintained a great friendship. He and I, along with a small group of investors, shared ownership of Ocean Radio, the first Cuban-owned radio station in Miami, which I've already recounted. Years later, we acquired Ocean View, a property in Windley Key, Islamorada, that my brother Roberto managed.

Carlos Benito's daughter, Kathy Fernández Rundle is Miami-Dade County State's Attorney and enjoys great prestige and admiration. She replaced Janet Reno in 1992 and has served our community for three decades. She has the admiration of Democrats, Republicans and Independents who recognize the difficult work she does so well. On several occasions she's been approached to run for Florida governor, but she's always declined, claiming that her obligation and responsibility is to the residents of our county. Undoubtedly, she's an example of public service.

Let's now return to our narrative, back to 1973. Ferré and I supported each other, as we had agreed, and Kennedy endorsed us. But, of course, we each concentrated on our own campaign, which was really exhausting, since we were both running against numerous contenders, most of whom were confident that the Cuban vote was not yet enough to win in Miami.

I gave myself no respite in that campaign and was very fortunate to have a very dedicated and enthusiastic team. We went up and down the streets of Miami, and I couldn't count how many doors we knocked on. In Little Havana I was received with great joy and with expressions of support, but it wasn't only there. Of course, the Cubans were the most enthusiastic, no matter which neighborhood of the city they lived in, but many non-Cuban voters greeted me warmly and demonstrated their support; and others, perhaps more reserved or perhaps committed to one of my opponents, listened to me politely.

In the buildings where low-income, mostly elderly, people lived, they hugged me and expressed their confidence in my election. On two or three occasions, they blessed me and promised me that they would be praying for my campaign's success.

Weekends were particularly complicated, as there were several Cuban organizations that had fellowship luncheons in party halls and parks scattered throughout the county. Different Cuban *municipios en el exilio* ("municipalities in exile," which were social and civic groups that exiles formed according to the towns in Cuba where they had lived, so that they could continue the relationships and activities they had enjoyed in their homeland), had their picnics at Tropical Park, Robert King High Park, and others. Numerous Miami voters attended all of these events. I tried to attend them all, and in all of them I was very well received.

Another very important part of the campaign was participating in local radio, especially in the Spanish-language stations. Almost all the programs had the same format: a first part in which the host of the program interviewed me and gave me the opportunity to explain my plans if I was elected to the Miami commission. That part was the least problematic, as the hosts were almost all supportive and their questions were not difficult to answer.

In the second part, the telephone lines were opened to allow the audience to ask their own questions and express their opinions. This was more problematic, because some of the other candidates had phone banks, through which their sympathizers or paid people would go on the air and ask questions that were difficult to answer, or simply spread lies and accusations to discredit the opponents, which was me, when I was the guest on the program.

I would fight them well and try to answer their diatribes with a loud and firm voice, but I would also try to lengthen the first part of the program as much as I could, so as not to leave too much time for the listeners' calls.

Either way, I enjoyed that interaction on Spanish radio and found it to be a very effective way to reach voters. I was also invited on English radio talk shows, although not as frequently as on the Hispanic stations. On those shows, generally, the host was more inquisitive and some of the listeners' questions exuded a deep xenophobic and racist hatred, but I handled them well and, a few times when the attacks were truly vitriolic, I successfully took on the role of these racists' victim, which won me the sympathy of many of the listeners who called in after the confrontations.

Tuesday, November 6, 1973, finally arrived, and Maurice Ferré was overwhelmingly elected as the first Hispanic mayor of the City of Miami. I came in first place among the 13 candidates for the commission seat that until then I had held by appointment. However, I couldn't avoid a runoff, scheduled for the following Tuesday, in which I would face my closest rival. When the day came, it wasn't difficult for me to defeat him.

So, on that November 13, 1973, I became the first Cuban to be elected Miami city commissioner and at the same time, the first to be elected to public office in the United States in the 20th century.

The news made national headlines. Please read below how *The New York Times* reported on that election:

MIAMI, Nov. 17—For the first time since the Cuban exodus to the United States began in the early 1960's, former Cuban refugees who are now American citizens have made their political influence felt here in local elections.

The Cuban vote has been termed the principal factor in the election last week of Maurice A. Ferre as Mayor of Miami and this Tuesday of Manolo Reboso as a City Commissioner.

Mr. Ferre, a 38-year-old wealthy industrialist, became the first Mayor of Puerto Rican extraction in a major city in the continental United States.

Mr. Reboso, a 38-year-old Havana-born engineer, is believed to be the first former Cuban refugee elected to public office in this country.

In Miami, mayors are elected for two-year terms, and commissioners, or councilmen, for four years. Although the city election here is nonpartisan, both winners are Democrats.

The victory of Mr. Ferré, a nephew of the former Governor of Puerto Rico, Luis A. Ferré, was overwhelming.

Running without the endorsement of the two local newspapers, The Miami Herald and The Miami News, he won all of the city's 82 precincts and received more votes than the combined total of his six opponents.

In file Tuesday runoff election, Mr. Reboso, also without newspaper endorsements, handily defeated James Black. In another race, for commissioner, the Rev. Theodore Gibson, a black minister, defeated a black businessman, Tom Washington. The terms of the remaining commissioners expire in 1975.

There were about 17,000 registered voters with Latin names among some 113,000 Miamians eligible to vote in the city election. Of the 113,000 total, slightly more than 32 per cent went to the polls on Nov. 6 and only about 20 per cent last Tuesday.

But an analysis of the election returns indicates that the Latin vote was proportionately much higher than that of other ethnic groups of Miami, which has a population of nearly 400,000, half of which is Spanish-speaking.

The New York Times didn't say it explicitly, but the inference was clear: things were changing in Miami: Cubans were the new political force in the city.

Chapter 17
"The Cuban-Born Commissioner"

> *There is no such thing as a great talent without great willpower.*
> Honoré de Balzac

In July 1972, when I was appointed to fill Commissioner Irving Christie's unexpired term, the City of Miami employed only 26 Hispanics, a derisory figure considering the high percentage of the population that we constituted by then.

The unexpected events that took place, such as Mayor Kennedy's suspension, the need to appoint an interim mayor, etc., and the short time that separated us from the elections, didn't allow me to develop a real work plan, but that discriminatory absence of our people in the local government payroll remained fixed in my mind as one of the most urgent priorities in what would be my work agenda if I managed to be elected.

And so it was that, already elected by the voters, I took on the task of repairing that injustice, since it was evident that our community deserved and needed greater representation. It was a problem that manifested itself in two different, but closely linked, ways. On the one hand, there was the labor force, strictly speaking, of the municipality, especially in administrative positions, those with the highest levels of responsibility and, accordingly, the best salaries.

On the other hand, there were the civic organizations that had great influence in the city's affairs and, at the same time, received appreciable benefits from the administration, as was the case of the Greater Miami Chamber of Commerce, the Orange Bowl

Committee, the University of Miami Board of Directors, the Jackson Hospital Board of Directors, etc. In these powerful organizations, Cubans, all Hispanics really, were conspicuously absent.

With such poor representation, it was very difficult to advance our community's legitimate interests; hence my interest in helping to change the existing situation.

I therefore set myself, whenever possible, to appointing Cubans in the different city departments. Of course, I only proposed Cubans who were truly qualified for the position to be filled, so that they wouldn't be promoted to those positions simply because they belonged to our ethnic group, but because they had all the necessary skills to perform their duties in an excellent manner.

Importantly, I didn't focus only on favoring Cubans and other Hispanics. Out of fairness and out of pure equity, I wanted to favor African Americans to a large extent.

When Paul Andrews was the city manager, I supported him in creating two positions that hadn't previously existed in the police department: a black commander and a Hispanic commander. Guillermo Zamora was the first Hispanic commander, and Leroy Smith, who was proposed by my colleague and friend on the Commission, Reverend Gibson, was the first Black commander.

Then there was the question of the presence, or rather, the *lack* of Cuban and African American presence, on the boards of the civic organizations I've already mentioned and others of the same kind, which, to a large extent, really controlled power in Miami but only served the interests of the white people. Among their leaders there was a strong resistance to diversify, to open up to the new realities of Miami, and above all, to leave behind their airs of discriminatory exclusivity.

Gibson and I agreed to see how we could open some space in those strongholds of traditional power in Miami. Those organizations received funds allocated to them in the city budget and in many cases, also from the commissioners' discretionary funds. When the time came to prepare the city budget, directors and lobbyists of these organizations would meet with the city manager and with the commissioners to present their petitions, advocate for their projects, etc.

At that point, I said to Gibson, "Now's our chance, Father."

Indeed, when representatives of these organizations began meeting with us about the upcoming budget, Gibson and I flatly refused to accommodate their requests. "We have no money for you," we would tell them.

This, of course, set off alarm bells in those boards, which were used to always being accommodated. Then, in a very subtle way, so that it wouldn't be interpreted as a quid pro quo, we would let them know of our displeasure at the absence of African Americans and Cubans on their boards of directors. That served as an effective remedy. Some of our people were incorporated into these power elites. There were few at first, but remarkably more later.

This is how people like Manolo Arqués, Leslie Pantín, Carlos Arboleya and many others were appointed to the different boards, and my greatest pride is being able to emphasize that all those who were appointed more than demonstrated their integrity and knowledge.

At the beginning of his term, Mayor Ferré didn't join us in our efforts to open up the circles of influence to Hispanics and African Americans. I mentioned earlier that, because of his background, Maurice then felt closer to Americans than to Hispanics. I don't know if it was a political calculation, or maybe he realized that Americans didn't see him as one of their own, but the fact is that he later joined Gibson and me, and this gave us much greater leverage in dealing with those centers of white power.

And on the whole, I think this was very positive for our city, which, as mere human beings, is rewarding.

Sadly, there are more than a few so-called community leaders throughout the United States who base their leadership and what they present as their struggle for justice and rights for their brothers and sisters in race, nationality or social status, on class hatred, a spirit of revenge and a brutal racism that becomes one of all against all.

Reverend Gibson and I, and later Mayor Ferré, made an alliance that was very effective without falling into extremism. We were firm in defending the rights of our people and in opening up opportunities for Cubans, African Americans and Hispanics to better themselves equally without trying to trample on those from whom we had to wrest that power. To those who kept trying to divide Hispanics and African Americans, we showed that we can work together and even more, that we can be true friends and at the same time extend an open hand to white people and those of any other ethnicity. Mutual respect, understanding and transparent honesty are the keys to coexistence, and this we were able to do in our small world, but not because it was small, less important, nor less exemplary.

This extended beyond the boundaries of Miami. In 1975, I received a call from Governor Askew. He asked me to recommend a Cuban lawyer because he wanted to appoint the first Cuban judge of industrial claims (now known as judge of compensation claims). I was very pleased to recommend Mario Goderich Jr., or Mayito, as he was known, for that position. A few years later, he would be appointed judge of the Eleventh Judicial Circuit. In 1990, he would also be the first Cuban judge at the Third District Court of Appeal, thus culminating a career in the judiciary that honored all Cubans. Judge Goderich, unfortunately, passed away in early 2022.

Of course, it wasn't all about staff appointments and attempts to change the outdated structures of the city administration; normally, the day-to-day work had to be taken care of and also, of course, the unexpected situations that arise everywhere.

In 1976, then city manager Paul Andrews resigned and therefore, we had to choose someone capable of fulfilling the requirements of this position, one that grew in complexity as Miami grew. We launched a national search and after the initial rounds, five finalists remained.

There were five finalists and there were five of us making the decision: the mayor and the four commissioners. So, we divided up the finalists, and each one of us went to their corresponding city to meet with the applicant we had been assigned to.

I got Joe Grassie, who was then in Grand Rapids, Michigan, and I went to visit him there. I spent three days in what appeared to be a beautiful and very quiet town, learning about Grassie, chatting with him, visiting the local newspaper, etc. In addition to other qualities, Grassie was bilingual, as he'd lived in Argentina, and this worked in his favor. Upon my return to Miami, I recommended that he be the new city manager, and Ferré and Gibson approved. J.L. and Rose Gordon voted for Don Hickman.

Those were years of feverish work. Hardly realizing the exact magnitude of it all, Miami was day by day becoming a great metropolis, with rapid growth. Ferré, Gibson and I, along with a number of far-sighted businessmen, encouraged the development of Downtown and the Brickell area, attracting to those areas companies and commercial firms that nurtured that development.

Little by little, huge skyscrapers, some of great architectural beauty, were rising in the center of the city, transforming Miami's skyline. The days when our city was a sleepy and unchanging small town were being left behind, present only in the yellowish images of some photo album.

Part of our work, in addition to promoting the growth and modernization of some areas, like Downtown, was the maintenance and improvement of the original Miami. Coconut Grove, for example, was a neighborhood that had been decaying over time. Something had to be done to revive the area, but it had to be done without stripping it of the charm of its village-like structures. It wasn't a matter of tearing down and rebuilding, but of maintaining and renovating.

We achieved this by simply investing in trees and vegetation, improving its parks and making its commercial areas more easily accessible, in such a way that I would say that this was the beginning of this place's amazing economic revitalization, in the heart of Miami.

This benefitted Ferré, who was accused by some of only caring about Downtown, because, they maliciously added, that was where his family's largest real estate investments were located. However, some promising results soon began to emerge to back up the most optimistic forecasts for the area's future, and we saw years later how almost everyone applauded "Ferré's vision of Miami as a great city."

One area that I was also very interested in was Miami's commercial and tourism relations with Latin America. I had the experience and many of the contacts I had gained as head of the International Bureau of the Florida Department of Commerce, and this served me well in trying to expand Miami's economic horizons.

I traveled extensively throughout the continent, always accompanied by Miami's civic and business leaders, and we were able, among all of us, to expand business ties with countries such as Chile, Argentina, Mexico, Venezuela, etc. Sometimes, as part of our Miami promotion campaign, we would declare our city and the capitals or important cities of those countries as "sister cities," which is what we did, for example, with Merida and Quintana Roo, in Mexico, and with Santiago, the capital of Chile. Establishing these bridges flattered our partners throughout the continent, and all of this led to broad benefits for Miami and for those countries.

With the President of the Junta de Gobierno, General Augusto Pinochet in Chile. I was invited by Gen. Gustavo Leigh, Chief of the Air Force and member of the Junta de Gobierno.

I realized that there were opportunities for us to strengthen those ties and do altruistic work with our neighbors at the same time. For example, our police department's cars are replaced every two years, when most of those vehicles are still in very good condition. I sponsored the initiative that these cars be donated to countries in Latin America, where they could be used for a long time. We were able to make it happen, and the governments of those countries welcomed this gesture. This, as it's easy to imagine, made their officials look very favorably on their relations with Miami.

In the second half of the 1970s, the rise of Cuban power provoked the emergence of a marked resentment in some sectors of Miami's white population. Bumper stickers began to appear that read: "Will the last American leaving Miami please bring the flag." Some small businesses identified themselves as "natives," which was nothing more than a way of identifying themselves as "non-Cubans," and some tried to portray Cubans as usurpers who were taking jobs away from African Americans.

That put a certain degree of tension in the city's affairs, something that my alliance with Reverend Gibson was trying to disprove. The situation didn't yet reach the levels of animosity that we'd see a few years later, after the Mariel crisis and the anti-bilingual campaign throughout Dade County. However, it was a situation that concerned me, because I saw how much we would all benefit if all us minorities worked together, which I'd experienced in my own election as a commissioner.

In 1973, I was elected with an overwhelming vote by white and African American voters, plus, of course, the support of Cubans, whose weight was beginning to be felt, although it was still far from being as decisive as it is today.

It was different then. Today there is a greater understanding of racial and community issues, but that wasn't the case in those days. Perhaps the white establishment had understood the need for minority representation in city government, but only as figureheads, what they call here a "token Cuban" or a "token Black." Of course, in our case, neither Gibson, nor Ferré, nor I, were willing to settle for that purely decorative role. The point was to get there, so that we could then exercise truly effective leadership.

But the fact that the people who controlled the votes in the Black community and among the white residents supported the mayors (Clark, Kennedy, etc.) and those mayors asked them to support us, helped us a lot. Likewise, the African Americans who supported the governor, also supported Mayor Clark and Mayor Kennedy, and for that, they supported me as well.

Another very important aspect of our political chess game was the role of the media. English-speaking public opinion was dominated by the *Miami Herald*, *The Miami News*, and some local TV stations. Cuban radio, as we've already seen, had a decisive influence among Hispanic people, especially among Cubans.

The relationship between Cubans and the *Herald* wasn't at all good at the beginning, because, in those days, there were still many in the world who viewed Fidel Castro sympathetically. They painted him as the guerrilla hero who had overthrown a dictatorship, the Robin Hood of that time. The *Herald* repeatedly did that and, of course, antagonized the Cubans in exile who fought Castro and his dictatorship. The *Herald* didn't view us with sympathy and continued to call him "Mr. President." They wouldn't name him as the dictator that he was; that took a long time to happen.

The fact was that the *Herald*'s attitude didn't contribute to friendliness among the different ethnic groups in Miami. To me, the paper kept its critical eye on me. Whenever I was referred to, I was identified as "the Cuban-born Miami commissioner," a term that helped to maintain many white voters' unhealthy animosity.

On one occasion, at an event at the OMNI hotel, I met the then-editor of the *Herald*, John McMullan. We greeted each other, and he asked me how I was doing and what I thought of the *Herald*'s coverage. I jumped at the chance:

"I'm doing well, and I think the Commission is doing a good job. As for the *Herald*'s coverage, I think it could be improved. I'm struck by the fact that you always identify me as 'the Cuban-born commissioner'."

"Does that bother you?" McMullan asked me.

"No, not at all," I answered. "On the contrary, it makes me remember Cuba and reminds me not to forget my status as an exile, which I'm very proud of. The problem you're going to have," I added, "is with Henry Kissinger."

"With Kissinger?" he asked, puzzled.

"Yes," I said, "because you never identify him as 'the German-born Secretary of State'."

McMullan laughed when I said that and didn't respond, but, from then on, the *Herald* stopped using that ill-intentioned reference when talking about me.

Chapter 18
The Fourth Power

> *We put too much faith in systems, and look too little to men.*
> Benjamin Disraeli

When talking about the media in Miami during those times when Cubans were fighting their first battles for a fairer participation in the local centers of power and for the representation they deserved due to their growing presence in all aspects of this city's life, it's necessary to remember that, although the *Miami Herald* and *The Miami News* exerted great influence on the ruling classes, the same was not true with respect to Hispanics in general and especially with Cuban exiles.

Generally speaking, Cubans were making progress in understanding and speaking the English language. Those who, like me, had had the opportunity to study in this country were almost perfectly bilingual, and we spent our lives serving as translators for our compatriots. And, for better or worse, we Cubans, as a rule, made ourselves understood – we "defended ourselves," as some would say.

While the majority of Cubans in the area were making progress, that fact was lost on the editorials and opinions of the two main newspapers in the area, the *Herald* and *The Miami News*. Then again, thanks to a string of discrepancies and misinterpretations, most of the exiles already considered these newspapers, especially the *Herald*, if not as enemies, at least as adversaries that sided with Castro most of the time and almost never with us. They say that generalizations are always unfair, and so it is, but that was the perception that existed and, certainly, the newspaper's management didn't do much to change it.

The situation went so far that some of our people called the *Herald* "the Sunshine Pravda." In the midst of such entrenchment on both sides, the *Herald*'s opinions bounced off Miami Cubans' indifference or antagonism; therefore, its influence among us was almost nil.

This was changing little by little, especially after the arrival of first *El Herald en español* and then *El Nuevo Herald*, and thanks to the fact that the voices of reputable journalists and print executives such as Roberto Suárez, Dave Lawrence, Alberto Ibargüen, Armando González, Sam Verdeja and Carlos M. Castañeda, among others, began to be heard in the newspaper's owners' headquarters. But this was a process that took many years, and there still remains, apparently, a certain degree of mutual distrust.

This contrasted sharply with the unforeseen influence of Miami's *periodiquitos*. These were tabloid-like weeklies, with either many or very few pages, all with a definite anti-Castro editorial bent, and some still framed within the old political structures of pre-Castro Cuba: pro-Batista, Authentic, Orthodox, etc. The *periodiquitos* were sustained thanks to Hispanic merchants' advertisements, official local government ads and the "paid political ads" of the electoral campaigns. Thanks to this, too, they were free for readers, who found them every week, without fail, on the shelves of almost all the commercial establishments of Miami, Hialeah, etc.

Some of the *periodiquitos* were managed by true masters of Cuban journalism, such as Armando García Sifredo and the poet Ernesto Montaner, among others, who sharply presented the exile community's beliefs and who carried more weight in public opinion than the big Miami newspapers, and those of any other place.

Diario Las Américas and its director, Dr. Horacio Aguirre, deserve their own chapter. This Nicaraguan journalist had been publishing his evening newspaper in Miami for several years before Fidel Castro appeared on the Cuban scene. Aguirre quickly grasped the totalitarian essence of the new Cuban regime and immediately became a supporter of the Cuban exile community. *Diario*'s pages were widely opened to illustrious Cuban journalists such as Guillermo Martínez Márquez, Humberto Medrano, José Ignacio Rasco, René Jordán, José Ignacio Rivero and others, and this made it acquire great prestige and influence, especially in exile intellectual circles.

So, the *Herald*'s antagonism didn't make much of a dent on the Cubans who were beginning to stand out in politics, since they had the backing of the Hispanic radio stations, the *periodiquitos* and *Diario Las Américas*.

In some respects, I'm pleased to see how things have changed in today's Miami. I'm very sorry for the depreciation of many of our old radio stations. I lament the irremediable absence of those greats of Cuban journalism, as well as that of Horacio Aguirre, and the disappearance of most of the little newspapers. But I'm pleased to see that the continued vitality of Cuban matters in our community is reflected in the remaining radio stations and on cable television, and on the local stations of the major Hispanic television networks. I'm pleased to see that *Diario Las Américas* remains faithful to its principles. And I'm especially pleased with the ostensible change in the editorial and reporting tone of the *Miami Herald* and *El Nuevo Herald*; now it's more in tune with the truth about Cuba and the feelings of the Cuban exile community.

Looking back to those times when I was starting out as an elected official in Miami, I can better grasp the main point, the detail that was the most important reason for the support I obtained at the polls. I personalize this a little, because it must be remembered that for a long time, I was the only Cuban elected by the voters for a political position.

This was several years before Raúl Martínez in Hialeah and Jorge Valdés in Sweetwater emerged. I was alone in the entire county.

The key to electoral success was in the person-to-person contact, in the direct relationship that I established with the voters – in many cases, from before, when they couldn't vote, a fact that almost none of them forgot.

I know that some critics refer disparagingly to the widespread practice among local politicians of visiting the *comedores* (senior centers), the low-income residential buildings and the events thrown by all kinds of organizations. I know that these activities are described as a joke on those voters, almost always elderly, who are supposedly told what they want to hear, photographed with the politician of the day, promised anything they ask for in exchange for their vote; and, after the elections, all those promises are forgotten.

It's possible that this happens in some cases, and I'd say that it's almost certain that those who act like this are the politicians who are never reelected. Bad politicians and stupid voters have existed since the first elections in the world were held, but neither the one nor the other are so abundant.

Those who say that voters are deceived by the politicians who hold meetings in the residential buildings for the elderly, who visit the community centers, and who attend local events, place very little value on the voters' level of intelligence. Those who promise and don't deliver are almost always punished by the votes of those who feel cheated.

First of all, it must be said that those gatherings – at least the ones I used to host – were, fundamentally, a display of friendship and closeness between the public official and the citizens, both his voters and those who weren't. It was about having a good time and coming together, and I hosted those gatherings at any time of the year, not only when elections were near.

So much so, that I didn't just go to those places where voters, almost always senior citizens, gathered, such as low-income buildings or community centers. I organized breakfasts for 30 or 40 people, twice a month, in different neighborhoods throughout the city. The guests were simply the neighbors, people from all walks of life. I would talk to everyone, greet them all, try to remember their names. Many of them would update me on the state of public services in the area, which gave me a very broad view of the city's problems. I would maintain contact with them, and they were kept informed of the steps we were taking to try to resolve issues.

I greatly enjoyed seeing the *viejitos'* (the "old folks") joy when we gave each family a turkey for Thanksgiving, or a bag of food for Christmas dinner, gifts that were almost always provided by local merchants. Of course, there too, some would take advantage of the occasion to ask for help, either with a problem in the building, or something personal, such as help with their immigration papers, etc. The reality was that, although there was always someone who wanted to talk to me about their problems, most of the people who attended those gatherings never overwhelmed me with requests of any kind.

A member of my team would take down names and phone numbers and within a couple of days would contact the person and help them resolve the matter. They were never asked for anything in return for the help we gave them, but most of them were grateful and very loyal people. I think it was a very appropriate thing to do, and I was very pleased to be able to help so many people in need in this way, directly.

Speaking of people in need, one of the problems in Miami that concerned me greatly was the state of poverty in which many families lived and, at the same time, the lack of opportunities for those families to overcome the limitations that prevented them from accessing a better standard of living.

In Liberty City and Overtown, in Little Havana, Wynwood, Allapattah and other places, there were pockets of poverty that were breeding grounds for crime and the ever-increasing deterioration of non-functioning families whose horizons seemed to be totally closed. Those were times when Miami was not yet the attractive city, full of opportunities, that was only emerging then. The big manufacturing firms in the country weren't interested in coming to Florida and, on the contrary, some of the textile companies established in Hialeah and Allapattah were slowly beginning to move their workshops to Asia or Central America in search of cheap labor. I felt so much helplessness, especially because I didn't see that this issue, which was very important to me, was of particular concern to other public servants, particularly at the state and federal level, which is where a problem of this magnitude could be solved.

Trying to alleviate the poverty of so many families, I tried to help some charities established in our city, which I knew worked hard to help the poor. One of those charities was Centro Mater, located in Little Havana near the river, where they took care of young children from low-income families so that their mothers could go to work. I greatly admired and was a friend of its director, a Catholic nun very dedicated to her mission, Sister Margarita Miranda. I always gave Centro Mater a good donation that came out of the commissioners' discretionary funds.

Another problem that had begun in the 60s, but which was gaining momentum in the 70s, was drug use. At this point, it was beginning to stop being stigmatized by the upper classes of the country and the world of the rich and famous and was becoming a national plague that had a terrible impact on poor neighborhoods. It was a very bad situation, and many families were suffering from it, but it was a national epidemic that was very difficult to try to control locally. Our police were doing a great job trying to keep our streets free of drug dealers, but the source of the problem was beyond our reach; these were federal crimes. It hurts to see that, today, this scourge has not only continued, but has spread to such an extent that many are indifferent to the ever-increasing statistics of overdose deaths from various types of narcotics, as well as to the shocking crimes committed under the influence.

And among the challenges we faced in those turbulent years, I cannot fail to mention something that occurred only in and around Miami, but which, like the drug issue, was not under local jurisdiction. Those were times when any chance for Cuba's freedom seemed to be completely closed. Against all odds, the Castro tyranny remained in power and that power seemed to be firmly established. The vast majority of exiles militantly committed to "the cause" (of freedom for Cuba) were very frustrated and felt abandoned by their former allies.

In such a state of mind, passions ran high, divisions between organizations and personalities were exacerbated, and some went to extremes, accusing anyone who deviated even slightly from the anti-Castro doctrine of being a traitor or an ally of Castroism.

This situation opened a productive field for Castro's agents in Miami, whose main function was to feed divisions, propagate defeatism and promote anything that could result in the projection of a bad image of the Cuban exile community.

Consequently, terrorist acts and attacks against individuals began to take place in Miami, which greatly contributed to Castro's supporters' objectives. In 1974, the engineer José Elías de la Torriente was assassinated in his Coral Gables home. Since the late 1960s, he had raised exiles' spirits with the "Torriente Plan," an initiative that had managed to unite many organizations and leaders and that had promised the liberation of Cuba in a relatively short time. Many assumed Torriente had strong backing from Washington; others accused him of having appropriated exiles' donations for his liberation plan. His death remained a mystery.

In 1975, Rolando Masferrer, a former confidant of Fulgencio Batista, a man of action with a reputation for courage and cold-bloodedness, was assassinated. In 1976, radio commentator Emilio Milián was the victim of a terrorist attack in which he lost his legs. In 1977, my dear friend and fellow member of Brigade 2506, Juan José Peruyero, was shot and killed. And they weren't the only ones; other Cubans were also victims of similar attacks. In addition, bombs exploded with some frequency in public places, whether it was a post office, or the premises of companies that sent packages to Cuba. There was a climate of insecurity and an atmosphere of violence that did nothing for the liberation of Cuba, the prestige of Cuban exiles or Miami's progress.

There were many who were of the opinion – me among them – that, if not in all cases, at least in some of them, those who carried out those violent acts were following directives from La Habana, some knowingly, others believing the opposite. Certainly, considering that the Castro regime was the only beneficiary of those events, it was very difficult not to come to that conclusion.

All this, of course, strengthened the arguments made by the white people and some African Americans who maintained a staunchly anti-Cuban attitude not only in Miami, but in all of South Florida. Some of them took those acts of political violence as justification for their accusations against the Cubans, saying they had turned Miami into a "banana republic."

Like it or not, in the political inner circles at the county and state levels, I was seen not only as just another Miami commissioner, but also as a representative of "the Miami Cubans." Some expressed this with a tone of irony, because they were trying to keep alive the worst stereotypes that presented us as a violent, fractious people, disrespectful of the laws; an ungrateful tribe that, far from assimilating into American culture, we tried to impose our customs over those of the United States.

Of course, it's only fair to point out that those who thought this way were extremists, who are almost always the most ignorant. I tried not to get into discussions on the subject, because I knew that they were closed-minded people with ready-made opinions, with whom arguing is a waste of time. I was careful, however, not to bow my head nor say anything that they might interpret as my validating their racist attitudes.

Many Americans, those who were more educated, those who read and were more aware of events inside and outside the United States, and those who experienced close dealings with Cubans, were far removed from those attitudes and were aware of particularities within the Cuban situation that escaped most ordinary people.

While all this was happening in "the Sun Capital," the calendar was running imperturbably, one day after another. And before I realized it, we were approaching 1977, the year in which Miami's voters would decide whether or not to give me another four years as their commissioner.

Chapter 19
More than 20,000 Votes – The "Dialogue"

> *Worry more about your character than your reputation. Character is what you are, reputation merely what others think you are.*
>
> John Wooden

It was 1977. There would be elections in November of that year, and although I felt confident in my chances of being reelected as city commissioner, I was very aware, at the same time, that in politics, nothing is set in stone. I knew that public opinion is fickle, that it's based on the impression that most voters have of the candidate at any given time, and that sometimes events beyond one's control can negatively affect one's image.

But, at the same time, I had already proven that if you are a consistent person, if voters see consistency between what you say and what you do, if you avoid corruption and the appearance of corruption, and if you are in tune with the thinking of the community you represent, it's difficult to be defeated in a reelection.

Now, although the above, i.e., conduct in office, is the key to seeking reelection, this doesn't exempt you from needing to remind voters of all this, highlighting your achievements, and skillfully pointing out the differences that make you the best among all the candidates. Hence, the political dynamic itself obliges you to develop a reelection campaign whose intensity may vary according to the circumstances, but where you can't take victory for granted, because in this, as in almost everything else, the danger lies in confidence.

All of the above, plus this *sine qua non*, which I remembered since the beginning of my first campaign, as I'd heard it said since I was a child, and I knew it was true: if the voters are Cubans, you cannot be "pesao" (annoying or a pain in the neck) because, according to the adage, Cubans forgive you everything, except being a "pesao."

I had to campaign, and that's what I did, although without neglecting the daily duties that I was obliged to perform as commissioner. Some aspects of the campaign were very different from what I experienced in 1973.

Then, although the support of Mayor Kennedy, Steve Clark and other highly regarded elected officials had made my path to the commission much easier, my personal effort to make myself known to the voters was labor intensive and extensive, requiring many hours of dedication. This time, the road to reelection was much less steep.

I already enjoyed a good degree of popular recognition. The almost 48 months that had passed since then had allowed me to establish important contacts throughout the city that, from the beginning of the new campaign, made the effort easier, both in terms of donations for campaign expenses and public attendance at pre-election events.

In the end, the result was so spectacular that I was filled with gratitude, proud, but at the same time humbled by the overwhelming victory that the people of Miami, and especially my community, had given me.

It was the first time in Miami that a commissioner got more than 20,000 votes. It was a landslide, not only in the number of votes, but also in the donations, which were massive, particularly those from Cubans who already had a certain economic status.

I was the first commissioner who dared to hold a campaign event at $100 per ticket. We held it at the Four Ambassadors

Hotel, and that event was attended by more than 1,200 people and more than a hundred had to stay in the lobby of the hotel, because there was no room for anyone else in the room. Four people ran against me, and there was no need for a runoff, so strong was the voters' support.

That invigorating electoral win made me enter my second term as commissioner with great confidence and great optimism. Ferré had also triumphed in his aim for reelection as mayor, and this put us both in what should have been our final stretch in the positions we held, he as mayor and I as commissioner. We were, then, four years away from the final phase of our pact, four years away from my mayoral aspiration and his aspiration to some higher position, not yet defined, in national politics.

But, as that moment arrived, Miami continued its dynamic growth and its constant challenges, some of them unique to our small but intricate cosmos, where domestic issues move alongside international intrigues, where nuclear submarines are sold in strip clubs, and no one forgets if the key to the city is given to the wrong person.

At the end of 1978, the atmosphere became so heated in such a bad way that I was affected as a Cuban, as a commissioner and as a simple human being – all because of a situation that made Cuba and Miami red hot, and about which, the truth is that there was very little we could do.

The proverbial simplicity of the then president of the United States, Jimmy Carter, who was anxious to reestablish full diplomatic relations with Cuba, and Fidel Castro's aspiration to become president of the Non-Aligned Movement (NAM) – a group dominated by Marxist enemies of the United States under a pretense of neutrality between Washington and Moscow and which Castro needed to improve his international image in terms of respect for human rights – led to the emergence of a rapprochement project between La Habana and Miami; that is, between the Castro dictatorship and the Cuban exile community. This process, known since then as *el dialogo* (the dialogue) has given the word "dialogue" the negative connotation that it still has for many Cubans.

The meeting was convened in La Habana between members of Fidel Castro's regime, which would eventually include the dictator himself, and a number of Cuban exiles, some more prominent than others. The announced objective was to improve relations between the Cuban government and the exiles, who were then referred to in the Castro-controlled press as "members of the Cuban émigré community" in Miami. One of the "collateral benefits" of that attempt at understanding would be, according to what was expected from the meeting, the release of Cuban political prisoners, whose number was then estimated at more than 3,000.

The project provoked one of the most bitter controversies of all those experienced in Miami. Most of us exiles rejected any rapprochement, even any conversation, with representatives of Castro's dictatorship. The reasoning was that Castro was the cause of evil and the one to blame for the existence of political prisoners in Cuba. What he should do, many said, was to free the prisoners and leave Cuba and for this, they argued, there was no need to talk to anyone.

Other Cubans reasoned, perhaps more pragmatically, that the regime was consolidated in power, that the exile community didn't have the means to change that situation and that, if the release of political prisoners could be achieved, it was worth exploring the situation, which, they argued, doesn't necessarily imply a surrender of our principles.

Such was Castro's interest in the possibility of an exchange that would benefit him by neutralizing the exile community, that he even allowed the U.S. media to interview some prisoners, almost all of whom agreed with the dialogue initiative. The big surprise came from none other than Eloy Gutiérrez Menoyo.

Menoyo had come to Miami in 1961, after being relegated to anonymity by Castro. Here he was one of the founders of Alpha 66, a militantly anti-Castro organization. In December 1964, he was captured during an attempted incursion into Cuba and had been imprisoned there ever since. His jailers allowed him access to visiting journalists to promote *el dialogo*, evidently certain that he would come out in favor of a Cuba-Miami-Washington understanding. But, as it turned out, the opposite was true.

Menoyo spoke concisely against the process: "There is only one jailer here, and that is Fidel Castro," – those were more or less his words. "He has the keys to all the dungeons in Cuba. If he wants to free us, all he has to do is open the doors. There is nothing to discuss with him."

That solidified the majority position of the exile community against *el dialogo*. But, on the other hand, the relatives of the political prisoners and many other exiles who saw the humanitarian side of the proposal didn't stop supporting the initiative. The tension in Miami was nothing short of explosive.

At the head of the group in Miami in favor of dialogue was a Cuban of Jewish origin, well known in the world of finance, and whose record showed nothing to do with Castroism. He was Bernardo Benes, who was called *el colorao* (the red one), not because of his political ideas, but because of the color of his hair and the color of his skin.

Benes had the Carter administration's approval and had traveled to Cuba on several occasions, where he had even met with Fidel Castro himself, trying to push for an agreement on the release of the prisoners.

In Washington, D.C., no doubt, there were many who were happy with the course of events; but in Miami, everything was radically different. The city was on fire and tension was high between those opposed to *el dialogo* and those in favor of it. The Hispanic radio stations were buzzing with controversy and there was talk of nothing else. Epithets were flying through the air. Anti-Castro organizations protested in front of Benes's offices, on SW First Street and 18th Avenue. The word *dialoguero* became the buzz word and, although not much was said about it, civilian and police authorities were concerned about the potential for violence.

Benes became the lightning rod for the exile community's wrath. And at his side was my partner, my friend, my brother Alfredo González Durán.

I knew Benes very superficially, although I had a good opinion of him. I was firmly against the project he headed and like most of my fellow exiles, I thought it would end in a political victory for Fidel Castro. Of course, I also wanted the prisoners' release, but I thought that it was all blackmail by Castro to gain political advantages, since, without changes in Cuba's government system, he would possess all the resources of power to be able to fill the Cuban jails again whenever he felt like it.

Another Cuban exile who was involved in those efforts was businessman José Orlando Padrón, owner of a brand of high-quality cigars bearing his surname. Padrón and I were friends; he always sent his famous Padrón No. 3 cigars to my office at city hall. Like Benes and Alfredo, he was strongly criticized and accused of betraying the Cuban exile community for his participation in *el dialogo*.

Anyway, in those days I tried to avoid Benes and Padrón, as I didn't want to have a personal discussion with either of them. With Alfredo it was different.

I didn't support him in his efforts, but above all was our friendship and my confidence in his patriotism and good intentions. It bothered me enormously that Cubans who had remained comfortably in Miami, while Alfredo was fighting in Playa Girón, questioned his loyalty to the cause of freedom and spoke harshly of him, forgetting his merits. And for me it was a very regrettable mistake and a great injustice that the Brigade decided to expel him from its ranks, together with other Cubans, also Bay of Pigs veterans, who didn't think as we did about *el dialogo*.

The fact was that, while Fidel Castro was determined to clean up his image as he eyed the meeting of the Non-Aligned Movement, soon to be held in La Habana, more than 3,000 political prisoners were released and went into exile, thanks in good measure to the efforts of Benes, Padrón and Alfredo.

In the long run, that didn't substantially change the confrontation between Castro's regime and the Cuban exiles, nor did it give any permanence to the improvement of relations between Washington and La Habana, since Castro never intended to change one iota of the bloodthirsty nature of his regime.

Unfortunately, however, it left permanent after-effects in Miami, where even today it's used as a reference to distinguish some as *dialogueros* and others as *de línea dura* (hardliners), neither of which term is completely fair.

Of course, all of this directly affected politicians and politics in Miami, since there were many who inserted Cuban issues into local affairs, mainly and almost always demagogically, in electoral processes.

This didn't affect me, and I was much more concerned about my friendship with Alfredo, which, thank God, never suffered. I got to know Bernardo Benes better years after that heated period. I reestablished my incipient friendship with him, and when we talked about *el dialogo*, I became convinced of his good intentions and his absolute anti-Castroism. I have no doubt that he was a good Cuban. Something similar could be said of Orlando Padrón.

Benes passed away in Miami, in 2019. Earlier, in December 2017, José Orlando Padrón had passed away.

I'm almost certain that non-Cubans reading these stories will be somewhat perplexed and may not fully understand the importance of Cuban events in Miami affairs. Some may wonder why what happens in Cuba and what Cubans in Miami think about everything related to the island has such a big impact, not only in the lives of thousands of people, but also in the electoral processes in South Florida.

One of the reasons that most notably affect this situation is Cubans' push to become U.S. citizens and receive their voter card. It must be kept in mind that the Cuban people never harbored anti-Yankee sentiments; on the contrary, they always considered themselves friends and admirers of the United States. They wouldn't trade their Cuba for anything in the world, but they were a people with an open heart for all. The anti-American rage of recent times had been imposed by Fidel Castro, but it didn't reach the hearts of Cubans.

So, Cubans saw no contradiction in loving both countries, understanding that both's true interests were the same, beyond the political misrepresentations of some demagogue like Castro. But, in addition, Cubans quickly understood that, to really influence Washington's decisions about Cuba, it was necessary to have electoral strength in this country.

Helping to liberate Cuba was one of the main reasons why Cubans became U.S. citizens and immediately registered as voters. And this, I repeat, without the slightest intention of using the United States in favor of our interests because, for us, defending Cuba's freedom is also defending freedom in the United States. Therefore, what's happening in Cuba and everyone's position on the matter has become a legitimate campaign issue in elections in this part of the world.

Returning to the unfolding of events in Miami, it's clear that, in the midst of the controversy over *el dialogo* that permeated everything, we had to continue with the day-to-day running of local affairs.

The tripartite political alliance we had – Ferré, Gibson and I – allowed us to move forward with different projects, many of which were of popular benefit and others that contributed to consolidating Miami's growing importance as a cosmopolitan, modern city – one suitable for doing business, setting up branches of large corporations, and underscoring its status as the "gateway to the Americas."

We won all these projects three to two, because the representatives of old Miami, J. L. Plummer and Rose Gordon, habitually voted against our proposals. They believed that good politics was about not spending money, saving, they said, taxpayers' money without risking it on big-ticket projects.

I tried to explain to J.L.: "Look," I told him, "I have traveled all over the Americas and whenever I arrive in a country, they show me their work. They tell me, 'this bridge was built by such-and-such mayor', 'this airport was boosted by such-and-such president', 'this road was widened by this senator'... I have never been told 'such-and-such mayor saved so much money', that's not what people need."

Neither J. L. nor Rose Gordon could understand the wisdom of making Miami a great city. On a personal level we were friends, I got along well with them, but I never got them to support any of our projects, which I lamented.

As if the events of 1978 in Miami were not so engrossing, there was, near and far at the same time, another scenario to which I was forced to pay attention, perhaps without thinking that what was happening there would have important repercussions in my personal life and in my political work. They were calling me from Nicaragua.

Chapter 20
Anastasio Somoza and Carlos Andrés Pérez

> *That men do not learn very much from the lessons of history is the most important of all the lessons that history has to teach.*
> Aldous Huxley

Like many of my fellow Cubans, I was very grateful to the president of Nicaragua, Anastasio Somoza Debayle. When almost the whole world turned its back on we Cubans who denounced the abuses that Fidel Castro's dictatorship committed against our people, Somoza, in his dominant role as head of the National Guard or, indeed, as president of his country, was one of the few who helped us.

That attitude of solidarity was made evident in a critical way, when he allowed the CIA to use Nicaraguan territory to place an airport in Puerto Cabezas for Brigade 2506. His solidarity remained even when the existence of that airport became an open secret and Nicaragua faced the possibility of a direct confrontation against Castro's well-armed and numerous military forces.

I got to know "Tachito" (as his close friends called him) personally through Manolo Artime, and we formed a good friendship that grew stronger when I, as head of the Florida Department of Commerce's International Bureau, visited that beautiful and welcoming Central American country. This continued later, when I was commissioner of Miami.

When a violent earthquake measuring over 6.0 on the Richter scale devastated Managua on December 23, 1972, I gave my myself wholeheartedly to the intense relief effort that took place in Miami. The earthquake was a catastrophe of biblical proportions: about 10,000 dead, 20,000 injured and more than 300,000 homes destroyed. The center of Managua was totally destroyed, an area of more than five square miles. I felt morally obligated to help those poor people and Miami, as always, stepped forward, with the generosity and good heart its people are known for. We raised $2 million in food and medicine. That help was something that Somoza greatly appreciated and something that helped strengthen our friendship. He asked me to go to Nicaragua with a group of executives and members of the exile media, and we went, accompanied, among others, by Luis Sabines, Manolo Arqués and Fusté.

With Nicaraguan President Anastasio Somoza following the earthquake that struck Managua in December 1972.

I knew then, as I know now, that when the name Anastasio Somoza Debayle is mentioned, a negative image immediately emerges, the stereotypical image of the old-style Latin American dictator, corrupt and bloodthirsty, whose vices and mistakes are exaggerated and whose virtues and successes are forgotten.

Without denying the defects he may have had, nor the mistakes he may have made, like any other human being, I must say, out of respect for the truth, that the man I knew was a warm and kind person, a good friend, a grateful man who, in his vision of things, tried to do what he believed to be the best for his country.

He was also a man of superior education. A graduate of West Point Military Academy, he had a larger vocabulary in English than in Spanish and was a true friend of the United States.

Some important factors weighed against him, such as his family's long tenure in the Nicaraguan presidency, his father's ("Tacho") fame as a "strong man," and the permanent state of poverty most Nicaraguans endured, in undeniable contrast with the vultures that, in all countries, grow rich as they circle the peaks of power.

I'll never forget something that the then U.S. ambassador in Managua, James Theberge, once told me: "Without a doubt," he said to me, "Somoza is the best president there is in Central America, but there's a consequence to his last name, and that's that it makes the people think of a dynasty, and the people don't like it. The Democrats themselves don't like dynasties, and they want change."

Changes that, as we've already seen - I say - are fatal most of the time. Like what happened in Cuba, when the people wanted to remove Batista, and despite the fact that Dr. Rivero Agüero had already been elected and was only 15 days away from taking office, Eisenhower forced Batista to leave the country. Rivero Agüero wasn't given a chance, and no consideration was given to all the factors that indicated that Castro would be worse.

The same thing happened in Nicaragua: Somoza has to leave power under pressure from the United States, and the people are happy with that and want a Sandinista government for the people, by the people, which will put an end to corruption... but they don't look at the new heroes' background and don't seem concerned about their intentions. We already know what happens: what happened in Cuba was repeated in Nicaragua.

And if that weren't enough, we saw the same thing in Venezuela: *Caldera is a weak man, we have to change... the Adecos are corrupt, COPEI has also been corrupted... everything is bad. Here there's a co- colonel; he's a paratrooper, he's charismatic, he's going to end corruption...* and there you have it: the people elected Chávez and what happened? Exactly the same as Cuba, the same as Nicaragua. It's sad that so much of the Cubans' suffering hasn't even served as a warning to other peoples, nor to open the U.S. State Department's eyes.

I don't mean to imply that when a situation is decidedly bad, one shouldn't try to change for the better. But it's vital in these processes to take all possible precautions so that, whether due to haste, lack of preparation or lack of knowledge, the change, instead of being from bad to good, doesn't end up being from bad to worse.

What prompts me to reflect upon this in the middle of this story? Well, the very course of events that have marked my life's history. In Nicaragua's case specifically, I was involved in some events that were decisive in that country's destiny, and this was due to my friendship with Somoza and my contacts within the U.S. Democratic Party, which gave me some access to the Carter administration.

I was advising Somoza, trying to make him see the need to improve the human rights situation somewhat, to control the excesses of some military leaders. Not only did I believe it was the right thing to do, but also because it was necessary to improve relations with the Carter administration so that he could keep trying to prevent the Sandinistas, whose links to Castro were obvious, from taking power.

Somoza accepted those recommendations willingly, began to move in that direction and in a short time, at the end of July 1978, he got a letter from President Carter in which he said that he was very pleased to note that there were some positive changes in Nicaragua, changes that his administration viewed very favorably.

That was a setback for the Left and the useful idiots in Latin America, and it paved the way for something that could perhaps be a graceful way out of the political chaos that was becoming uncontrollable.

Talking one day in Caracas with Miguel Ángel Capriles, he mentioned to me the possibility of talking to the president of Venezuela, Carlos Andrés Pérez, who was, at that time, like the standard bearer of the Latin American democratic left. He was receptive to this proposal, precisely because it came from Capriles. The idea was to set up a meeting between him and Somoza in order to reach an agreement for a political transition in Nicaragua, which included Somoza's departure from power.

And it included this condition because Somoza himself had confided to me his desire to hold elections in Nicaragua under the auspices of the OAS, to hand over the presidency to whoever was elected and whoever was not imposed by the Sandinistas, and to come to the United States, at least for a while. He was tired of the political tension that had enveloped most of his life.

So far so good, but, upon telling Somoza about Capriles's suggestion and our meeting with Carlos Andrés and his willingness to meet with him, Tachito began to shake his head. He agreed to meet with any other major Latin American figure, but not with Carlos Andrés, whose word he didn't at all trust, even though Capriles's intervention in the matter gave him hope.

I didn't know what to do in the face of Somoza's refusal. In my opinion, if we began that process by snubbing Carlos Andrés, we were off to a bad start. Trying to find a way to convince Somoza, Julio César Quintana, who was then his foreign minister, came to my aid and told him: "President, I think Manolo is right. We lose nothing by trying."

Somoza agreed, and I felt a great relief and a comforting hope. I didn't want Nicaragua to suffer the same fate as Cuba, and everything indicated to me that we were on the right path to avoiding such a disgrace. Somoza sent his first cousin Luis Pallais, president of the Nicaraguan Congress and the vice minister for foreign relations, to Venezuela to set the date and place of the meeting.

The meeting was set for Sunday, July 30, 1978, on the island of La Orchila.

La Orchila is a beautiful islet located in the Venezuelan Caribbean, just north of Caracas. It houses a military base and the summer residence of Venezuelan presidents, all in the midst of a beautiful, peaceful landscape.

We had had the invaluable help of my friend Miguel Ángel Capriles, the great magnate of the Venezuelan press. He was the owner of the *Novedades* newspaper and other influential publications. I had a very strong relationship with him because one of his daughters was married to David Brillembourgh, brother of my roommate at Georgia Tech, Rene Brillembourgh. Capriles and I had become very good friends. Every year he would invite me to his beach house in Venezuela and one curious detail I remember is that he had named his beach house "Varadero" because his wife was Cuban.

Miguel Ángel accompanied Carlos Andrés to La Orchila. There were six of us in all: Somoza and Carlos Andrés, each accompanied by his foreign minister, Capriles and me. We arrived at nine o'clock in the morning, under a torrential downpour.

The two presidents met until noon at the presidential house. The Nicaraguan Foreign Minister, Julio César Quintana, his Venezuelan colleague, José Alberto Zambrano Velasco, Capriles and I stayed in another house within the same compound.

At twelve o'clock we were told to go to the main house, and there we had lunch. Carlos Andres sat at the head of the table, with Somoza to his right and his minister Zambrano to his left. Capriles sat between Somoza and Quintana, the Nicaraguan foreign minister, and me next to him. I remember, I couldn't ever forget, that the main course was a delicious Australian rabbit, which I had never tasted before.

At a moment when we were able to speak alone, before sitting down, I had offered Somoza my leave from the conversations. After all, I had no official position; I was there only because of my friendship with him and my interest in avoiding a repetition of Cuba's unfortunate experience in Nicaragua. But I didn't want Somoza to feel obligated to having me participate where it wasn't my business to be. Somoza was emphatic: he wanted me there because he trusted me and, besides, he told me: "You are an American citizen. With you here, as a witness, Carlos Andrés will not dare to play a trick on me. We are in his territory, don't forget that."

Lunch lasted three hours as well, because, in fact, conversations continued there. Carlos Andrés Pérez said he had found in Somoza an open president. Somoza reiterated that he should talk to the Nicaraguan opposition so that their leaders would meet with him to set a date for the presidential elections, and he also reiterated that he would hand over power to whoever was elected. Carlos Andrés could not have been more pleased and assured Somoza that in a week's time the opposition leaders would come to see him, that they would meet with him.

We left there at three o'clock in the afternoon, all satisfied and I, in particular, happy. We had saved Nicaragua from becoming another Cuba.

Or, at least, that's what I thought.

Over the following days that illusion was destroyed, making it clear that Carlos Andrés Pérez had made a mockery of us, that he had shamelessly lied to us.

Two weeks later, Somoza sent for me.

"This is not working, nothing is happening," he told me, visibly upset.

I went back to Venezuela and talked to Capriles, and we went to see Carlos Andrés, who assured me that in the course of that same week the Nicaraguan opposition would go to meet with Somoza. That week passed, and nothing happened.

After a month had passed, and the situation in Nicaragua was getting worse every day, Somoza called me one night at one o'clock in the morning: "Take the LANICA flight, the one at seven in the morning and come here. We have to review this, because I don't like it."

So I did. I arrived in Managua, on August 22, 1978, and went, as usual, to the Intercontinental Hotel. At twelve o'clock I arrived at the bunker, to have lunch with Somoza. When I arrived, Colonel Porras told me to come in, that the president was already at the table. We greeted each other and had a drink. Somoza always drank vodka with tonic water.

That drink also had a history between us. Somoza had had a heart attack some time ago, and he had come for treatment here in Miami Beach. While he was recovering, I went to see him every day. The doctor asked him, "General, what do you drink?" Somoza replied that he drank scotch, one called White Horse, which wasn't black label but more like a hard whiskey. The doctor then advised him to stop drinking scotch and to drink vodka and tonic water instead. I, listening, took the advice for myself and from then on vodka has been my favorite liquor.

Well then, that day in the bunker we were already drinking our respective vodkas. Lunch had not yet been brought when Colonel Porras suddenly entered and, unable to hide the apprehension he felt, said to the president: "Boss, the Sandinistas have taken *Palacio*."

Palacio was the National Palace, where the nation's Congress met. A Sandinista commando, under the command of Edén Pastora, known as *comandante Cero* (Commander Zero), and *comandante Número Uno* (Commander Number One), Hugo Torres, had taken possession of the Palace and were holding hostage all the congressmen, senators and other officials, a total of around 3,000 people, demanding from the government a series of concessions, among them, the release of political prisoners and a ransom of $10 million.

The situation could not have been more serious or more tense. In their demands, the Sandinistas also asked that a series of documents be disseminated in the national press and guarantees for the commandos' exit from the country.

The Catholic Church quickly offered to mediate, to avoid the massacre that would ensue if a confrontation between the National Guard and the Sandinista commandos took place. Both parties accepted and the mediating commission was comprised of the Archbishop of Managua, Monsignor Miguel Obando y Bravo, who seven years later would be elevated to the rank of cardinal by Pope John Paul II; the bishop of Granada, Leovigildo López Fitoria; and the bishop of León, Manuel Salazar y Espinosa. The ambassadors of Costa Rica and Panama, Virgilio Chaverry and Carlos Boyd, respectively, joined them later.

When the three prelates arrived to speak with Somoza, I got up to leave, but he asked me to stay and this allowed me, without my seeking it, to become an eyewitness of those historic events.

Somoza had quickly assessed the situation: the Sandinistas had acted with boldness and precision and had in their hands the lives of those 3,000 people, among whom were relatives of the president himself, such as his cousin Luis Pallais Debayle, his nephew José R. Somoza, and others, as well as some of his closest collaborators. Somoza wasn't willing to sacrifice their lives nor to run the risk of bringing about the massacre that the Sandinistas were undoubtedly willing to carry out.

The crisis lasted less than 48 hours and at the end of it, the Sandinistas got almost everything they asked for and scored a resounding coup. Somoza ordered the release of all the prisoners they were demanding, including some of his best-known leaders such as Daniel Ortega and Tomás Borge; the documents the guerrillas wanted to release were released; they were provided with the means for the entire commando to leave the country without problems; and they received $500,000 in cash.

I returned to Miami with the sad conviction that Nicaragua was already irremediably condemned to become a second Cuba.

Chapter 21
The Resignation and the Pact – Tragedy is Repeated

Truth suffers, but never dies.
St. Teresa of Ávila

In Miami, many things awaited me: the day-to-day work of the commission and the realities of my private life, my family and my business. I was also approaching what was to be the beginning of my mayoral campaign.

Not many days passed without Somoza resuming his efforts to find a way out of the political situation in Nicaragua. He was still willing to leave power, but at the same time he wanted to prevent the Sandinistas from gaining access to power. The harsh impact of the Palace takeover by Edén Pastora and his guerrillas apparently passed quickly and failed to convince him that the situation was rapidly and hopelessly slipping out of his hands.

At the beginning of 1979, Somoza firmly asked me to drop everything else and dedicate myself full time to helping him in what should be his last battle, which was none other than to get the United States to fully support his efforts to prevent the Marxist guerrillas backed by Fidel Castro from taking over the country.

That put me in a very difficult situation. My mind told me that it was virtually impossible to stop the Sandinistas' march towards total political control of Nicaragua, but my heart refused to give up completely and not make a last effort to avoid the catastrophe that this would mean. Was there any chance left to make President Carter and his advisors face this reality?

Another aspect of the choice that lay before me was my plan to run for mayor of Miami. I was sure of my future victory in that race, but if I accepted Somoza's offer, I would have to resign from my position as city commissioner and inevitably disconnect myself a little from activities in Miami, just as I was entering what should be the most intense part of my campaign.

What should I do?

My heart knew that I would never forgive myself if I refused to make that last effort for Nicaragua. And my heart won.

I resigned from the Miami Commission in early 1979. In stepping down as commissioner, I was leaving a better, more inclusive city with broader horizons.

Cubans, other Hispanics and African Americans had made great strides up the social ladder, in integration, advancement and inclusion in government and in local power groups, thanks, in good measure, my joint efforts with Rev. Gibson and Ferré. I remember that when I was sworn in as commissioner, only 26 Cubans were employed by the City of Miami. When I retired from that position, there were more than a thousand compatriots on the official payroll, and some of them had reached the centers of power, where decisions were made.

I had also contributed to broadening Miami's horizons and to its progress on the road that would lead it to becoming the most important city in Latin America. Downtown and the Brickell Avenue area were taking on a new, taller, more modern and progressive silhouette. And many of our people were being given well-deserved opportunities to leave the ghetto of *La Pequeña Habana* (Little Havana) and integrate into more prosperous areas.

I had the peace of mind that I had done all I humanly could to help the less fortunate, not only Cubans, but of all backgrounds. Looking back, I felt calm and content, without any arrogance or false pride. On the contrary, I gave thanks to God, who had given me that opportunity to serve and had helped me fulfill my mission without a guilty conscience.

I now had to concentrate on a larger and more challenging assignment. Most of my work would have to be done in Washington, D.C. It was lobbying work and my main target was Robert (Bob) Pastor, who was in charge of Latin America in President Carter's National Security Council, which was headed by presidential advisor Zbigniew Brzezinski.

Bob Pastor and I had met through Diego Arria, then governor of the Federal District of Caracas and with whom I had very good relations. Pastor was married to Robert McNamara's daughter. McNamara been Secretary of Defense in the Kennedy and Johnson cabinets. He had also served as president of the World Bank.

Visit as vice mayor of Miami to Caracas, Venezuela, where I was received by Governor Diego Arria, later the Venezuelan Ambassador to the United Nations.

Diego Arria, for his part, was a diplomat of such importance that he would become president of the United Nations Security Council in the early 90s. He was governor of Caracas, Minister of Tourism and Venezuelan Ambassador to the United Nations. In my opinion, no one is currently as well prepared as he is to be president of Venezuela.

Diego had a summer house on Mustique Island and often lent it to Pastor. Bob Pastor was no slouch and had been in charge of negotiating the treaties by which sovereignty over the interoceanic canal was transferred to Panama.

But it was too late. Events in Nicaragua had taken on a dynamic of their own. The government had shown its vulnerability by caving in to the demands of the Sandinista assailants; global public opinion was raging against Somoza and his family; the Carter administration continued in its frivolous fantasy of the false redeemers of Latin America. And the Nicaraguan people, eager for a fairer fate, were experiencing with the Sandinistas the same revolutionary debauchery that we Cubans had experienced 20 years earlier with Fidel Castro and his henchmen. In Cuba it had been *los barbudos* (the bearded ones) and in Nicaragua it was *los muchachos* (the boys).

Unfortunately, this was never understood in Washington. When, many years later, a series of previously confidential Carter administration documents were declassified, a memorandum that Bob Pastor himself wrote for his superiors in the National Security Council came to light. In it, he recounted a conversation between him and me that took place in Washington on April 5, 1979.

In that conversation I impressed upon Pastor Somoza's willingness to bring about a peaceful transition of power and leave Nicaragua and conveyed to him a request from Somoza to meet with him. Bob Pastor did not take Somoza's offer seriously, and although he acknowledged Fidel Castro's involvement in the

Nicaraguan situation, he mentioned the possibility of talking to Somoza "at some future point... six to eight months from now... which will permit genuinely free elections in 1981." Such was the prevailing disinformation in Carter's inner circle.

On July 17, 1979, a little more than three months after that memorandum, Somoza had to leave his country for permanent exile. Nicaragua had been lost, just as Cuba had been lost before.

Fourteen months later, on September 17, 1980, Anastasio Somoza Debayle was assassinated as the target of an attack perpetrated by the Sandinistas in Asuncion, Paraguay. Days later, his body was transferred to Miami, where his burial took place. His relatives asked me to give a eulogy, which I did with sincere sorrow. As if ordained by the hand of God, three years earlier, at the request of Adelaida, his widow, I had also had to eulogize my dear and esteemed friend Manuel Artime, the great leader of Brigade 2506, who, coincidentally, was the one who had introduced me to the Nicaraguan president.

After Somoza's fall, I logically had to readjust my priorities. I was no longer on the city commission, although, through my contacts, I kept very much abreast of everything regarding local politics, eyeing my upcoming mayoral campaign. Without neglecting this, I concentrated a little more on my business and avoided falling into a major financial crisis. At the same time, I was paying careful attention to what was happening on the national political landscape, where the engines were already heating up for the impending battle for the presidency in November 1980.

Jimmy Carter was up for reelection, and on the Republican side, the candidacy of former California governor and former Hollywood star Ronald Reagan was emerging with overwhelming force.

I didn't think twice. After what happened in Nicaragua, where it can honestly be said that Carter was the one who had put the

Sandinistas in power, and seeing the state of affairs in the world, which were not at all encouraging at that time, I was greatly concerned about the idea of Jimmy Carter being in the White House for four more years.

Carter, to be sure, is a good man. He's a very religious man who said he had never told a lie, didn't drink and didn't smoke, and was contrite in admitting that he had once been unfaithful to his wife, albeit only in thought. None of this is bad, nor does it bar him from a position of authority. But Jimmy Carter said all this with a dangerous naiveté that made him unfit to sit down and debate with the Soviet leader Leonid Brezhnev, who did lie, who drank, smoked and probably had as many women as he wanted. It was the fight of the unwary against the cynical, where the United States had everything to lose. Jimmy Carter was perhaps the president who did the most for human rights. But, in my opinion, the role of president of the world's leading power was too big for him.

In 1977 at the White House with President Jimmy Carter

I quickly founded a group that we called "Democrats for Reagan," and it was a success because there were many members of the Democratic Party who thought the same as I did. Reagan had been a member of the Democratic Party in his youth and had been president of the Hollywood actors' union. He was a great communicator, and he proposed a government program full of common sense. He was the leader that not only the United States, but also the West, needed at that time. Cubans, moreover, saw in his presidency a renewed hope of freedom for Cuba.

That election was a political tsunami. Reagan swept the whole country and specifically in Miami, his victory was overwhelming. The Cuban vote was practically all his. Moreover, Carter's presidency was a determining factor in the exodus of a large number of Cuban voters to the ranks of the Republican Party. This was a very unfortunate decision in my opinion, but very understandable, given the circumstances.

Reagan took office in January 1981 and, if I remember correctly, I believe it was in that same month that Maurice Ferré and I met one morning for breakfast at Monty Trainers, the popular restaurant in Coconut Grove, located next to Miami City Hall. As you may recall, he and I had made a pact regarding the mayoralty. His second term as mayor was in its final stages, and it was now up to him to support my candidacy, just as I had supported his in 1973 and 1977.

I asked Maurice what he had in mind.

"Precisely, I wanted to talk to you about this issue, because… things have changed and I have decided to run for mayor again in November," he said.

"That's not the agreement you and I had," I reminded him.

"Yes, I know, and I'm sorry," he told me then, "but, since you left for Nicaragua, I thought you renounced politics here."

"Mauricio," I replied, "you know very well that the Somoza era ended in 1979, and I returned here immediately. And although I've been traveling, I have never left politics here and I still intend to run for mayor this year."

"Then," he told me dryly, "I think we are going to run against each other."

"Well, that's the way it will be," I said. "I'll see you in November."

That certainly didn't surprise me. A few years earlier, Maule Industries, which was the center of the Ferré family's economic power in South Florida, had been declared bankrupt. The family's huge financial problems had been picked apart by the local and national press, and its expected economic recovery was apparently not coming. Maurice Ferré's public persona was suffering from all this, and although he maintained much of his political power in Miami, he didn't seem to be in a position to aspire to a higher political office.

I immediately began to reach out to all my contacts about my mayoral aspiration, and when I officially announced my intention to become the first Cuban mayor of Miami, Ferré began a strong smear campaign against me, insinuating or saying explicitly that I had resigned from the Miami Commission because I was forced to by the *Herald*, to prevent the newspaper from publishing information that could destroy me politically.

The falseness of all this became evident a few months later when the *Herald* surprisingly endorsed me for mayor. The support they had always denied me as commissioner, they were now giving me for mayor of the city, against Ferré.

And it wasn't only the *Herald*. If there is one thing I can boast of, it's the outpouring of solidarity that my mayoral aspiration aroused. Raúl Masvidal and Leslie Pantín Sr., two leading figures in South Florida, were the co-chairmen of my campaign. I had support from CAMACOL, the Interamerican Businessmen's Association, and Hispanic professionals. Exile organizations, some of which could not be involved in local politics, supported me implicitly. I also had the support of our newspapers, radio and television press, including important executives like Joaquin Blaya and the people of Univision, where I had had a weekly program.

Everything indicated that I would sweep those elections. I had the white vote, thanks to the backing of the *Miami Herald* and prominent politicians like Steve Clark, Dave Kennedy and Reubin Askew. Harvey Ruvin was backing me as well, and all this was important for English speakers. Sergio Bendixen, the pollster, who was an assistant to a Congressman from North Miami of Jewish origin, asked for two months' leave to work with me, and this helped me a lot with that community.

I believed I was solid with the Black vote as well, because of the connections I had with T. Willard Fair and because I had the support of Rev. Gibson and other prominent leaders in the African American community whom I had helped from my position as a commissioner.

On the other hand, the campaign fundraising was truly massive. I raised far more than Ferré, both from wealthy donors and from ordinary citizens who enthusiastically supported me.

And as if all this weren't enough, I also received the explicit support of President Reagan. The local press gave great coverage to the letter he sent me from the White House, where, among other things, he said to me: "Just as you helped me, I now have the opportunity to help you."

THE WHITE HOUSE
WASHINGTON

November 5, 1981

Dear Manolo:

It was good to see you today on your visit to Washington, and I enjoyed reminiscing about those hectic days last fall when you served as the Dade County Democrat Reagan Chairman.

Now the situation is reversed, and you are the candidate. Well -- just know that I understand what you're going through, and I'll be thinking about you.

With warm personal regard and my best wishes,

Sincerely,

Ronald Reagan

Mr. Manolo Reboso
Manolo Reboso for Mayor
  Campaign Committee
Post Office Box 45-0931
Miami, Florida 33145

THE WHITE HOUSE
WASHINGTON

5 de noviembre, 1981

Querido Manolo:

Fue muy agradable verte hoy en tu visita a Washington y disfruté recordando aquellos días activos el pasado otoño cuando tú servías como Presidente de los Demócratas Por Reagan del condado de Dade.

Ahora la situación es a la inversa, tu eres el candidato. Quiero que sepas que yo entiendo por lo que estás pasando y que estaré pensando en tí.

Un saludo personal y mis mejores deseos.

Sinceramente,

Ronald Reagan

Mr. Manolo Reboso
Manolo Reboso para Alcalde
Comité de Campaña
Apartado Postal 45-0931
Miami, Florida 33145

Letter from President Reagan, November 1981

With President Ronald Reagan in the Oval Room at the White House in November 1981.

The elections took place on November 3, and Miami had to choose from a total of eight mayoral candidates. Ferré received 40% of the vote and came in first place. I followed closely behind with 36%, which put us into a run-off election to be held in a week's time.

Those elections, and in particular the run-off between Ferré and myself, had aroused the interest of the mainstream press in the United States, since two candidates, neither of whom had been born in this country, were running for mayor of a major city. In addition, it was a litmus test to measure the true scope of the much-talked-about "Cuban power" in Miami.

A UPI cable, dated November 8, 1981, highlighted the high level of voter participation, estimated between 45 and 50%, and also emphasized that this was the most expensive election in the history of Miami, with the two candidates spending between them almost $600,000. It repeated that the pollsters did not dare make predictions, due to the virtual tie shown in the pre-election polls.

Likewise, that cable, and others on the same subject, pointed out the ethnic issue as something of great weight in the race. They quoted Ferré accusing me of trying to attract the Cuban vote by attacking him for not being Cuban, and they quoted me accusing Ferré of having made ethnic comments in the white and African American media.

Those seven days that separated the first and the second round of elections were seven red-hot days.

And finally came that defining Tuesday, November 10, 1981.

Chapter 22
A Hispanic Mayor – The Cuban American National Foundation

> *Life is 10 percent what you make it,*
> *and 90 percent how you take it.*
> Irving Berlin

Maurice A. Ferré was reelected mayor of Miami that long day in 1981.

I was convinced that I would win until the very day of the election. I felt I could win without problems and didn't even expect a close vote. It was what the opinion polls told me; it was what was in the air in the city; my candidacy had what they now call momentum. However, throughout the night, as the official tallies came in, that momentum began to unravel.

Where had my calculations and those of my campaign advisors gone wrong? The numbers had the last word: I had won the Hispanic vote with 76% of the total; the white vote was very tight, but I won it too, this one with 54%. Maurice Ferré won 97% of the African-American vote, and that was the determining factor.

What had happened to the African American vote? Wasn't there a sincere alliance between Miller Dawkins and me? Hadn't I always supported measures that favored that community? And why was there such an abysmal difference between my votes and Ferré's?

The Miller Dawkins situation was a case in itself, one of the greatest displays of disloyalty and ingratitude I have ever received. When he was running for the Miami Commission and had no chance of being elected, I decided to help him. I asked my friends Luis Lauredo and Virgilio Pérez Jr. to take care of his campaign's publicity, and they did it to the best of their abilities. And thanks to this, to a large extent, Dawkins was elected against all predictions. Logically, I expected him to reciprocate by drawing his community's votes to me. Not only did he not give me those votes, but he also didn't even thank me. The trust I placed in him was betrayed.

But that wasn't all. There was another factor, a very important one, of which my friends in the African-American community had warned me beforehand, but which I played down. I couldn't believe that this single factor would erase my entire performance in the Miami Commission, but it did: "Your relationship with Reagan was what turned the Black population against you."

Founding "Democrats for Reagan," campaigning for him and having my picture with him in the White House published on the front page of the *Herald*, as well as the letter in which he endorsed my candidacy for mayor of Miami, triggered a visceral reaction against me, some analysts said, and I think they were right.

Along with all of the above, there was another very important factor, an ancestral evil that infected a good part of Miami's African Americans and which, at election time, was decisive. This must be acknowledged out of respect for historical truth:

The Black vote, at that time, was controlled. Ferré had allied himself with Charlie Hadley, who was the most powerful vote dealer in the Black neighborhoods; he had complete control over the ballots. With him there were two or three other people who controlled the vote among members of his community. Athalie Range was one of them; she had huge control over the vote. She also never forgave me for not wanting to support her for interim mayor at the time of Dave Kennedy's suspension.

When an African American ran for office, you had to give them contributions, but Hispanics didn't get contributions from them. I never did, and I don't think Ferré did either.

I don't say this intending to offend or upset anyone, much less an entire community. This has changed quite a bit, for the good of all. There were influential people among African Americans, like Carrie Meek, Barbara Carey and others, who broke the corrupt ones' hold, which I sincerely welcome and hope is indeed a thing of the past.

That defeat was a very hard blow for me, but I quickly accepted reality. That same night I went to Univision, congratulated Ferré and mentally, I set out to properly and with time prepare myself for a new fight for mayor of Miami in 1983.

Life goes on, I told myself. Life has to go on. In spite of that difficult electoral setback, I felt good about the massive support I had gotten both in my community, the Miami Cubans, and in the white community. I think I have already said that one of the rules that governs my life is that everything happens for the best, so I concentrated on my private business, on construction.

One of my least successful adventures in the construction field was the purchase of several hotels in Miami Beach, right on the now world-famous Ocean Drive. Some friends asked me if I had gone crazy, because back then the south end of the beach was a row of old hotels, whose front porches were filled with sleepy old people who, according to the popular saying, came from the northern states to die here, so they called the place "the elephant's graveyard." I was being advised at the time by Rob Parkins, whom I had known and supported since he was a young man, when he was a City of Miami policeman and wanted to go into administration. He worked his way up to become Miami Beach's city manager. He predicted that what we now call South Beach would fabulously become "Coconut Grove with a beach," and time confirmed his keen vision. Nevertheless, I didn't fare well with my investments there and had to sell the properties before that vision became real.

I had two partners at the time: Juan Calderoni and Tomás Roberts, Spanish-Argentine investors. We managed to get the Banco Industrial de Venezuela to give us a loan of $43 million for the construction of its Miami headquarters at 1101 Brickell Avenue. We were very excited about this project, and it also helped me see that Maurice Ferré, the reelected mayor of Miami, still had me in his crosshairs.

Ferré got a prominent Venezuelan senator, Luis Piñerúa Ordaz, to, through him, carry out a campaign to discredit me. This senator claimed that I had squandered the $43 million that the Banco Industrial de Venezuela had lent me for the construction of its offices in Miami; he claimed that the bank had lost its investment. Irresponsibly and without further investigation, the *Herald* published those diatribes on its front page.

My friend Miguel Ángel Capriles came all the way from Venezuela to see how everything was going. He trusted us, and we went ahead with the construction project. When we finished the project, Banco Industrial de Venezuela received an offer of $88 million from investors in New York.

Then Capriles published in his newspapers *El Mundo*, *Últimas Noticias* and *Novedades*, in Venezuela, that he wished all the investments made by the Banco Industrial de Venezuela were as good as this one in Miami, thus discrediting those who had tried to discredit me.

Ferré was sure that, if I ran against him again in 1983, he would lose the election. He had lost the Cubans' support, which he would never regain, and he knew that the number of Cubans registering to vote was growing rapidly every year. A victory for me in 1983 was something that, looking at my numbers in the '81 campaign, seemed inevitable.

However, shortly thereafter, I decided that continuing in politics and running again for public office was not in my best interest, and I let my family, friends and allies know it. There is a time for everything, according to an oft-repeated biblical phrase, and I felt it was time to say goodbye to the political arena.

Eventually, I made peace with Ferré. We had been friends, we had shared many hours together in politics, working almost always in agreement, and I'm not one to hold grudges. He said that I had "screwed him" with the slogan *cubano, vota cubano* (Cuban, vote Cuban), which had become popular at that time, and that I had invented it. But the truth is that no, I didn't invent the phrase. I'm almost certain that the phrase came from Tomás García Fusté's wit.

To many analysts' surprise, Maurice Ferré's political career stalled within a few years, and he was never able to take off again. After his first eight years as mayor, many of us thought he was ready to run for governor of the state, or for the Senate. But he, for whatever reasons, insisted on continuing as mayor of Miami, after which he suffered a series of consecutive defeats that sank his career. The highest level of office he was able to achieve was county commissioner, which was considerably lower than what was expected of him early in his career. He failed to retain the favor of Cuban-American voters, and that was a key factor in his political life.

After my decision not to run again for mayor of Miami, Xavier Suárez, a young Cuban-American lawyer, entered the political arena and a world full of opportunities opened up before him, a world that began, precisely, with the Miami mayor's office.

And coinciding with the appearance of new characters in Miami's political arena, like Xavier Suárez himself, there also appeared, with no link between them, a new Cuban entity that would change the *modus operandi* of the activities towards Cuba's liberation and whose weight would also be strongly felt in the exile capital's politics. And although they were very different worlds, on more than one occasion these worlds collided. Sometimes harmoniously, sometimes not so much.

The Cuban American National Foundation was born in Miami, and I want to tell you how this happened, because the true story is somewhat different from what others have told.

When a new president of the United States is elected, members of his campaign team, people close to him and experts on different matters, quickly form a Transition Committee, whose objective is to set in motion the process of the transfer of powers, the formation of the new presidential cabinet, the appointments of new officials in important positions, etc.

Ronald Reagan was no exception to this unwritten rule and, as soon as he was elected by an impressive landslide on November 4, 1980, his Transition Committee began its work.

Carlos Salmán, who had been Reagan's campaign treasurer in Florida, wanted his friend and colleague Raúl Masvidal, a man extraordinarily qualified for the position, to be appointed secretary of commerce in Reagan's Cabinet. To achieve this, it was appropriate to have someone advocate for Masvidal within the Transition Committee. This was done with the inclusion of Mario Elgarresta, then a very capable young man who was taking his first steps, with notable successes, as a political consultant.

Elgarresta took the necessary steps, but the desired appointment couldn't be obtained. Instead, Masvidal was going to be offered a position as assistant secretary of Commerce, which he turned down. Elgarresta made friends with several members of the transition team and one of them was Richard Allen, who would become national security advisor to the Reagan administration. On one occasion when they were talking about the Cuba issue, Allen said to him:

"I think you Cubans are wasting your time in Miami, talking about Fidel being a communist, about what's going on in Cuba – all that stays among you. You need a lobby or a foundation here in Washington, like the Israelis have; a foundation that lobbies senators, congressmen, ministers, here, at this point in time. That would be the most effective thing you could do."

When Elgarresta returned to Miami, he told Raúl Masvidal and Carlos Salmán about that conversation. They met and decided to organize what would become the Cuban American National Foundation. The address that appears in the Foundation's original registration papers is Raúl Masvidal's apartment.

It so happened that after they founded and registered it, they both realized that they didn't have time to devote to the Foundation. Masvidal suggested that they talk to Jorge Más Canosa to see if he was interested in the project, which they considered to be a brilliant idea with great possibilities.

All said and done, Más Canosa liked the idea, and the rest is history.

But history has its twists and turns that are important to know. The Foundation was created in 1981. In 1985, Raúl Masvidal was running for mayor of Miami against Maurice Ferré, who was trying to be reelected again, and Xavier Suárez, who had already entered the political arena. As I understand it, Raúl Masvidal was the Foundation's most generous donor, but despite this, Más Canosa decided not to support him in his mayoral aspiration, citing some reasons that turned out to be quite inconsistent. A great division ensued.

Apparently, the real reason for Más Canosa's refusal to support Masvidal was that Pepe Hernández, his second in command at the Foundation, supported Xavier Suárez, as he had done before, in 1983. Pepe, a good Cuban, a companion of mine in Brigade 2506, had a great influence on Jorge Más, and this was the reason why the Foundation refused to support Masvidal.

There's an agreement to hold a meeting to try to settle differences and avoid disunity. Raúl (Masvidal) asks me to represent him, since he's so angry with Más Canosa that he doesn't want to see him. So I go to the meeting and ask Julito González Rebull to accompany me. Más Canosa brought with him his colleague and friend Pedro Roig, also a member of the Brigade. The meeting took place during a breakfast in South Miami.

I spoke of the situation with Jorge, reminding him of Raúl's role as founder and contributor to the Foundation. Jorge replied that he understood that very well, but that the Foundation has a policy not to support any candidate.

I then asked him how long that policy had existed, because the previous year, 1984, at an event that took place at La Carreta on SW 8th Street and 36th Avenue, he himself had made a vehement speech supporting Steve Clark for county mayor. I didn't mention then, as it would've been counterproductive, that at that time Jorge was trying to obtain a zoning change for some of his properties and Clark was helping him with that matter. Jorge replied that this had changed later, and the Foundation's policy was to not support any candidate.

The meeting didn't achieve its objective, and Más Canosa and Masvidal remained enemies forever. I didn't understand this, since I thought that, because it was a political issue, there should've been a reconciliation. And I think that now there should be a reconciliation between Más Canosa's children, Jorgito and his brother, and Raúl Masvidal himself, since they are all highly esteemed people in our community and should not be estranged.

In the end, those elections strongly shook the local political world. Maurice Ferré couldn't even make it to the runoff this time and lost forever Miami as his political stronghold. Raúl Masvidal was defeated by Xavier Suárez, who then became the first Cuban mayor of Miami. And, in case anyone doubted it, the

Cuban vote was established as the most important electoral factor in South Florida.

To me particularly, those elections also left me with the bitter taste of division, of the political disagreement between Más Canosa and Masvidal. And this reminded me of an anecdote, perhaps not entirely fair, but very close to reality about a common fault that has permanently plagued the Cuban exile community.

When I was commissioner, I was invited to almost all exile events, and so was Dr. Carlos Prío Socarrás, former president of Cuba. Whenever I had the opportunity, I would sit next to Dr. Prío, because I always learned something good from him.

Once, we were both at a graduation of the Interamerican Military Academy, the school that Pedro Roig had on NW 7th Street and 35th Avenue. I asked Dr. Prío what, in his opinion, was our problem. Despite having Fidel Castro as our common enemy, we Cubans had 400 different organizations, and the divisions among us had reached such extremes that, for many so-called leaders, it seemed that Fidel had taken a back seat, and they aimed their cannons, instead of at him, at their rivals in exile. Something similar happened with the little wars between the radio stations, which divided public opinion, and between one and the other, it was never possible to put together a unified front to fight for Cuba.

I remember that Prío looked at me with some sadness in his eyes and told me: "Manolo, the exile community is like a bucket of crabs. If one crab wants to climb up to escape from the bucket, the crab beneath it pulls it down, so that it cannot leave."

That answer from the former president of Cuba has always remained in my memories.

Chapter 23
Ronald Reagan – Politics and Politicians in Miami-Dade

> *A politician is a man who understands government. A statesman is a politician who's been dead for fifteen years.*
> Harry Truman

After that election season, I concentrated a little more on my construction company, although I didn't stray too far from the local political scene. During that period, as time went on, my disenchantment with President Reagan grew.

Yes, he was a good president. Many of his policies were successful, but there was no evidence that he had any plans to revitalize U.S. policy towards Cuba, nothing that would lead to the end of the Castro regime. The Foundation had brought him to Miami one year to celebrate May 20th. He had worn a fine guayabera made especially for him by Ramón Puig; he had had lunch at the popular restaurant *La Esquina de Tejas*; the Dade County Auditorium had heard the *¡viva!* to a free Cuba – but that was it.

Worse still, as early in his presidency as 1982, Vernon Walters, his special envoy, had met for six hours in La Habana with Fidel Castro. He also held secret talks with Carlos Rafael Rodríguez, one of the grey eminences of Cuban communism, in Mexico, in what appeared to be a search for appeasement, since no other action was apparent on the Cuban front.

Unlike many of my compatriots who rushed to change parties, trusting in the Republicans' promises, I, seeing that time went by and Reagan didn't make a move on Cuba, kept my membership in the Democratic Party. This didn't prevent me, for example, from liking Bush Sr. during his first term as president.

As for Miami, Xavier Suárez wasn't the only example of young Cubans who stood out in local politics, which confirmed that a new generation of our own was emerging and little by little winning public offices, as has happened in all human activities throughout the centuries.

One day in mid-1987, my friend Hermán Echevarría, then president of the Hialeah Chamber of Commerce, came to my office. Hermán was a political powerhouse in his own right. He had been a Hialeah councilman and was a strong ally of Mayor Raúl Martínez. All the politicians wanted him as a friend because he had a very sharp mind, an accurate political instinct and was a magnificent fundraiser for the campaigns in which he was involved.

He was also very successful in business, thanks in part to his political connections, from which he always sought benefits for his companies. Hermán introduced me to a skinny, intelligent-looking young man who accompanied him. He was 24 years old, his name was Alex Penelas, and he had recently graduated as a lawyer.

Penelas was running for Hialeah City Council and Hermán asked me to help him by putting him in touch with the radio commentators of the moment. I liked the boy and decided to give him a hand. I introduced him to Fernando Penabaz, Fusté and other local radio figures. The elections would be in November 1987, and I decided to help him.

Hermán and Penelas were part of a trio of friends completed by Jorge Luis López, who a few years later would become one of the most important lobbyists in the political arena. He and Alex Penelas had studied together and together they had decided to get into politics, with the commitment that when one of them ran, the other would be his campaign manager and vice versa. I believe, but don't know for sure, that they flipped a coin and Jorge Luis López was the first to run.

Jorge Luis ran for the state House of Representatives and Alex ran his campaign, but luck didn't smile on them that time. It was then Penelas's turn to run, and he decided to run for the Hialeah commission. Jorge Luis ran his campaign and success was theirs this time. Alex became a Hialeah City Councilman in 1987 and was reelected in 1989. Jorge Luis was his Chief of Staff. I was glad to have helped them.

For the 1992 elections for county commissioners, our group, which was a very small group, decided to help Alex run for the seat held by Jorge Valdés.

Valdés was an excellent person, a decent, capable and very popular politician. He had been the first Cuban elected as a Dade County commissioner and had the support of people and organizations of great political weight, such as the Latin Builders, CAMACOL, etc. Sergio Pino, who was one of the most important people in our community, was his campaign treasurer.

For us, that was an uphill race, but we decided to run it anyway. We won, and that's how Alex Penelas emerged as a political power at the county level.

Alex didn't rest on his laurels. He moved very well within the county's political corridors; he is a very good speaker; he was incredibly charming in the radio programs where he was frequently invited; he is disciplined. All of this convinced even the most skeptical of his strong chances, in 1996, for county mayor. Besides, Alex was the darling, the delight, of the Cuban *abuelitas*; they all wanted to adopt him.

Another important quality in Alex Penelas is one that I had only previously noticed in Reubin Askew: Alex was not only honest, but also projected that honesty, which quickly earned him the goodwill of voters.

And in the inner workings of politics, in the art of negotiation, in what in Cuban slang is called *el talle politico*, Alex had nothing to envy the old masters of the profession.

Despite all of the above, it wasn't at all easy to run for that position in those elections, because his opponents were all very strong candidates. In addition to Alex, former Miami mayors Maurice Ferré and Xavier Suárez, as well as county commissioner Arthur Teele, who was deeply established in the African-American community, were running for county mayor, making the campaign a very intense one and one that required abundant resources.

There were more than a few so-called election gurus in South Florida who didn't give us a single chance of winning. They said that Alex was too young, that he didn't have experience comparable to the other three contenders; but, despite all those gloomy predictions, we won. Of course, in those circumstances a runoff was inevitable and that was, to the surprise of many, between the youngest of the Hispanic candidates and Arthur Teele, the African-American candidate. Curiously, in that race the roles were reversed: Penelas, the Cuban American, was a member of the Democratic Party. Arthur Teele, the African American, was a member of the Republican Party. It's well known that in our area local and county elections are not partisan, but it's also known that the candidates' parties, whether they're a Republican or a Democrat, influences the voters.

Alex Penelas became the youngest mayor of any political body comparable to Dade County.

That year, 1996, would also be of great significance in my personal life. Nora and I had divorced, and in November I married again, this time to my current wife, Nadia Leets, from Nicaragua.

Meanwhile, the political world in South Florida continued its always-hectic course. Penelas was running a successful mayoralty in the county and, come the year 2000, he decided to run for reelection. Triumph was his again, and this time it was an easy win, as he had already proven his great ability.

Having won his reelection, Alex decided to celebrate by taking a vacation to visit his wife's family in Spain. Nadia and I accompanied them. We were in the Basque country, which at that time, at the end of 2000, was dangerous because of the presence of ETA, the terrorist organization of the region's pro-independence movement. After two weeks there, we decided to go to Madrid. We were on our way back to the United States, but Alex wanted us to invite Felipe Valls, the county's restaurant industry czar, owner of Versailles and La Carreta, among others, and a great friend of mine, to join us in Madrid. I called Felipe and he and Natty, his wife, loved the idea, and they promptly joined us.

It got a little complicated, because both the mayor of the city of Madrid and the mayor of the community of Madrid each offered us dinners, so our stay in Spain was extended for three weeks. We returned only one week before the general elections here.

In Spain with Madrid's Mayor Manzano, Miami-Dade County Mayor Alex Penelas and Felipe Valls.

Alex had a successful second term as county mayor. Among others, it was his initiative to change the name of the county from Dade to Miami-Dade, with the approval of the voters, but his political star was later eclipsed. In 2004, he couldn't run to continue as county mayor due to term limits, so then he launched a huge electoral adventure, where he didn't do well at all. He ran for U.S. senator and finished third, behind Betty Castor and Peter Deutsch. Alex had problems with the Democratic Party establishment, and this deprived him of the support he would've needed to win that election.

He then retired to private life, to his legal profession. In 2020, he attempted a return to politics, aspiring once again to the office he'd previously held, county mayor; but by then he had to win the vote of a new generation that was not familiar with his previous performance and was looking for new paths. On the other hand, the coronavirus pandemic had already broken out, and this greatly limited personal contact with the voters, visits to the senior centers, etc.

The current mayor of the county, Daniella Levine Cava, and the current mayor of Hialeah, Esteban Bovo, went to a runoff, from which Alex was left out. Ms. Levine Cava became the first woman to hold the highest executive position in Miami-Dade.

As for Arthur Teele, his life and political career came to a tragic end. In 2005, a series of investigative reports published by the *Miami Herald* led to Teele's indictment on charges of embezzlement and unlawful compensation, which in turn prompted then Governor Jeb Bush to suspend him from his position as city commissioner. He was convicted, and Teele faced the likelihood of a lengthy prison sentence.

On July 27, 2005, Teele went to the newspaper building, which was then in downtown Miami, next to Biscayne Bay, and there, in the lobby of the *Miami Herald*, he took his own life by shooting himself in the temple.

Two years later, in a post mortem appeal that his widow obtained, his case was reviewed by the court. His previous conviction was overturned, and he was acquitted of the charges against him.

This was a true tragedy that shook South Florida, especially its political landscape. Teele was a highly respected leader, not only by his community, but by all who knew his resume. He had been discharged from the Army with a brilliant military record and was a successful lawyer, and before entering local politics, he had been appointed by President Reagan to a high position in the Department of Transportation.

No doubt Teele was hit hard by the accusations made against him and by the unjust sentence imposed on him. He entered the lobby of the *Herald* carrying a gun, and I understand that he asked for a specific person, so it's been left in doubt whether, in addition to committing suicide, he also intended to hurt someone. Teele left nothing in writing, no farewell note, so his specific motivations have been left open to speculation.

I got along very well with him and respected him. I think his case stands as a sad reminder of the balance that must be struck between freedom of the press and respect for the truth and the good name of individuals.

Another thought about Arthur Teele is that his death left a very large leadership void in the African-American community, so large that I believe no one has yet been able to capably fill it. At one time it was thought that Kendrick Meek would fill that space, but, in my opinion, Kendrick turned out to be too passive for South Florida's political dynamics.

In recounting these experiences that I've lived and which, at the same time, are part of Miami's history, I have mentioned many people who are, equally, part of what's been lived by this community of ours, and when I speak this way, I am not only referring to the Cuban community, but to the diverse, multicultural and multiethnic *Miamian* community.

I mentioned, for example, Xavier Suárez and Raúl Martínez, without whose names our history in the United States cannot be written. Xavier was, as I already mentioned, the first Cuban mayor of Miami, and that is a distinction that will always accompany him, since it wasn't by chance that he achieved that honor, but by the talent he displayed at the beginning of his political career.

I've known him since he graduated from Harvard. He went to City Hall one day, met with me and confided in me his intentions to go into politics, and he was successful. He was in the right place at the right time, but, that success didn't last long. Since then, he's been going from one position to another, running for different positions, and those are things that to me give the impression that you want to live on political positions all your life; people who run and run again, and don't know when to stop.

I don't mean by this that people who don't know when it's time to retire from public life are not good or intelligent, but it's evident to me that they lose their sense of reality.

I also mentioned Raúl Martínez; my friend Raúl, a true political engine, whom I value very much. Whoever remembers the Hialeah in the 60s and 70s, when cows still grazed by the train line, and Henry Milander took off his butcher's apron to sit for a while in his mayoral chair, must recognize that the vibrant and modern city that is the Hialeah of today has a father, and that father is Raúl Martínez.

In 1989, Raúl was running for the seat in the U.S. House of Representatives that had been vacated by the death of Dante Fascell, for which State Senator Ileana Ros-Lehtinen was also running. Ileana's husband, Dexter Lehtinen, was then U.S. Attorney for South Florida, and Raúl was indicted on several corruption charges before a grand jury. Legal proceedings entailed three separate trials and stretched over several months, which completely derailed his congressional aspirations. In the end, those accusations could never be reliably proven. Raúl was acquitted of one extortion charge, and a new prosecutor dropped the remaining charges because of a hung jury. Raúl returned to political life, where he remained for a long time.

Raúl is a *sui generis* case. In our Spanish language, the word "political" has more than one meaning. One of them is to be a skillful speaker, capable of not letting your true feelings show and of saying only what will not bother anyone. If someone says to you "you are very political," that is what they are telling you. Raúl is the opposite: he says what he feels without thinking twice, he's not tactful, and he never shies away from a good controversy. His way of being is a big part of the reason why those who elected him mayor of "the City of Progress" for 24 years remain loyal.

As I write these words, the political landscape in Miami, in Hialeah, in all of Miami-Dade County is at a point of great uncertainty, perhaps a moment of transition; although, if so, I don't think there are many who can say where that transition is going.

In the past, there was a time when it was said that a Cuban would never become mayor of the county, because of the resistance of Americans, both white and black. Later, when the numerical dominance of our people prevailed, it was said that, given the growth of the Cuban community, no American, black or white, could ever again become the mayor of Miami-Dade. Despite all those calculations and all those predictions, a woman is currently mayor of the county: a white, American, Jewish woman, Daniella Levine Cava.

Her rival in the election she won, Esteban Bovo, now mayor of Hialeah, is a skilled and efficient politician, well prepared for the job and widely supported by Cuban and not a few white American voters. What prevented him from succeeding in his bid for the mayoralty?

It's true that the current mayor had the white Democrats' support and the massive support of the Jewish vote. But, in my opinion, which is also that of several independent analysts, former President Donald Trump's support was a curse for Bovo; it was a decisive factor in his defeat. The same thing happened to him as happened to me in my 1981 Miami mayoral bid, in which my support for Ronald Reagan and his support for me caused almost all Black voters to vote against me.

In Bovo's case, Trump lost him not only the Black vote, but also non-Cuban Hispanic voters, most of whom are Democrats. And, in addition, he also lost the vote of many Independent voters who, at present, vote for anyone not associated with Donald Trump.

Rarely in the history of the United States has what happens at the national political level affected state and local politics as much as it has in these, the 20s of the third millennium. How will this affect us in the short term here in South Florida and specifically in the capital of exile? That, of course, remains to be seen. I only pray to God that common sense and true patriotism will prevail. If not, there will be more than reasonable cause for concern about the future of democracy in the United States, which we'll talk about later.

Chapter 24
Return to Nicaragua – The Two Statues

> *It almost always happens that the greater part defeats the better one.*
> Tito Livio

My wife Nadia had relatives in Nicaragua, so when Arnoldo Alemán was president, we began to see possibilities of going there to spend some time with them.

This had become possible due to the events that had occurred in that country, which I love so much. There had been political changes that would've been impossible to predict when Somoza was overthrown on July 17, 1979.

With the departure of Somoza, the Sandinistas took power with the creation of a National Reconstruction Junta, with Daniel Ortega at its head as coordinator. Ortega consolidated his power by being elected president in elections held in 1984, which gave speed and depth to a very radical government program aimed at changing the entire political order in the country.

As soon as the Sandinistas came to power and their leftist ideology became evident, many Nicaraguans, little by little at first and more rapidly afterwards, began to become disenchanted first and then to reject the new order of things. The Reagan administration in Washington, determined not to allow another adverse enclave in Latin America, took matters into its own hands by helping to create and finance anti-Sandinista guerrilla forces that would become known as the Contras. These forces became a serious challenge to Daniel Ortega and his regime, and the situation practically turned into a civil war. In 1989, with the conflict bogged down and facing intense international pressure, the disputing parties agreed to negotiate their differences. They agreed to gradually demobilize the Contras and ratified a call for presidential elections in February 1990.

Ignoring Fidel Castro's fierce opposition, Ortega agreed to hold those elections. His opponents managed to unite in a coalition called UNO, which had as its presidential candidate Violeta Barrios, the widow of the most respected anti-Somoza leader, journalist Pedro Joaquín Chamorro, who was assassinated in Managua in early 1978. All polls pointed to an easy victory for Daniel Ortega.

But despite these polls, Violeta Chamorro won the election by a wide margin. Once the election results were known, many Nicaraguans declared that they had lied when answering the opinion polls, fearing possible reprisals.

Under the presidency of Doña Violeta, a political process began that seemed to indicate that democracy was being institutionalized in Nicaragua.

Arnoldo Alemán, the former mayor of Managua, had been elected as the new president at the end of Doña Violeta's term. It was then that Nadia and I decided to move to Nicaragua. We went to the city of Granada, which we liked very much, and that's where we settled. We spent the first six months in a hotel and then we moved to a house, but we always considered it a temporary situation, because we never thought of staying there permanently.

In 2001, a new electoral cycle for the Nicaraguans arrived and, among others, the engineer Enrique Bolaños aspired to the presidency. Bolaños was elected president, and we remained in Nicaragua. Plain and simple, we liked it there.

After Enrique Bolaños, in 2007, Daniel Ortega was again elected president of Nicaragua and has remained in that position until the present, something I will elaborate on a little later.

To understand this in the Nicaraguan context, it's necessary to know some details that are not often found in history books, nor in all the reports that are written about it.

With my wife Nadia and Sancha in Nicaragua

It's necessary to know, for example, the influence that the Venezuelan president Carlos Andrés Pérez had in that period of Nicaragua's history. Carlos Andrés was backed by the pressure he had exerted at the time to bring about the end of the Somoza regime, something we have already seen in previous pages here. Afterwards, he enthusiastically supported the Sandinistas in power, and it was only when this support became counterproductive for him and his own ambitions in Venezuela that he began to look for a democratic alternative to the Nicaraguan problem.

He found that alternative in the candidacy of Doña Violeta Barrios. Carlos Andrés was the person, the Latin American ruler, who gave Chamorro's widow the most support and, of course, after her victory at the polls, she felt morally obligated to him.

That help, however, came at a very high price and made it clear that the Venezuelan president hadn't given up his old determination to become the arbiter of democracy throughout the continent. Carlos Andrés asked Doña Violeta to keep Humberto, Daniel Ortega's brother, at the head of the Nicaraguan armed forces. Doña Violeta, forced by these circumstances, accepted that proposal which, to a certain extent, bound her hands, preventing her from carrying out some of the changes that were essential for her own government's stability.

The supposed closeness of the Venezuelan president to the extreme left-wing movements in Latin America was, in the opinion of many who knew him well, a great hypocrisy, since his tastes were those of a capitalist millionaire and nothing like those of a blue-collar man. The ADECO leader (of Venezuela's Democratic Action Party) liked Cristal champagne; if he was offered one of inferior quality, he wouldn't drink it. When he visited Madrid, he stayed at the Ritz, and if there was no room available there, he would leave Spain. Humility was not one of his attributes.

For her part, Doña Violeta, in spite of her limitations and considering the problems she had to face, formed a good government and demonstrated her patriotism and her great willingness to serve others.

As I have already mentioned, Doña Violeta was succeeded by the former mayor of Managua, Arnoldo Alemán, of the Liberal Party. At that time, he was very popular throughout the country. Alemán developed an inordinate taste for power and devised treacherous ways to ensure his eventual return to power once his presidential term was over.

As if that weren't enough, Alemán carried out a Machiavellian plan to weaken his own party by making his followers within it split off and found a separate party, which would serve him as a political façade so that he could satisfy his ambitions.

Alemán was succeeded in the presidency by the engineer Enrique Bolaños, who had been his vice president. Bolaños was a completely different man, an honest politician, conservative, despite being at the head of the Liberal Party, which wasn't at all contradictory in Latin America.

The new president offered Alemán two ambassadorships for him to choose from: Spain or the Dominican Republic. If Alemán had accepted Bolaños's offer, he would've left as ambassador and returned four years later. It would've been very easy for him to become president of Nicaragua again; he would've won in a landslide. But he preferred to stay in Nicaragua, to continue serving as president.

Meaning, he wanted to be above Bolaños and humiliated him whenever he could. I was there, and I lived through it. When he was somewhere and Bolaños arrived, or they were both at some public ceremony, Alemán, who boasted of being a good singer, would order the musicians to play "El Rey," that well-known ranchera that says in part, "I am still the king," and he would sing it to make fun of the president. Under those circumstances, Bolaños was facing great difficulties due, among other factors, to the division of the Liberal Party that Alemán was stoking by staying in the country.

Bolaños undertook an intense anti-corruption campaign, the most impressive result of which was the indictment and conviction of the now former President Alemán, who was sentenced to 20 years in prison for scandalous incidents of embezzlement.

Bolaños promoted remarkable measures that favored the national economy, but his presidency was permanently sabotaged by Alemán's followers.

In 1977, the U.S. Ambassador to Nicaragua, James Theberge, an old friend of mine, introduced me to the then mayor of Granada, Alvaro Chamorro, with whom I have maintained a good friendship. In 2006, Nadia and I went to Alvaro's birthday party in Granada and, with the country in the midst of an election, Daniel Ortega and his wife, Rosario Murillo, also attended.

With Daniel Ortega in 2006 when he was running for President of Nicaragua.

Ortega was then projecting himself as being democratic, on the basis of having held free elections in 1990 and, having lost them, handing the position, without problems, to his rival, Violeta Chamorro. Ortega and I talked about his totally social democratic form of government and took a picture together.

As it was, Daniel Ortega was again elected president of Nicaragua in 2006, with 38% of the vote. He took office on January 10, 2007, and two years later, the highest court in the country, which was totally controlled by the Sandinistas, overturned Arnoldo Alemán's conviction. Daniel Ortega has remained in power ever since.

This was the result of agreements between Ortega and Alemán that would have been unthinkable in the Nicaraguan political landscape. Alemán invited Ortega to his home, and Ortega was accompanied by Dionisio ("Nicho") Marenco, then mayor of Managua. To both of their surprise, Alemán proposed to Ortega the evil plan of the two of them taking turns being president. Since the Sandinista National Liberation Front never obtained more than 36 or 37 percent of the votes, and the minimum to win the presidency was 45 percent, Alemán lowered that requirement to 35 percent, in order to smooth the Sandinistas's access to the highest office in the country.

This, however, was not enough. It was also essential to divide the Liberal vote, a task that was left in Alemán's hands, the dirty work of dividing his own party.

In Nicaragua there have been, in reality, two revolutions: the Sandinista one in 1979 and the Ortega one in 2007. The Sandinistas should erect a statue to Jimmy Carter; the Orteguistas should do the same to Arnoldo Alemán.

While this was unfolding in Nicaragua, Nadia and I kept going back and forth smoothly, which helped me to keep abreast of the political situation in Miami.

Perhaps some readers will wonder why, in what is a person's memoirs, in this case mine, it's necessary to include a detailed narration of a country's history. This is something that may not be well understood by those fortunate enough to have never had their lives, their family, their personal history directly affected by the political developments in their respective countries. They should thank God for that.

Chapter 25
Politics, Yesterday and Today

> *I have come to the conclusion that politics are too serious a matter to be left to the politicians.*
> Charles deGaulle

Returning to Miami for good renewed my interest in the city's and the county's affairs. I had never really lost interest, since my life had previously been between the two cities, Managua and Miami.

Inserting myself again in South Florida's day-to-day political matters brought no surprises to my life, but seeing the changes that have occurred since I was appointed interim commissioner in 1972 has given me some food for thought that I must share with all the people who love this corner of the world, where so many men and women of a thousand different origins have found a new home and a way to live dignified and free lives.

I am one of those who believes that sterile nostalgia, remembering the past for no other purpose than nostalgia itself, does us no good, because it can disconnect us from the present moment in which we have to live. Remembering the past is useful if it helps us examine the mistakes we've made, so as not to repeat them in the present, and it helps us remember the lessons we've learned.

At the same time, I have to admit that when one has already lived a lot, as in my case, comparisons between what we have lived and what we are living are inevitable.

So, in my opinion, the great contrast that exists between the way politics was practiced in not-so-distant times, say in the second half of the last century, and how it's done today, is obvious.

My active political life unfolded in an era that was different in many ways from how we live today. For me, the biggest difference lies in certain ethical values that now seem to be in decline and whose lack makes the political environment very inhospitable. I'm not referring specifically to politicians' handling of taxpayer money, because there have been thieves in all social spheres since the world began to turn and they continue to exist, unfortunately, in all countries of the world. It's important to remember that the abundance of evil can never be used as an excuse for not fighting it.

I am speaking rather of human relations, because today, the way people deal with each other, especially when they are in competition with each other, seems to have lost respect for certain taboos that existed in the past and whose existence protected coexistence. In the past, people's private lives were respected, the family was respected, epithets were avoided in political disputes, and there was at least a minimum of cordiality between adversaries. This is what in Cuba we called *buena educación* (good education or manners), which had nothing to do with academic degrees, but with one's conduct towards others; a politician who was rude was condemned to failure.

Today, a good portion of politicians and almost all the press ignore those parameters, and when you dedicate yourself to politics you lose a lot. You lose privacy in your life; you have to become an open book; they can ask you any questions they want; they can call you at any time they want; and you must always be available to give explanations, sometimes on issues that have nothing to do with your public performance.

It's very difficult to be a politician, because the press doesn't pay attention to the ways it obtains information, and that is why many people refuse to participate in politics. For example, *Fortune* magazine publishes every year its famous list of the 500 most successful corporations in the United States, and those corporations abound with executives who are more than ready to be president of the United States. However, those executives don't get into politics, because they know that it would require them to have a perfect record in all aspects of life. They investigate you, and if they find that when you were in kindergarten you took the crayons from the little girl sitting next to you, they make such a scandal out of it that they disgrace your life. Many talented men and women, who don't want their private lives meddled with, stay away from politics and leave the destiny of nations to the mediocre.

This has been getting worse over time. I would say that after, perhaps, Franklin Delano Roosevelt, the United States has not produced true statesmen, none of the stature of Winston Churchill or Charles de Gaulle or of Adenauer. The presidents of the United States have been people who have not shone much, who don't seem to have had great intellectual gifts. Jimmy Carter, who grew peanuts in Georgia; Bill Clinton, a good lawyer; Ronald Reagan, a movie actor. Obama is another one: neither as a state senator nor as a federal senator could he pass a single law, and yet he became president.

I'm not saying that they were bad people, nor that they didn't have some stellar moments as presidents, but if, due to the political circumstances of their time, they had not become president, what legacy would they have left to humanity? Would anyone remember them?

On the flip side, many people believe that one of the great things about this country is precisely that anyone can be president, which one can argue ad infinitum whether this is a virtue or a defect of democracy. See, we have Donald Trump, the most pathetic example of "anyone can be president of this country."

Of course, to be fair in these assessments, it's necessary to recognize that the deterioration of civic values to which I've referred is not an evil that afflicts only the United States; it's seen across the world. If we remember that just 20 or 30 years ago, presidents were untouchable, not only in the United States, but in almost the entire world, we can see the difference. Presidents' private lives were respected. That more or less ended in John Kennedy's time, perhaps because he and his wife, Jacqueline, were given an aura by the press itself as if they were Hollywood stars.

I can see the positive side of this phenomenon, the one that informs and shows the leaders for what they are as people; the negative side is that there seem to be no limits. One should remember, for example, that during Clinton's presidency, when news of his affair with Monica Lewinsky came out, some media described how the girl's blue dress had been stained. Was that necessary?

As for relations between political adversaries, chivalry has gone on vacation and doesn't seem to want to return, and there are so many examples that they need not be mentioned. It's enough to recall the most recent electoral campaigns, from local to national, to see that the outlook is not at all encouraging.

I don't intend, neither in this topic, nor in any other, to offer myself as an example of virtue. That's not my style; I don't overvalue myself, nor do I forget the saying "tell me what you boast of and I will tell you what you lack." If I speak of myself on issues such as civic and human values in politics, it's only because of the value of the personal testimony of what I've experienced and demonstrated.

In my personal experience, it's possible to go run for office, it's possible to have different visions regarding public administration, it's possible to win or lose an election, without denigrating the opponent, nor establishing everlasting enmities.

My dealings and my relations were always cordial with everyone. Although Rose Gordon and J. L. Plummer, my colleagues on the

Miami commission, almost never voted in favor of my proposals, my personal relationship with them was always very good. They had their reasons and we, Rev. Gibson and I, had ours and we respected each other. We wanted to move forward, both on the Hispanic side and on the African American side and they, as white people, were trying to serve those who were then the dominant power in Miami, the white establishment, something we could all understand without anyone getting upset about it.

Likewise, I had good relations with county commissioners, with state officials and legislators, with governors, even with governors of other states and also with some foreigners, such as the presidents of the Central American countries, almost all of whom I knew, and likewise with the governors of southeastern Mexico, with the mayor of Madrid, and so on.

I had a good friendship with the local leaders of the Republican Party, with Carlos Salmán, Al Cárdenas, Lincoln Díaz-Balart, Ileana Ros-Lehtinen and others. We never let partisan issues divide us, as we see happening today with many people.

And as for electoral rivalries, which I had, almost all of them were within a framework of decency and reciprocal respect. So much so, that I have forgotten the names of almost all those who ran against me. In my most difficult campaign, which was the Miami mayoral campaign, which had some very heated moments, I've already told how Ferré and I never really stopped being friends.

I have proven that it's not difficult at all to get along with people, and it's also advisable, because you never know who you'll need in the future.

And the future, let no one forget, depends on the new generations, some of whose members will be the leaders and activists of the political parties and who, in due course, will become governors, legislators and officials of all kinds. I wonder if those young men and women who show interest in politics are being adequately prepared for their integration and development in what should be the beautiful world of public service.

In saying this, it seems to me that I'm focusing on the main cause of the deterioration of politics these days. I don't know if in the schools where our young people study law, political science, etc., the concept is stressed to them – is instilled in their minds and in their hearts – that *politics is public service*; that a politician is a servant of the people, and every young person who envisions his or her future in the world of politics should have that concept very clear in his or her mind.

I can't help but worry about the future when I contemplate, at times, the movements of almost all politicians, just to cite one example. Let's say that a politician of any level, be it municipal, county, state or federal, goes to a radio or television station where he/she is going to be interviewed or arrives at a public space where a project is going to be inaugurated. Just look at the entourage that accompanies him!

Before the politician arrives at the place, two or three of his assistants, all young people, who are or appear to be in charge of his personal security, arrive at the place, armed with their corresponding cell phones and, in some cases, walkie-talkies. They are polite, generally speaking, but they emit a certain bully-like attitude, or, at least, that's the impression they give. If they are in the lobby of a building, one of them will approach the receptionist and ask her, in a low voice, that as soon as the politician arrives, he needs to be let inside the studio or office where he's going, because he cannot wait in the lobby where he would be subject to the greetings, comments and requests of the people who see him there. They stand around the door through which the politician must enter. They don't sit down; they give the impression of being very busy.

The politician finally arrives, surrounded by other members of his group, all of them with cell phone in hand, some with a folder full of papers, all elegantly dressed, very well groomed, impeccable hair, manicured nails, some of them very close to the politician whispering something in his ear. When he enters the studio or office, one or two of his assistants will enter after him, two or three will stay in the corridor, near the entrance... It's a whole show, which seems to be performed to underscore *the great importance* of the politician in question.

Many future politicians generally come out of this unserious entourage. It's certain that, back at the politician's office, some of these assistants will be busy helping citizens who have come to them with a request. Many, I would like to believe, will make an effort to resolve those cases. Others will be more concerned with making the politician look good, without making a real effort to serve those who come to him. Are these young people being trained as public servants, or are they simply being taught how to engage in politicking? This is my great concern.

From my own experience, I can say that most of the young people who enter the political arena do so without having a clear idea of what the problems are that affect the community they are supposed to serve. I would say that, first, the person who aspires has to learn to know that community well, has to get involved in how his community works, what it has, what it lacks, and has to examine himself honestly to see if he can be an influence in solving the problems.

He should not do it, plainly and simply, as many politicians do, to live from their position. There are many who are there for *saecula saeculorum*; they get into politics and never leave it because that is their *modus vivendi*. That's their job, to be in an elected position and to be reelected every four years. That's not the right thing to do. I believe that those who get involved in politics should do so because they are concerned about the problems of their community and seek in politics the means to solve those problems.

In my youth I had a strong interest in entering politics because I saw it as a vehicle to improve our community. I served for eight years and when I realized that I had done my part, that it was enough. I resigned and left the field open for someone else to take my place. Over time I received many offers, in the best sense of the word, to run for other positions, whether as state senator, county commissioner, etc., but I declined those propositions, because I had already fulfilled my role in politics.

And although I sometimes miss some of the more satisfying aspects about politics, I know that my time has passed and it's now up to me to help, encourage and pave the way for those who come after me.

Chapter 26
Family and Friends – Leaders, Past and Present

> *If you confer a benefit, never remember it;*
> *if you receive one, never forget it.*
> Chilon of Sparta

This exercise of writing my memoirs is very beneficial for me in a thousand different ways, and one of them is that it gives me the opportunity to put into perspective events and experiences that perhaps, at the time, I wasn't able to assess in their proper measure.

My parents and grandparents instilled in me the traditional values of our Catholic-Spanish culture, values that were reinforced by my Cuban upbringing and to which were added our very Cuban sense of humor and our Caribbean spark.

Needless to say, in our upbringing, there is nothing more valuable than the family, nor is there a credo as unanimous as the one instilled in us since we're born and that we in time instill in our descendants: the family is the most important thing. And, though we're human and therefore not perfect and though we make mistakes, we put our best efforts into the welfare of the family.

So, I would like to begin this chapter by thanking all my relatives. I'm indebted to them for so much that they've given me, and they are my truest pride. My grandparents and my parents taught me, by their example, the lessons that equipped me to walk a clean and honest path throughout my life. They didn't know much about child psychology, but they knew the value of respect for oneself, for traditions and for family honor. They passed on to me a healthy pride in a job well done, no matter how humble it may be, and they taught me to appreciate people, not for their race or their distinction nor for what they have, but for who they are.

I had the satisfaction of seeing my younger brother Roberto grow and develop within the parameters of these virtues, and I could see the respect and admiration that all those who knew him felt for him.

With my brother Roberto

Tengo seis hijos que me llenan de sano orgullo. Cuatro de ellos son abogados muy bien acreditados. Ninguno se hizo médico, que es lo que yo necesitaría a esta edad que tengo, pero me satisface mucho el hecho de que los seis son personas de bien, excelentes seres humanos.

With my children Irma, Robert, Melissa, Alex, Noreen and Manny

Alex, the oldest, earned his bachelor's degree from the University of Miami. He continued his studies and received his law degree from Georgetown University in Washington, D.C. He is married to Kiki and has two children, David and Ali. David is father to Mila and Gavin. Ali is mother to Sebastian and Andrea. Alex currently practices law and specializes in personal injury.

Roberto Luis, the second, graduated with a degree in Business Administration from the University of Miami and then moved to Spain, where he worked in the banking system for two years. Back in Miami, he worked in the City of Miami Beach for several years. He is currently retired, single and lives in Coconut Grove.

My third daughter, Irma, graduated with a law degree from the University of Miami. She is the widow of Mario Solares, who passed away in 2016. She has two children, Gabriela and Mario Luis. Gabriela is married to Peter Cirera and Mario Luis is single. Irma practices law at a reputable law firm in Miami.

Noreen, my fourth daughter, is a graduate of Florida International University (FIU) with a degree in Business Administration.

She is married to Albert Balido, and they reside in Tallahassee, where they own a major public relations company.

The fifth, Melissa, is an attorney. She graduated with a law degree from Florida State University (FSU), and is married to Eduardo Lombard. They have two daughters, Sofie and Lily, and also reside in Tallahassee.

The sixth, Manny, also attended law school. He received his law degree, also from FSU. He is married to Camile, who is a medical doctor specializing in pediatrics. They have two children: Eva and Manny Jr. Manny Sr. worked for two years in the court system, seven years in the state attorney's office, and for the last three years he's been a federal prosecutor.

In all, I have six children, eight grandchildren and four great-grandchildren. Needless to say, I'm a happy and proud father, grandfather and great-grandfather of these beautiful offspring that God has allowed me to have.

My first two marriages ended in divorce. I will always be grateful to my two ex-wives, Irma and Nora, for the children they gave me. Nadia and I were married on November 7, 1996, and I thank her for the many good things she has brought into my life, all of which I happily appreciate and cherish.

With my wife Nadia

Within those Spanish-Cuban and Catholic values, after family, gratitude occupies a top place, because all the men and women of my generation were taught that being grateful is one of the most important virtues in good people.

I always tried to show my gratitude to those who deserved it, not because I felt obligated to do so, but out of a sincere feeling. Today, as I look back on my life, I'm even more grateful to so many people who were with me, helping me in one way or another in the different stages of my life and who guided and supported me on the different roads I've traveled.

There are many such people, family and friends. But with my life as a public servant, as a politician elected not so much to govern as to serve, being such an important part of this memoir, there's in my heart a special place that's full of gratitude to those who helped me to fulfill that mission, because, if today I can, without lacking modesty, feel proud of my public work, it's due in large measure to those who unselfishly helped me.

I'm not referring now to the friends who introduced me to the world of politics and helped me win elections and proposals, people like Governor Askew, Steve Clark, Dave Kennedy, Alex Penelas, Reverend Gibson, etc., whom I've already mentioned and thanked in previous pages. I refer now to those whom we call friends, true friends, and others, friends too, whom we consider "civic leaders of the community," because, indeed, they were.

Among intimate friends, the closest ones, I must first mention two people, a man and a woman, who each exemplified the meaning of that phrase in its fullness: Felipe Valls, Sr. and Alelí Puig.

One cannot write the history of Cuban exile without talking about Felipe Valls. He arrived in Miami in 1960, with his wife Aminta and two children born in Cuba: Lety and Felipe Jr. Jeanette would be born later in Miami.

At only 27 years of age, Felipe left a fortune in businesses and properties in Cuba, after realizing early on that the new regime was Marxist. He simply left in search of freedom.

Both here and there, he always described himself as a businessman, not a politician. He created a gastronomic empire in Miami and was blessed with children and grandchildren who helped him, listened to him and continue to actively participate in the business organization that Felipe Jr. leads today.

With Felipe and Lourdes Valls and my wife Nadia

I always considered Felipe Sr. more than a friend; he was a brother. For more than 60 years he aided the cause of Cuban freedom and helped every compatriot who needed him. Throughout the many years of our fraternal friendship, I heard only one regret: that of not having been able to see his beloved Santiago de Cuba once again, in a free country.

With my other brother Felipe Valls

Having finished writing this book, I have had to rewrite this part, because my dear Felipe sadly passed away in November 2022, leaving a great void in his family, among his friends and in the Cuban exile community.

As for Alelí Puig, all the good things that can be said about the best human being could be said about her. Fernando Puig, her husband, was, like me, a member of Brigade 2506. Although we were both in Guatemala during training, I didn't meet him then, as he was at the air base that was on the ground at sea level, and I was at the Trax Base, at the heights of the volcano.

It was in Puerto Cabezas, Nicaragua, before boarding the ships for the mission, that our mutual friend Julio González Rebull introduced me to him. Fernando was impressive for his stature and corpulence. Years later, in Miami, we met casually, but we didn't establish a friendship until 1972.

It was then that I met Alelí, his wife. She was perfectly bilingual, very intelligent and excellent in public relations. When I was appointed Miami commissioner on July 6, 1972, I made her my office manager and she soon became my "right-hand woman," earning my trust through her loyalty and diligence.

Alelí held that position until 1979, when she received all kinds of praise and congratulations for her efficient performance and for the effective and prompt help she always provided to all those who came to her. Later, she was in charge of other city departments, always successfully. When Fernando passed away, she took over managing the family business. Alelí passed away on March 10, 2020.

They were people genuinely interested in the welfare of our community and in making the prestige of Cubans in exile as high as possible, as well as showing, with deeds more than with words, our love and gratitude to the United States for having welcomed us and given us the opportunity to live in freedom. They were also convinced that if we could establish ourselves as a strong, prosperous and law-abiding community in this country, we could influence Washington's policies and decisions regarding Cuba.

I have to mention people like Leslie Pantín, and his son, Leslie Jr., Raúl Masvidal, Eduardo Padrón, Carlos Arboleya, Luis Botifoll, Luisa García Toledo, Manolo Arqués, Luis Sabines, Guarioné Díaz, María de la Milera, William Alexander and many others. They were people who stood out in the private sector because they were very successful in the business world or in their specified fields. And when a crisis arose, or there was a serious problem in any of the municipalities that make up the county, they spared no time, effort, contacts or money and joined the local authorities to find fair and quick solutions.

At the same time, they paved the way for others to move forward. We have, just to give an example, Raúl Masvidal's time on the State University System of Florida, the body that appoints the presidents of the state's public universities whenever it's necessary. Masvidal had the opportunity to appoint Modesto

Maidique as president of FIU, and this was a tremendous achievement because Maidique was very successful as the head of this important educational institution.

Another shining example is that of Luis Botifoll, who, from his position at Republic National Bank, the first Cuban-owned bank in the United States, helped a large number of Cuban entrepreneurs and businessmen, providing them with loans and strengthening their credit so that they could start their businesses since the early days of exile. On many occasions the loans were backed only because Botifoll guaranteed them, since he knew them from Cuba and trusted their integrity. That trust was never taken advantage of.

Luisa García Toledo was a shining example of dedication to the community, and when I say this I'm referring both to the Cuban community and to everything concerning our Miami and the best interests of the United States. She was an exemplary patriot, very active, in Cuba, in the MRR (Movimiento de Recuperación Revolucionaria); here she belonged to several institutions, all dedicated to serving the community, and whenever she was called for a just cause, she was there.

The same can be said of Manolo Arqués, leader of the businessmen's association, who also used all his resources and all his influence not only to carry out any endeavor that benefitted his colleagues, but also to help our community, whenever it was necessary. Manolo traveled with me on several occasions when it was necessary to expand Miami's commercial horizons.

Carlos Arboleya gained great prestige in the Boy Scouts of America, and through this organization he greatly helped a lot of Miami's children and young people. I was able to get a city park, precisely where the Boy Scouts trained, named after Arboleya, who was another of those leaders who got involved in community affairs, always willing to help.

Maria de la Milera is a tireless worker, always ready to serve. She worked for the county, but it wasn't just that she performed her duties well; she gave one hundred percent in everything she did. She never refused me her support.

With Luis Sabines we would have to make a separate chapter, because he was an exceptional leader. Luis was a man of basic education; he didn't speak English; he wasn't guided much by social etiquette; but he won everyone's affection for his open and frank manner that held no slyness. He created the Latin Chamber of Commerce of the United States (CAMACOL) with a remarkable group of Cuban grocers and turned it into a positive force, not only for Hispanic merchants, but for the entire community. Luis and I became great friends, and he always remembered that the first $50,000 that CAMACOL received was given to him by me, from the discretionary funds that the commissioners had.

With County Mayor Alex Penelas and the President of the Little Havana Chamber of Commerce, Luis Sabines

Whenever it was necessary, whenever there was a worthy cause, Luis Sabines mobilized CAMACOL's membership and used his clout, and there was no problem that wasn't solved. I traveled with him many times to several Latin American countries and also to Europe, and I could see how useful his people skills were to making good friends in all those countries, all of which resulted in good business for Miami.

There's not much to say about Dr. Eduardo Padrón, founder, soul and life of Miami Dade College, because not only our community, but the entire world of education recognizes his extraordinary work as the head of the academic institution with the largest Hispanic enrollment in the United States. His well-deserved fame never prevented him from participating in all the efforts made to help our people.

The same can be said of Guarioné Díaz, who is well known for his community work and who has helped hundreds of families and has promoted the interests of our people at the national level.

The importance of this type of person, from the private sector who is conscious of their civic duties, could be clearly seen in Miami a year after I resigned as commissioner, in 1979. In 1980, we experienced the Mariel exodus, through which more than 120,000 Cubans arrived on our shores over a short period of time, all in precarious circumstances and all in need of help.

The efficient manner in which Miami processed that huge immigration crisis that posed a huge strain on the social services that could be offered to the newcomers was something that spoke very well of our community. Some media have said that before the first penny of federal aid arrived here to help with the situation, our public and private entities, working together, had everything under control. I don't have the exact information, but I believe that this was the case, and those civic and religious leaders stepped forward and efficiently helped the then city manager, César Odio, who did an excellent job in the face of that human avalanche.

In saying this, I have to mention another leader, this one from the public sector: Tony Ojeda. Tony was fantastic in getting the situation created by Mariel back on track, and I saw his skill and willingness as my own, because when the county created a position for a Hispanic, County Commissioner Mike Calhoun asked me to help choose the best person. I was given the resumes of the 25 finalists. I spent a weekend reading them all and recommended Tony, who was then in San Antonio, Texas, and that's how they chose him. When he came here, I was in charge of taking him to different places, introducing him to the different exile personalities and putting him in contact with the civic leaders we had at that time. He didn't disappoint me, as he was always a positive influence in all the positions he held in Miami-Dade County, until his retirement.

Another positive consequence of politicians working together with these and other community leaders on the issues that affect us all could also be seen in the aftermath of the Mariel exodus, an example on which I'd like to dwell.

Let's remember that, in his diabolical evil, Fidel Castro emptied his prisons and psychiatric wards and infiltrated a remarkable number of violent criminals and mentally ill among the thousands of Cuban families who arrived here in those unforgettable days of April and May 1980. The dictator's objective was to tarnish the reputation of Cubans in South Florida and create chaos with that wave of refugees.

He almost succeeded and this provoked a strong anti-Cuban sentiment that had been brewing since before due to the resentment of many "Americans" who felt displaced by the Cubans.

However, that soon passed and had no major consequences because by then our community already enjoyed sufficient economic and political power, and it wasn't easy to impede our advancement. And this was thanks to the vision of the pioneers who understood that we had to take action in local affairs and participate in U.S. politics.

That's changing for the worse, and it worries me. Today we have too many politicians who don't exercise any leadership and too few civic leaders. Today there's a proliferation of commissioners, councilmen, mayors, state representatives and senators, each with their more or less large share of power, some who can't hide their desire for prominence. And while I don't doubt the good intentions they surely have, I believe that the community as such is lacking the balance of private sector leaders who, if there are any at this time, are not making their presence felt.

The men and women who are currently prominent in professional life, the leaders of commerce, banking, real estate, education, etc., don't seem to be interested in public affairs, nor in being a positive force in terms of the community's problems and needs.

Politicians need the advice, opinions and input of those who, precisely because they don't aspire to any political office, can contribute their knowledge, experiences and relationships; those who can, without raising suspicions of having political ambitions, point out when elected officials forget that they also have their limitations, both human limitations and those of the law and common sense.

Where are the Luis Botifoll and the Luisa García Toledo of today? Where is the Luis Sabines of these times?

To illustrate this, I'd like to mention, even briefly, some of the many civic, political, professional and all kinds of associations to which I've belonged during my political life, and, in some cases, up to the present. They are all organizations that invited me to join for two main reasons: to have access to and influence over local or state political power, which is very valid, and also for the opportunity to offer their vision in civic affairs and public policies and contribute their opinions about and endeavors toward the problems and crises that every society has to face from time to time.

I was or am a member, among others, of the following associations: Governor Reubin Askew's State of Florida Advisory Committee, member of the Bay of Pigs Veterans Association (Brigade 2506), member, in addition, of: Florida Council on International Development, Florida State International Board, Inter-American Alliance, U.S. Conference of Mayors, Dade County Criminal Justice Advisory Council, Dade County League of Cities, Miami Ecology and Beautification Committee, Loyal Order of Moose, Bay Height Homeowners Association, Dade Young Democrats Club, Latin American Democratic Club, Latin Chamber of Commerce, Latin Builders Association, Club Bancario, Unicorn Clubs International, Safety Council of Dade County, José Martí International YMCA, Performing Arts Society, Florida-Colombia Alliance, Tiger Bay Political Club, Association for Tenant Safety, Parks and Recreation Task Force, Cuban-American Government Council, Spanish-Speaking Democratic Club, Dade County Rapid Transit Study Committee, Association of Latino Democratic Officials, etc. In some of these organizations I held leadership positions; in others I was only a member. In all of them I saw the desire to participate in public affairs, both those that directly affected their interests and those that were important to the general population.

As a curious fact, in 1977 I was appointed Grand Marshal of the picturesque Disneyworld Parade, which I remember fondly.

May the people who today excel in their local areas of activity, Cuban Americans and of all ethnicities, realize that their lives will not be complete, nor will their achievements be lasting, if they don't add to their work the civic component, the joy and obligation of serving the less fortunate around us; in other words, public service, which shouldn't be limited to elected officials. It's everyone's obligation.

I cannot close this chapter without mentioning several friends who, beyond their positions in our community and the leadership role that many of them have in their different fields, have always shown me their sincerity and their willingness to serve and who, over time, have earned, through both commonalities and differences, the title of friends.

I must first mention some of those who have lived up to the title of "friend" so fully and completely, and who, sadly, are no longer with us in this world. Among them: Felipe Valls, Sr., Manuel Artime, Roberto Pérez San Román, Ramón Mestre, Jorge Más Canosa, Teok Carrasco, Carlos Salmán and Ricardo Gómez.

Thank God, there are also many others who have been and still are excellent friends, such as Sergio Pino, Joe Sánchez, Felipe Valls, Jr., Pedro Peláez, Camilo Padrera, Gustavo Villoldo, Armando Codina, Emilio and Gloria Estefan, Norman Braman, Manny Diaz, Benjamin Leon, Julio González Rebull, Jr., Freddy Balsera, Tomás de San Julián, Sergio Bendixen, Alex Penelas, Roberto Rodríguez Tejera, Tomás Regalado, Oscar Haza, Juan Bido, Raúl Martínez, Humberto Cortina, Luis Lauredo, Néstor Carbonell, Luis Conte Agüero, Ricky Gómez, Armando Gutiérrez, Jorge Luis López, Gerry Tobin, Mel Martínez....

At this point I must, in fairness, dedicate a few lines to a very special friend: Harvey Ruvin. I met him in November 1972 when he was elected Dade County Commissioner. I had already been a Miami commissioner since July of that same year, so our friendship lasted for more than 50 years. An exemplary public servant, he was a commissioner for 20 years, during which he was recognized worldwide as a true authority on everything related to the environment, a pioneer in the field. In 1992, he ran for and was elected County Clerk, a position he held for 30 years. Harvey was admired and respected by Democrats, Republicans and Independents alike; but, more important than all this, a better friend could not be had. Sadly, Harvey passed away on the last day of 2022, at the age of 85.

With Hon. Harvey Ruvin, beloved and respected by all

I can't forget officials from other countries who became true friends, such as the governor of Yucatan, Carlos Loret de Mola; the governor of Tabasco, Mario Trujillo; the governor of Quintana Roo, David Gutierrez; and the governor of Campeche, Carlos Sansores. Likewise, the trustee of Buenos Aires, General Osvaldo Cacciatori; the mayor of Santiago de Chile, María Eugenia Ozarzún; and the mayor of Rancagua, Chile, Patricio Mekis. Also, the mayor of Madrid, José María Álvarez del Manzano.

I would like to express my gratitude to all of them and, in advance, apologize for any omissions I may have inevitably made.

At this point, and as we approach the end of this memoir, some questions arise in my mind that are very similar to those I've asked of the civic leaders of the community, and these have to do with other leaders, those we should have both in the efforts for Cuba's freedom and in U.S. politics.

My life has had two aspects, two causes, two motivations, that have defined it: political activity in the United States and the struggle for Cuba's freedom, which reached its culminating moments in my participation in the Bay of Pigs mission, but which has always been alive in my heart, as I believe is the case with most Cubans of my generation.

That is why I can't help but wonder, what is happening to Cuba, after more than six decades of slavery? Where are the Miró Cardona and Tony Varona of today? Where are the Manuel Artime of these times? And also: Where is the United States going? Is the democratic system in danger? Where are the leaders for times of crisis?

I believe that this account of my life and my endeavors, which are very similar to those of hundreds of thousands of my compatriots, deserves a final look at these two topics – Cuba and the United States – which have been and are of such importance to me.

With three former Presidents of Brigade 2506, Juan Pérez Franco, Miguel Álvarez and Pedro Encinosa

With members of Brigade 2506: Oscar Carol, Julio González Rebull, Pedro Roig, Humberto Cortina, Fernando Puig and others.

With Frank Sinatra, Anselmo Alliegro, Eddy Silva and *brigadistas* Jorge Herrera and Julio González Rebull.

With Lincoln Díaz-Balart and Carlos Benito Fernández

With Freddy Balsera public relations consultant and businessmen Mitch Villalón and Pedro Peláez.

With my brother Roberto, Jorge de Cárdenas and the *brigadistas* Raúl Masvidal, Pedro Roig and Julio González Rebull

Chapter 27
Cuba and its Exile – Democrats and Republicans

> *If you want to find a helping hand, look for it at the end of your arm.*
> Napoleon Bonaparte

I am writing these, the last chapters of my memoirs, at the end of January 2023 and, as I look towards Cuba and its exile, the panorama I contemplate is radically different from the one that appeared before my eyes as I approached the island aboard the *Lake Charles* in April 1961, when we saw Cayo Guano del Este, ready to disembark and fight in an armed confrontation that sought to liberate Cuba from an incipient communist dictatorship, which revolved around a charismatic, intelligent and intrinsically ruthless leader named Fidel Castro.

It was then a battle of conventional methods, between two armies, if that's what we could call our small expeditionary force. We thought we would emerge victorious from this battle, because we were confident in our fighting abilities, in the determined support of our people and, above all, in the backing of our great and powerful ally, the United States government.

We were wrong in our estimations. We were defeated, and Fidel Castro and his tyranny emerged strengthened from that bloody episode. Our people were not in a position to offer us substantial support even if they had wanted to give it. Our ally, incredibly, left us in a lurch, and from then on, Washington's policy towards Cuba and Miami changed radically and also changed the course of the lives of those of us who dreamed of returning to a free and democratic Cuba.

As I now look towards Miami, not as the American emporium that it is, but as the "capital of Cuban exile," I also contemplate a very different panorama from the one that opened before my eyes when I returned here from Puerto Cabezas, my soul and my sense of things shocked then by the fresh and bitter taste of the great disaster we had just suffered.

Cuba is today a different country, to its own detriment. Defying all predictions to the contrary, the regime imposed there by Fidel Castro has survived even the death of the dictator himself, as well as the mediocrity of his most visible successors, his brother Raúl, first, and now Miguel Díaz-Canel, who is supposed to be limited in his powers by the supremacy of the military leadership, which is the one that, in reality, runs the country.

The island has become a pit of misery located in the backyard of the third world. The lack of rights and misery suffocate the population while the dictatorship has lost all restraint and proves daily that its permanence in power is based only on the fiercest repression and the most absolute disregard for human rights.

The internal opposition, extremely commendable for its tenacity in the face of tyranny, has also changed. The small groups organized as such have almost all disappeared, and their leaders are now imprisoned or in exile. But the eruption in Cuba of the Internet and its social media networks has marked a great positive change for the unorganized opposition, which has grown abundantly and, at this moment, is showing signs of a great potential to challenge the regime. All of this constitutes a new element to be taken into account in any analysis regarding Cuba, its present and its future.

This was clearly demonstrated in the widespread popular protests of July 11, 2021, in which thousands of Cubans spontaneously took to the streets across a good number of cities and towns, protesting against the lack of freedom and the impoverished living conditions they face day after day. The cries of ¡Libertad! and ¡Patria y Vida! gave a clear testimony of the nature of the demonstrations, after which the regime unleashed a fierce wave of repression. As a result, the current number of political prisoners, which includes women and adolescents as well as men of all races and conditions, is estimated at more than one thousand. All of this was carried out with an ostensible exemplary intention, that's to say, to set an example.

In spite of this, as I write this chapter, the people continue to protest and demand a change of regime, taking advantage of the blackouts to try to escape from the Castroist cruelty and continue the protests in the dark. Meanwhile, the Internet continues to be the forum where the population denounces the abuses and shows a Cuba that seems to be overcoming fear and taking the initiative of its own liberation.

The Cuban exile community has experienced no less remarkable changes. The patriotic demonstrations no longer cover long stretches of SW 8th Street, or fill stadiums. They are concentrated mostly in front of Versailles restaurant and are convened – not by leaders like those who have passed away over time – but also through social media. They are apparently unstructured, and driven by so-called "influencers," rather than by anti-Castro leaders in the old style.

There don't appear to be any organized lobbying groups as such. Some of the traditional radio stations whose programming focused mainly on Cuban issues have disappeared. Very reputable voices in local journalism, such as Roberto Rodríguez Tejera, Tomás Regalado and Oscar Haza, to name a few, maintain very popular programs in which the Cuban issue continues to be the main topic.

But a good part of the discussion about Cuba seems to have moved to the partisan struggles of American politics, where, like a sad hothouse flower, it languishes and only receives some attention at election time.

We made two very similar mistakes that today we can consider happy mistakes. The first came from U.S. academic and journalistic sources, but was accepted and shared by more than a few pessimistic Cubans. It was the one that told us, at the beginning of our exile and sporadically from time to time thereafter, that after a few years, we Cubans from South Florida would be assimilated by the American mainstream, and that only the folkloric aspects of our culture would remain. Because of our rapid integration in the United States, they predicted that our children and grandchildren would not speak Spanish, and that Cuba would remain in our memories as a nostalgic reference, not as a cause.

The inaccuracy of this prediction is so obvious that I don't think it's necessary to refute it. Today there are many more Americans who eat black beans than Cubans who drink root beer, as an example.

The other prediction was foretold by us exiles, and it was as much a fear that distressed us as a possibility born of the sad experiences accumulated in our endeavors at freedom. Almost all of us believed that the struggle for Cuba's freedom would end with the death of those of us who had been exiles in the early days of the regime, let's say the generation of the 1940s and the following one, the Playa Girón generation. We said that the island's young Cubans, born and raised under the dictatorship, and that our children and grandchildren, born and/or raised in the United States, would not feel their *cubanía* (the personal want to be Cuban) as we feel it and, even worse, they wouldn't believe they had a commitment to Cuba's freedom, as those of us who today are in the winter of our lives have.

"We have no one to relieve us," we used to say, with sad conviction.

And here we are, in the third decade of the 2000s, watching the videos taken in Cuba and seeing that the political prisoners and those who fill the destroyed Cuban streets demanding their rights and mocking Díaz-Canel are almost all young people in whom the Marxist indoctrination backfired when compared to the harsh reality of our homeland. And also looking at how, in their great majority, those who protest on the sidewalks in front of Versailles or in front of the White House are equally young Cubans: the recently arrived along with the children and grandchildren of Cubans born outside Cuba.

This obligates us all to continue our relentless efforts: Cuba must be free. But how? What can we exiles do at this point in history?

It's not so difficult to answer this, because I believe that in our minds and in our hearts we all have an idea of what would be, ideally, the road to follow. What's really difficult is the how, how to implement what we understand needs to be done.

It would be presumptuous of me to try to appear here with recipes for freedom; that's not the purpose of this book, nor am I capable of designating myself a leader of the exile community, which I'm not, nor do I pretend to be. But I do believe that I can share with you some suggestions that could be useful now, on the steep hill of our dreams for Cuba.

As in any endeavor of national scope, when it comes to achieving an already difficult goal, we could do with a little closeness and coordination among the different factors that are currently giving life to the opposition against tyranny. What's left of our organizations, artists, intellectuals, influencers, independent press, bloggers, activists of all kinds: we should establish points of contact, we should get to know each other, we should share ideas and dare to try initiatives together. If disunity has been our great sin, we should at least seek a minimum of unity, which can't harm us in any way.

There is, within the exile community, a specific area of the Cuban problem that I would especially like to mention, because I have navigated those waters and I know their depths. I am still a

Cuban in love with the dream of Cuba's freedom, and I am also a Cuban American with a certain amount of experience in the political intricacies of the United States. Allow me, then, to state some truths and make some suggestions, intending only the best development of our efforts regarding Cuba.

I said earlier that the discussion of the Cuban problem has been transferred, almost completely, to the sphere of partisan struggles in American politics. I must now add that this sphere, in itself, almost never offers a clear and transparent view; on the contrary, what goes on in the shadows is almost as much as what is perceived with the naked eye. And the worst part of the situation is that, in the midst of party interests and electoral struggles in this country, we Cubans find ourselves at a great disadvantage. Despite the importance attributed to the Cuban vote in state and national elections, all that the top political leadership does, in reality, is to manipulate us to obtain our votes, without seriously compromising its policy towards Cuba.

This is fundamentally due, in my opinion, to the fact that the Cuban exile community has put all its eggs in the Republican basket, without demanding concrete actions and real support for the liberation of Cuba, while having burned all our bridges with the Democrats, without even the space to listen to each other with common respect. Therefore, the Republicans, in reality, have no reason to seriously help us with Cuba, since they take our votes for granted; and the Democrats are hardly concerned about reviewing their policies towards Cuba, since they already consider the votes of the Cubans as lost. In my opinion, this unilateral accommodation of the Cuban vote greatly limits our possibilities of obtaining measures from the U.S. government that are truly aimed at weakening the regime and the emergence of an alternative opposition that could capitalize on the growing discontent of Cubans on the island.

And, please, let's not allow ourselves to be entertained any longer with measures of much commotion and little effectiveness. The limits on remittances do not work, because most of the remittances are sent to Cuba through relatives or mules that travel there; the sanctions against companies and consortiums that do business with the dictatorship don't seem to be effective for Spanish hoteliers, nor for the many Latin American governments that under the guise of the "Cuban medical missions" provide the regime with millions of dollars without stopping to consider the mockery that this makes of the labor rights of doctors who work as slaves abroad. Many, perhaps not all, of these sanctions seem designed for the gallery, to entertain exile voters, rather than to actually punish the Castro regime.

How to change the dynamic between Washington and Miami? How do we get real help for the cause of Cuban freedom?

First of all, by making ourselves respected by Republicans and Democrats alike. Organizing ourselves seriously with a minimum of unity and coherence and giving clear signs that we are aware that it's our duty and nobody else's to free Cuba and bring to it democracy. Then, dealing with the American establishment from positions of mutual respect, and, in the best sense of the expression, selling our votes at a high price.

In this regard, we exiles have a good precedent, a magnificent example to follow, and it was given to us by Jorge Más Canosa. In its better days, the Cuban American National Foundation supported politicians who, in turn, supported our interests regarding Cuba, whether they were Democrats or Republicans. Recall how, when George Bush, Sr., who had liberated Panama from the dictator Noriega during his presidential term, did nothing, however, for the freedom of Cuba in the very years when the communist world was being liberated and the Soviet Union was disintegrating, the Foundation switched sides and gave its support in 1992 to the Democratic candidate, Bill Clinton. Bush Sr. was unable to win a second presidential term and Clinton, as president, did not insist on the appeasement policies of his Democratic predecessor, Jimmy Carter.

With President George Bush Sr.

We should keep in mind that in the long time since Castro's rise to power in Cuba, the United States has had seven Republican presidents who have been in the White House for 34 years and six Democratic presidents who have held the presidency for a little less than 30 years. Eisenhower, the first Republican on the list, bears the responsibility for facilitating Castro's seizure of power in Cuba by pushing for Batista's departure without seeking alternatives to the bearded man's troubling unknowns. Kennedy, the first Democrat on that same list, bears most of the blame for the failure of the Bay of Pigs Invasion. Neither they, nor the other presidents on that list, can show really effective actions in support of their "Miami allies."

As for Donald Trump, the penultimate on the list and the one who seems to have captivated a good part of my compatriots in exile with his sly rhetoric, it's worth remembering that shortly before deciding to run for president, associates of his were visiting Cuba exploring business opportunities with Castro's people. It's worth remembering that many of his sanctions against them were more noise than substance and that, like all the others, during his time in the White House and in spite of his boastful promises – let us remember that, regarding Cuba and Venezuela, "all options were on the table" – he did nothing significant to overthrow the dictatorship, perhaps, like all the others, to have something with which to cajole his "Miami allies" and secure his votes for a second term that he lost, unquestionably, to Joe Biden.

We should've taken into account that, as long as Vladimir Putin protects Cuba and Venezuela, Trump was not going to do anything about it, and this could be proven in his four years in office. It is something, moreover, that he's invariably maintained, so much so that, despite Russia's invasion of Ukraine, Trump has not dared to criticize Putin even once.

To sum up, if there's one thing I could say to all Cubans in exile, it would be, simply: let us leave behind our divisions and come to the reality that bringing freedom and democracy to Cuba is our responsibility and ours alone, not that of the U.S. Marines, who, like us, are flesh and blood. Let's stop blaming others for the things that happen to us. In more than 60 years of exile, very few Cubans have done nothing, many have done very little and very few have done a lot. Everything would be very different if every Cuban did his or her part, no matter how modest it may seem.

Let's look at the Jewish people in the United States and we'll see that, compared to them, we have nothing. They control a large percentage of public opinion in this country; they have newspapers, radio and television stations, etc. They have a large percentage of public opinion in this country. We could have the same if we organized effectively. This is fundamental in the struggles of these times.

In the end, the Cuban cause would benefit extraordinarily if, instead of constantly arguing among ourselves, we would remember with conviction that phrase in our national anthem that encouraged the heroes of our independence: *Morir por la patria es vivir* ("To die for the homeland is to live").

With this, I don't seek to dictate guidelines, nor to be controversial. I only hope to make those who, like me, still dream of Cuba's freedom, think.

Chapter 28
Miami's Future – Necessary Changes

> *Life is a compromise between conservative tradition and renewing influences. To live is to get used to it.*
>
> Le Dantec

Thanks to the fact that I've lived for many years – almost nine decades at the time of writing these memoirs – and to the not-very-pleasant circumstance that most of the men and women with whom I shared the civic and political scene in this part of the world now rest in peace, it happens now with some frequency that friends and acquaintances, some journalists and also some political neophytes approach me and ask my opinion about issues that affect us in one way or another, almost always in politics.

Of course, they don't do so because they believe that I'm a fountain of wisdom, which I'm not, but rather because they recognize my experience in the matter and, also, because they know that at this stage of my life, I don't harbor political ambitions and don't aspire to any position, and this gives me a clear vision and strengthens my objectivity.

Something that almost everyone asks me is my opinion about the future of Miami. I always answer that the future of Miami is very much like the Miami of today. Our geographic location and the growth already achieved almost assure the continuity of the status of this beautiful corner of the world as the gateway or capital of Latin America. Our melting pot of cultures; the fact that we have a large population that is as comfortable in English as it is in Spanish; the ease of communication in both languages, but also with a touch of Portuguese, Creole and other languages, are not so readily available in other large cities. The existence here of international finance and banking, the large international companies and corporations, the extended network of diplomatic representations of so many countries – all this and much more will continue to be a magnet, a tremendous allure for the area's economic strength.

The flow of money from other countries to Miami should continue, as everything seems to indicate. If we apply a bit of cynicism to this aspect of the area's economy, we could say that, as long as leftist governments continue to appear from time to time in Latin America, Miami will continue to receive capital from those countries.

However, what's not taken care of deteriorates, and this also applies to the attractiveness of Miami as a whole. There are some issues to which local leaders, along state and federal ones, will have to pay more careful attention if the future is to be at least as inviting as the present.

There is much room for improvement in inter-city transportation. I know we're all somewhat skeptical when it comes to transit in Miami, but, as difficult as the solutions may seem, it's necessary to insist upon the urgent need for an efficient public transportation system; it's necessary to direct efforts towards the elusive goal that the automobile ceases to be a necessity of the first order to live in Miami, where at present, vehicular traffic is already a major nightmare.

And it's also imperative that everyone – government leaders, businessmen, etc. – stop thinking only about the glamour of Miami and its status as a tourist and business mecca. There are a great number of families, workers, the elderly, etc., who are oblivious to the glamour of Miami because its resources keep them in poverty, and they have very limited opportunities for advancement. Communities that forget their poor tempt the breakdown of social peace and eventually retreat from prosperity, because either prosperity is for everyone, or prosperity is not.

With that in mind, there is no more urgent need than that of affordable housing for the majority of the population. The very high cost that makes the American dream impossible for large segments of the population, and the exaggerated rents, if they continue their current rapid upward spiral, will eventually drive away many of those who today could enrich our community with their work and talents.

Another thing – not only of the future, but also of the present – is the need to take seriously climate change, which is already manifesting itself in the frequency of flooding in areas where it didn't previously occur and in the relentless rise in ambient temperatures. Everything that has to do with the environment in which we live demands intelligent attention without any more time being wasted.

There are other areas that demand attention, and among these, the issues of policy and governance are unavoidable.

For example, in the not-so-distant days when the current mayor of Miami, Francis Suárez, promoted the initiative to change the status of his office and provide the city with a "strong mayor," many people asked me for my opinion on the matter. It wasn't the first time that this idea circulated in local political circles, and invariably, my response has been the same:

This is something that would have to be studied very well. The pros and cons would have to be conscientiously evaluated, because it's something dangerous. How good or bad a strong mayor could be depends on how good or bad the person occupying that position is; it depends on the person's maturity and ethics, and I don't think we need to run that risk.

If we're talking about reforms to the system of government in Miami, if we're looking for greater efficiency, if we really want to take a step towards the future, it seems to me that we should look a little bit further, not only to the city of Miami, but to Miami-Dade County as a whole.

At present, Miami-Dade County consists of 34 municipalities, plus what we call the unincorporated area. In other words, we have 35 mayors (including the county mayor's office) and 35 teams of commissioners, with multiple police and fire departments; 35 top-heavy bureaucracies with departments of all kinds. All this to cover a continuous area, with similar needs and a citizenry accustomed to the interaction between neighborhoods and cities, since almost everyone lives in one municipality, works in another, attends events in its four cardinal points and most of the time doesn't know, nor care, if at any given moment they are, territorially speaking, in one municipality or another. When, being outside South Florida, a resident of any of our municipalities is asked where he or she lives, the automatic answer is Miami and, in the rest of the world's view, no one is from Opa-locka or Medley or Virginia Gardens: we are all from Miami.

Imagine how much money we would save, how much our taxes could be lowered, if instead of the present duplication by three-and-a-half dozen government entities and their respective officials and employees, we had a county mayor with 34 city commissioners, each one representing his respective city, and one police and fire department each at the county level with its 35 captains. Imagine how much simpler the necessary paperwork to apply for permits, inspections, etc., would be.

Let's think about elections and campaign expenses, how much they would be reduced by eliminating positions that would be unnecessary as a result of a political reorganization such as the one I'm outlining here, which would also include, as in New York, the county school board.

There should also be a reform of the judiciary. At present, any lawyer with campaign money can be a judge. For many, the system of electing judges by popular vote, as political officials are elected, is a major mistake, allowing the evils of politics to infiltrate the judiciary. A system based on the merit and knowledge of aspiring judges, governed by judges of the highest courts, would give the public a better chance of having the best-qualified judges for the very delicate task of dispensing justice.

That Miami-Dade would practically become a republic within the state of Florida? Maybe, and why not? What we should be concerned about is the welfare and progress of the citizenry, not the maintenance of an inefficient and stagnant status quo.

Of course, what I'm setting forth here is a project that I'm describing in broad strokes. It's something that would have to be studied and discussed in all its aspects, and would require a great vision of the future and an adequate dose of boldness on the part of our politicians – which doesn't seem to abound in these times.

Another aspect of our system of government that is crying out for more attention from everyone is the role that members of the state legislature have and should have with their respective districts. In today's times, the relationship of each state representative or senator with his or her constituents is reduced, in practice, to the electoral issue: this is my district, because the people of my district are the ones who can vote for me.

I don't see, after the electoral period, any interaction between the legislator and his or her constituents. There is no mechanism that makes the representative in Tallahassee appear before the people he or she supposedly represents there. The only time they are accountable for their performance is in the following election period, if that legislator aspires to reelection. It doesn't seem that the way this works – or doesn't work – those who represent us in Tallahassee can be very aware of the needs and opinions of the people in their districts.

At the same time, it would be necessary to create an organization where, with a certain frequency, area mayors and commissioners could meet with the corresponding state legislators, so that joint solutions to the problems and needs of the areas of common government could be coordinated. I believe this would provide better tools for the search for solutions to the needs of the population. The reasoning is simple: if the mayor and commissioners of my city were to meet consistently with the representative and senator of my state district to put into perspective the needs of the place where I live, they could find solutions to the problems more effectively, by coordinating in a single effort, what each one can contribute according to their jurisdiction.

The same does not happen with representatives and senators at the federal level, because in their case, the issues are different and everything revolves more around partisan politics and national issues, and also the politicians' interaction with voters is very different. However, it wouldn't hurt for our representatives in Washington to check more frequently with voters' sentiments; I think policymaking would flow more harmoniously if they did so.

Speaking of reforms, there are some that are long overdue, but not just for our area, but for the United States as a whole. Therefore, these are not up to our local politicians, but to the nation's Congress.

One – perhaps the most urgent – is that of campaign finances, which, in its present design, has become a form of legalized bribery, corrupting the democratic system of government and serving the interests of the powerful rather than those of the nation and its people in general.

In the present system, electoral campaigns are paid by politicians with the money they receive as "campaign donations" from companies and conglomerates of various kinds, some of which aren't even identifiable, since they hide behind the so-called PACs – which, in my opinion, constitute a complete negation of the democratic system of government, a system that's supposed to be characterized by its transparency. For example, oil companies contribute thousands of dollars to the advertising campaigns of representatives and senators who aspire to be elected or reelected. When these politicians achieve their goal and are already in office as legislators, will they pass laws that, in order to protect the environment, would force the automobile companies to depend less on oil as a source of energy for their products?

We see the same, unfortunately, with the National Rifle Association's contributions to election campaigns, how many politicians demagogically invoke the Second Amendment of the Constitution to protect the indiscriminate sale of assault rifles to whomever chooses to buy them. This is a macabre commercialization of the death of innocents, and all because of politicians' dependence on the "donations" of these merchants. We should ask if they are really donations or a thinly disguised form of bribery: I give you so much, and you vote for what I want.

Let's take into account how, for the election of a candidate to a position that pays less than $50,000 a year, the aspirants to that position raise millions of dollars. A proportional limit must be placed on the salary to be earned.

In most European Union countries, the state finances the campaigns of all candidates for elected office. Time limits on the duration of electoral campaigns and spending limits are established, and this has considerably cleaned up the electoral processes and political lives in these countries.

I'm not at all optimistic about the possibilities of something like this happening in the United States, but I think it's worthwhile to bring up the issue and raise awareness about it, because it seems to me that it's fundamental for the health of our democracy.

Another issue of national scope that should be studied is the reform of the U.S. Senate. In its original conception, drawn up at the beginning of the integration of the 13 original colonies to form "a more perfect union," times in which the representatives of each of the colonies jealously guarded the rights and interests of their respective territories, the formula of two senators for each state was adopted to put them all on an equal footing in the Upper House. More than two centuries have passed and today the concept of the United States as a nation is firmly established, which, I believe, provides an opportunity to introduce changes that are possible today without jeopardizing national unity.

In my opinion, the Senate, like the House of Representatives, should be constituted in direct proportion to the number of inhabitants of each district or constituency, one senator per certain number of inhabitants. This would result in a fairer representation and a greater opportunity for voters' voices to be heard. It makes no sense that states like California, with over 39 million people, or Texas, with almost 30 million, have the same number of senators, i.e., two each, as Vermont and Delaware, the former with 643,000 and the latter with 989,000 people.

Finally, while I'm talking about things that are ideal, there's another aspect of the laws by which this country is currently governed that's crying out for elimination. I'm referring to the existence of the Electoral College, which is, ultimately, what decides who wins the presidency of the United States, discarding, at times, the will of the voters as expressed directly in the popular vote. To cite just two recent examples, let's recall that, in 2000, Al Gore, vice president under Bill Clinton, lost the presidency despite having obtained more votes than his Republican rival, George W. Bush, because the latter was favored by the Electoral College's votes. Likewise, in 2016, former Senator and former Secretary of State Hillary Clinton was stripped of her triumph, even though she obtained almost three million more votes than Donald Trump, who was declared the winner by the Electoral College. Is this not a mockery of the voters and a profoundly undemocratic move?

I know that none of the changes I've outlined, which I believe to be very necessary, could be easily adopted, but this doesn't diminish the urgent need for them in our democratic system of government. And since we're talking about the health of our democracy, it seems to me opportune and beneficial that all those who have acquired this book and have read it up to this point should have a deep and serene meditation on these subjects, which are, or should be, of critical importance to every citizen.

In the following chapter, I will elaborate a little more on these topics, because I believe that in the immensity of this country, our community, Miami-Dade, the one composed of Cubans, Nicaraguans and Venezuelans in particular, holds the greatest number of people who have had in their lives and have felt in their own flesh the stings of totalitarianism, of the lack of democracy, of the curse of caudillismo – in short, of the great difference that exists between living under the rule of law and living under a dictatorship.

It seems to me that this is a subject on which we should seriously reflect.

Chapter 29
Fidel Castro and Donald Trump

> *Man is the only animal that trips twice over the same stone.*
> Popular wisdom

I believe that we would be betraying ourselves, and we would very badly serve the country that has welcomed us and given us endless opportunities to decently and fruitfully advance our lives and our families, if we don't stop in its tracks the political discourse that's heard and repeated more frequently these days at the national level; if we don't meditate objectively on the content of that discourse; and if we don't look critically at our own behavior and all that some pretend to give us as a political creed, as a matter of faith and loyalty to our most just and dearest principles, when, in fact, the opposite is true.

Beware! Lest by our words and actions we're contradicting all that we've previously described as the reasons for our presence in the United States.

I would like to refresh some memories, as it seems that many exiles – mostly Cubans, Venezuelans and Nicaraguans – have forgotten a good part of the experiences we've lived and which have shaped our lives. The worst part of the matter is that, on the whole, it doesn't seem that many of those who allow themselves to be swept along by the political wave *du jour* realize the grave dangers to democracy in the United States, and that they're not precisely the dangers that they're made to see, but those related to the acceptance of beliefs and loyalties of some who seek to seize exclusively the title of patriots and defenders of democracy, when, in fact, they themselves constitute the antithesis of democracy by regressing to a tribal totalitarianism such as has not been seen before in the United States.

I was born in a Latin American country where, in the mid-1950s, most of its inhabitants thought that everything was going wrong. Demagogues and politicians with some power of convocation clamored against everything and everyone, proclaiming that everything in the country was infected by corruption, that political parties and institutions only harbored bandits and liars, that everything was a fraud to the citizenry.

Certainly, we weren't perfect. There were injustices to repair, values to rescue, institutions to clean up. But all was not lost, nor, as the defamers proclaimed, were there more bad guys than good guys. The country was moving forward and prospering, and most of the citizens were still good, virtuous people. But we preferred to listen to the cries of the alarmists. The voices calling for civility and sanity – Cosme de la Torriente, Carlos Márquez Sterling, Jorge Mañach, etc. – went unheard and were drowned out by the refrains of hatred.

We preferred to place our faith and hopes in a convincing manipulator, unknown to most, whose lack of scruples was hidden behind a tremendous histrionic ability and a total lack of respect for the truth. We gave him political power, and he took all the other powers.

All those who didn't submit completely to him, all those who pointed out any fault or mistake, were part of some sinister conspiracy hatched by "imperialism" and, therefore, could not be believed or even paid attention to.

As he said that all the press was corrupt and full of lies, he appropriated the entire press, so that his "truth" would be, simply, the only truth. Since political parties were dens of vices and lies, he suppressed political parties and allowed only one, his own.

First, he told us that all elections had been fraudulent, then he promised us free and authentic elections, and in the end he told us, "Elections? For what?"

On television, he mocked his adversaries: he baptized the great journalist José Ignacio Rivero as "Pepinillo"; he called the priests "henchmen with cassocks," he ridiculed all the civic and political hierarchies and put the whole nation at the level of a dunghill.

He dismantled an entire republic that was salvageable and turned it into his little kingdom – the one where he was the supreme patriot, the supreme leader, the custodian of truth and, in the end, the only one with the right not only to govern, but to breathe freely, to think for himself, and to be the arbiter of the vices and virtues of every citizen's life.

Never has a people paid more dearly for its foolishness, its submission to a liar, its forgetfulness of the elemental commitment of every human being to the rights of its fellow human beings. Never has the smearing against the country's institutions and then their destruction been so costly as it's been for my people. Never has political fanaticism, following a man and not reason and common sense, had a punishment of such painful consequences and such long duration.

The fanaticism that Donald Trump demands from his followers is the white American version of the fanaticism with which Fidel Castro was elevated by his followers. It's the American version of third world totalitarianism – it's the same collar on a different dog.

I believe that anyone who remembers Fidel Castro's speeches, especially those from his early days in power, when he still denied being a communist, and compares the tone, the mood and even the gesticulation of the "Maximum Leader" with the rhetoric and style of the 45th president of the United States won't be able to deny the striking similarities, which also reveal a great similarity in their egocentric personalities.

More worrisome than this, however, is the similarity in discourse. The same arrogance, the same evasion of responsibilities, everything is the fault of "the enemies," the same or similar lies, everything adverse that happens to him is because of some sinister conspiracy against him, the same attacks and diatribes against the free press, the same disparagement of institutions. For Fidel Castro, the CIA was the mother of all evils; for Donald Trump, it's the FBI. For Castro, criticism of his government was the talk of detractors who wanted to stop "revolutionary justice"; for Donald Trump, opinions contrary to his own come from the Democrats who don't want him to "make America great again" and try to impose "the new world order." For Fidel Castro, the United States and the western world were his enemies and Russia, the best ally. For Donald Trump, the western world and NATO, are, in reality, crafty enemies of this country; Vladimir Putin is always right. Fidel Castro didn't admit defeat, he didn't know how to lose. Donald Trump still claims, against all evidence, to have won the 2020 presidential election, a claim rejected by more than 60 courts, many of them presided over by judges appointed by Trump himself.

The reality is that a large number of voters in the 2020 presidential election voted against Donald Trump rather than for Biden.

I remember how the vast majority of Republicans who today idealize Donald Trump loyally supported and emphatically praised George W. and Jeb Bush, Mitt Romney and other leaders of their party, all of whom have been denigrated by Trump. His unbridled ego denigrated even a Vietnam war hero, the late John McCain, and even his second-in-command, the Republican he chose as his vice president, Mike Pence.

As if all this were not enough, it's already been proven ad nauseum that Donald J. Trump tried to stage a coup d'état in Washington, on January 6, 2021, a thing unheard of in the more than 200 years of existence of this, the best republic in the world. So much so that I think the United States should erect a statue of Mike Pence in the Capitol, because, in refusing to please Trump, who asked him not to certify Joe Biden's win, he prevented the coup d'état, saving democracy and the Constitution.

What more does Donald Trump have to do to make his followers see his falseness and the danger he poses to democracy and freedom?

It would be a great gift to me and a blessing to all if the Trump admirers reading this would stop any quick and angry response that comes to their lips and before repeating any of the many false arguments that are part of their caudillo's stock responses, take time to reread what has been presented here, none of which is a lie, and think carefully and sincerely if an individual like him deserves to be entrusted with the future of the "the land of the free and the home of the brave."

What will happen in November 2024? The presidential election that will then take place is, in my view, the defining event of America's future as a rule-of-law state and a true and functioning democracy.

I trust in the patriotism and common sense of the vast majority of the citizens of this country, Democrats, Republicans and Independents. If we put this first, I'm sure that wonderful times will come for this, our second homeland.

So sure am I of this that, in the next chapter, which will be my last, I will dare to predict, without hesitation, the outcome of those elections.

Chapter 30
The 2024 Elections: A Prediction

> *If you know the past and understand the present well, you will be able to predict the future.*
> An exiled poet

I said in the previous chapter that, in the 2020 presidential election, most voters did not vote for Joe Biden, they voted against Donald Trump. This same principle has been expressed by political analysts, sociologists and pollsters. And taking into account the Republican's performance during his four years in the White House, as well as what he's been doing and saying from then to date, it seems to me that this is an inescapable conclusion for anyone who can see and interpret the facts dispassionately.

Certainly, the shortcomings that could be wielded against Biden during his presidential bid were minimized by the magnitude of the danger that Donald Trump's character flaws, ethical shortcomings and narcissism represented then and represent today for the preservation of the rule of law and the health of democracy in the United States. And it's a well-known fact that people are more motivated to vote against a person than for another one.

If anyone is convinced that Donald Trump lost the 2020 election fair and square, it is Trump himself. He and those who surround him in his business are numbers people, and they know that numbers don't deceive. For them, Joe Biden's legitimate triumph in those elections is clear.

It's necessary to take the above into account before we dare to try to unravel what to expect in the next presidential elections, on November 5, 2024. In addition, we must take into consideration some other data that have an impact on the U.S. electoral landscape:

African Americans massively voted against Donald Trump, and that's not going to change in the foreseeable future. Hispanics in all states vote overwhelmingly Democrat, and this will not change in 2024. The exception to this rule is the majority of Miami Cubans, who have moved from the left of Mao ("Fidel, this is your house") to the right of Genghis Kahn ("Trump won"). Women will vote in large numbers against Trump, as a large part of them feel threatened by his misogyny. Democrats will vote for their party's candidate, as will many Republicans if their party's candidate is Donald Trump, as Republican Congresswoman Liz Cheney has said.

Therefore, the logical inference is that the Democratic Party will win the White House in 2024; it has no chance of losing. And that victory for the Democrats is guaranteed... by Donald Trump.

Ideally, neither Trump nor Biden would be the candidates in the upcoming race. Democrats have the possibility of avoiding Biden's reelection candidacy at that year's convention. Although difficult, this isn't impossible. The Republican Party does not have this option. If they manage to stop Trump's candidacy at their convention, he will run as an Independent candidate. This would split the Republican vote and give the win to the Democratic candidate even more easily. This happened in the 1992 election, when Ross Perot's candidacy made it possible for Bill Clinton to beat George Bush, Sr.

Recall that, in 2016, Trump won not only the presidency; he also won the majority in the Senate and the House. In the following four years he lost the House, lost the Senate and lost the White House. Donald Trump is one of the biggest losers in the electoral history of this country.

It's somewhat ironic, but very true, that, on two occasions the Democrats tried to impeach Trump, thus giving the Republicans a chance to get rid of him. They didn't, and now they're at a dead end: the monster they created is about to devour them.

Let's wait for 2024. Those who have read this will see that there are no surprises. As Julius Caesar would say, the die is cast.

November 26, 2022 with my children, grandchildren and great-grandchildren

Index

A

Adams, Tom, 157
Adenauer, Konrad, 277
Aguirre, Horacio, 207
Albizu Campos, Pedro, 60
Alejos, Carlos, 76
Alejos, Roberto, 76
Alemán, Arnoldo, 267-268, 271-273
Alemán, José Manuel, 51
Alemán Valdés, Miguel, 137, 157
Alexander, William, 290
Allen, Richard, 252
Alliegro, Anselmo, 44, 47, 73, 301
Alonso, Leonel, 32
Alonso, Miriam, 32, 133
Álvarez del Manzano, José María, 298
Álvarez, Belarmina, 25-26, 70
Álvarez, Miguel, 300
Ameijeiras, Efigenio, 53, 64-65
Anderson, Howard F., 83
Andrews, Paul, 196, 199
Andrews, Wilbur, 43
Arango, Eddy, 59
Arboleya, Carlos, 197, 290-291
Arce, Rafael, 79
Aronovitz, Sidney, 175-179
Arqués, Manolo, 149, 197, 226, 290-291
Arria, Diego, 237-238
Artime, Adelaida, 239
Artime, Manuel, 14, 100, 116, 225, 239, 297, 299
Askew, Reubin, 14, 134, 139-144, 146-151, 153, 157-158, 161, 164, 170-171, 186, 198, 243, 259, 287

B

Balaguer, Joaquín, 157
Balbis, Manuel, 67
Baldor, Aurelio, 28
Baldor, Francisco, 28
Balido, Albert, 286
Balsera, Freddy, 297, 302
Barba, Carlos, 184
Barquín, Ramón, 27, 49-50
Barreto, Berta, 61, 117-118
Barrios de Chamorro, Violeta, 268, 270-271, 273
Batista, Fulgencio, 19, 24, 27, 30, 33-34, 45, 47, 49-52-55, 58, 61, 71, 73-74, 85, 105, 115, 130, 212, 227, 310
Bello Álvarez, Esperanza, 25, 43, 49, 52, 64
Bello, Francisco, 25
Belt, Guillermo, 61
Bendixen, Sergio, 243, 297
Benes, Bernardo, 219-222
Betancourt, Virginia, 118
Biden, Joe, 311, 326-327, 329-330
Bido, Juan, 297
Bissell, Richard, 89

333

Blanco Navarro, Manolo, 74, 124
Blanco Navarro, Nelson, 124
Blanco Navarro, Renaldo, 54, 59, 65, 74, 123-124
Blaya, Joaquín, 184, 243
Bolaños, Enrique, 268, 271-272
Borbonet, Enrique, 49-50
Bordón Machado, Víctor, 65-66
Borge, Tomás, 234
Bosque, Gilberto, 67, 69-70
Botifoll, Luis, 290-291, 295
Bovo, Esteban, 262, 265-266
Boyd, Carlos, 233
Braman, Norman, 297
Brezhnev, Leonid, 240
Brillembourgh, David, 230
Brillembourgh, René, 230
Brito Mérida, Casilda, 21-22
Brzezinski, Zbigniew, 237
Bundy, McGeorge, 89
Burke, Arleigh, 89, 115
Bush Jr., George, 320, 326
Bush Sr., George, 258, 309-310, 330
Bush, Jeb, 262, 326

C

Cabell, Charles, 89
Cacciatori, Osvaldo, 298
Caíñas Milanés, Armando, 54, 62-63
Calderoni, Juan, 250
Calviño, Ramón, 115
Calzadilla, 70, 126-127
Campanería, Virgilio, 83
Candela, Hilario, 39-40
Cantillo, Carlos, 52
Cantillo, Eulogio, 29
Capriles, Miguel Ángel, 229-232, 250

Carbó, Ulises, 120
Carbonell, Néstor, 116, 297
Cárdenas, Al, 279
Carey, Barbara, 249
Carol, Oscar, 300
Carrasco, Teok, 297
Carreras, Jesús, 55, 58
Carroll, Mons. Coleman, 178
Carter, Jimmy, 141, 217, 229, 235, 237, 239-241, 273, 277, 310
Carter, Jimmy, administration, 219, 228, 238
Castañeda, Carlos M., 206
Castor, Betty, 262
Castro, Fidel, 14, 18-19, 24, 27, 33, 46-47, 50, 52-54, 57-64, 69, 72-73, 80-81, 83, 85, 87-88, 90, 93, 95, 101-107, 109, 113, 115, 117-121, 123-127, 129, 131-132, 173, 203, 205, 207, 211-212, 217-222, 225, 227, 229, 235, 238, 253, 255, 257, 268, 294, 303-304, 310, 323, 325-326, 330
Castro, Raúl, 19, 50, 54, 63, 70
Chamorro, Álvaro, 272
Chamorro, Pedro Joaquín, 268
Chaverry, Virgilio, 233
Chávez, Hugo, 228
Cheney, Liz, 330
Chibás, Eduardo, 118
Chiles, Lawton, 163
Christie, Irving, 163-164, 166, 195
Churchill, Winston, 277
Cienfuegos, Camilo, 50-51, 53
Cienfuegos, Osmani, 109
Cirera, Peter, 285
Clark, Steve, 133-138, 141-143, 157, 161, 172-174, 202, 216, 243, 254, 287

Clay, Lucius, 123
Clinton, Bill, 277-278, 310, 320, 330
Clinton, Hillary, 320
Codina, Armando, 297
Collazo, Mirto, 76
Conte Agüero, Luis, 297
Cortina, Humberto, 297, 300
Couto, Carlos M., 163
Cushing, Cardenal Richard, 123

D

Davidson, Mina, 169
Dawkins, Miller, 247-248
de Cárdenas, Jorge, 302
de Diego, Felipe, 116
de Gaulle, Charles, 275, 277
de la Milera, María, 290, 292
de la Torriente, Cosme, 324
de la Torriente, José Elías, 211-212
de San Julián, Tomás, 297
Dean, Tanny, 178
del Pino, Rafael, 61
del Pozo, Justo Luis, 61
Deutsch, Peter, 262
Di Maggio, Joe, 13
Díaz-Balart, Lincoln, 279, 301
Diaz-Balart, Rafael, 33, 60
Díaz Lanz, Marcos, 46-47, 51-52
Díaz Lanz, Pedro Luis, 46, 50-52
Díaz Tamayo, Martín, 73, 75
Díaz Tamayo, Rosaura, 73
Díaz-Canel, Miguel, 304, 307
Díaz-Hanscom, Rafael, 83
Díaz, Guarioné, 290, 293
Díaz, Higinio (Nino), 86
Díaz, Manny, 297
Díaz, Miguel, 40
Diaz, Nora, 169, 260, 286
Donovan, James B., 118, 123

Dulles, Allen, 89, 115
Durán, Alfredo, 27, 44-45, 47, 121, 147-148, 164, 220-221

E

Echevarría, Hermán, 258
Eisenhower, Dwight, 19, 84-85, 93, 99, 105, 107, 128, 227, 310
Eisenhower, Dwight, administration, 84-87, 89, 105-107
Elena, Martín, 100
Elgarresta, Mario, 252-253
Encinosa, Pedro, 300
Escribano, Julio, 40
Estefan, Emilio, 297
Estefan, Gloria, 297
Esterline, Jake, 89
Estorino, Julio, 11
Estrella, Evelio, 130

F

Fair, T. Willard, 243
Faircloth, Earl, 144, 146
Fascell, Dante, 129-130, 142, 264
Fernández, Carlos Benito, 184, 187-189, 301
Fernández, Conchita, 117-118
Fernández, Eufemio, 83
Fernández Reboso, Sebastian, 285
Fernández Reboso, Andrea, 285
Fernández Rundle, Kathy, 189
Ferré, Luis, 174
Ferré, Maurice, 14, 135, 174-179, 181-187, 189, 191-192, 197-200, 202, 217, 223, 236, 241-243, 245-251, 253-254, 260, 279
Fleites, Armando, 58-59, 61
Freyre, Ernesto, 116-118

G

Gaitán, Jorge Eliécer, 61
Galindez, Ignacio, 30
García Fusté, Tomás, 173-176, 178, 182-184, 226, 251, 258
Garcia Sifredo, Armando, 206
García Toledo, Luisa, 290-291, 295
Garrido, Alberto, 27
Gibson, Rev. Theodore, 164, 172, 176-178, 192, 196-199, 202, 223, 236, 243, 279, 287
Goderich Jr., Mario (Mayito), 198
Goizueta, May, 27
Goizueta, Roberto, 27
Gómez, José Miguel, 29
Gómez, Ricardo, 297
Gómez, Ricky, 297
González Mayo, Cristobal, 150
González Rebull Jr., Julio (Julitín), 297
Gonzalez Rebull, Julio (Julito), 83, 158, 169, 254, 289, 300-302
González, Armando, 206
González, Osiel, 32
Goodman, Murray, 169-170
Gordon, Rose, 163-164, 172, 175, 177-179, 199, 223, 278
Gore, Al, 320
Graham, Bob, 14, 142, 150-151
Grassie, Joe, 199
Grau San Martín, Ramón, 33, 51, 130
Grau, Abdón, 184
Guerra, Fernando, 28
Guevara, Alfredo, 61
Guevara, Ernesto (Che), 19, 50, 66, 80, 107
Gutiérrez Menoyo, Eloy, 54, 58-59, 61-62, 65, 123, 219
Gutiérrez, Armando, 297

Gutiérrez, David, 298

H

Hadley, Charles, 248
Hall, Chuck, 136, 144
Haza, Oscar, 297, 305
Hernández Corzo, Rogelio, 83
Hernández Tellaheche, Arturo, 54, 62
Hernández, Pepe, 253
Herrera, Jorge, 301
Hickman, Don, 199
Huguet, Rafael, 40
Humphrey, Hubert, 134

I

Ibargüen, Alberto, 206

J

Johnson, Lyndon B., 131, 237
Jones, Carlos, 112-113
Jones, Jorge (Yoyi), 112
Jordán, René, 207
Juan Pablo II, 233

K

Kefauver, Estes, 43
Kennedy, Dave, 134-135, 138, 142-144, 161, 163-164, 166, 169-171, 175, 185-187, 189, 195, 202, 216, 243, 248, 287
Kennedy, Jacqueline, 124, 278
Kennedy, John F., 17-18, 43-44, 86-89, 105-107, 124-126, 128-129, 131-132, 237, 278, 310
Kennedy, John F. administration, 17-18, 77, 84-86, 89, 106

Kennedy, Robert (Bobby), 14, 109-123, 129, 131-132
King Yun, Jorge, 115
King, Jr., Martin Luther, 36
Kirk, Claude, 143-144, 146
Kirkpatrick, Lyman B., 78, 90, 93
Kissinger, Henry, 204

L

Lamas, Tony, 27, 65-66
Lauredo, Luis, 248, 297
Lawrence, Dave, 206
Lehtinen, Dexter, 264
Leigh, Gustavo, 201
Lemnitzer, Lyman, 89
León, Benjamin, 297
Levine Cava, Daniella, 262, 265
Lewinsky, Monica, 278
Lindsey, John, 140
Llaca, Enrique, 118
Lluberes, Guarionex, 157
Lombard, Eduardo, 286
Lombard, Lily, 286
Lombard, Sofie, 286
López Fitoria, Leovigildo, 233
López, Jorge Luis, 258-259, 297
López, Ramón, 184
Loret de Mola, Carlos, 298
Lynch, Grayston, 111

M

Maceo, Antonio, 100
Machado y Morales, Gerardo, 24, 30
Maidique, Modesto, 290-291
Mañach, Jorge, 324
Marenco, Dionisio, 273
Marina, Evaristo, 130
Márquez Sterling, Carlos, 324

Martín Pérez, Roberto, 62
Martin, Frank, 169-170, 186
Martínez Márquez, Guillermo, 207
Martínez, Mel, 297
Martínez, Raúl, 208, 258, 264-265, 297
Más Canosa, Jorge, 253-255, 297, 309
Más Santos, Jorge, 254
Masferrer, Rolando, 212
Masvidal, Raul, 242, 252-255, 290, 302
Mathews, Irma, 46, 64, 70, 73, 75, 110, 169, 286
Mathews, Jack, 144
McCain, John, 326
McMullan, John, 203-204
McNair, Angus, 83
McNamara, Robert, 237
McRaven, William H., 14
Medina, Pepín, 79
Medrano, Humberto, 207
Meek, Carrie, 249
Meek, Kendrick, 263
Mekis, Patricio, 298
Mestre, Ramón, 297
Milander, Henry, 264
Milián, Emilio, 182-183, 212
Miranda, Sister Margarita, 210
Miró Cardona, José, 14, 100, 115-116, 299
Montaner, Ernesto, 206
Morgan, William, 54-55, 58, 65, 68, 123
Murillo, Rosario, 272

N

Nixon, Richard, 128, 163
Novell, Angela, 120

O

Obama, Barrack, 277
Obando y Bravo, Mons. Miguel, 233
Odio, César, 294
Ojeda, Tony, 294
Oliva, Erneido, 116, 118, 125
Orr, Jack, 133, 172, 174
Ortega, Daniel, 234, 267-268, 270, 272-273
Ortega, Humberto, 270
Ortega Reboso, Camile, 286
Oswald, Lee Harvey, 131-132
Ovares, Enrique, 54, 59-61, 65, 67, 69
Ozarzún, Maria Eugenia, 298

P

Padrera, Camilo, 297
Padrón, Eduardo, 290, 293
Padrón, José Orlando, 220-222
Pallais Debayle, Luis, 230, 234
Pallais, Nadia, 11, 260-261, 267-269, 272-273, 286, 288
Pantín Jr., Leslie, 290
Pantín Sr., Leslie, 197, 242, 290
Parkins, Rob, 249
Pastor, Robert (Bob), 237-238
Pastora, Edén, 233, 235
Peláez, Pedro, 297, 302
Penabaz, Fernando, 258
Peñalver Sr., Rafael, 150
Pence, Mike, 326
Penelas, Alex, 258-262, 287, 292, 297
Pepper, Claude, 129-130, 142
Perez Cisneros, Guy, 61, 117
Pérez Franco, Juan, 300
Pérez Heredia, Arturo, 116
Pérez Jr., Demetrio, 164
Pérez Jr., Virgilio, 248
Pérez Roura, Armando, 184
Pérez San Román, Roberto, 111-112, 116, 297
Pérez, Carlos Andrés, 14, 225, 229-232, 269-270
Pérez, Tony, 111
Perot, Ross, 330
Peruyero, Juan José, 212
Piñeiro, Federico, 27
Piñerua Ordaz, Luis, 250
Pino, Sergio, 259, 297
Pinochet, Augusto, 201
Plummer, Joseph Lionel (J.L.), 164, 172, 176, 178, 199, 223, 278
Porras, Rafael, 232
Pozo, Luisito, 61
Prío Socarrás, Carlos, 33, 74, 130, 255
Puig Miyar, Manuel Lorenzo, 83
Puig, Alelí, 287, 289-290
Puig, Fernando, 289, 300
Puig, Ramon, 257

Q

Quintana, Alfredo, 38
Quintana, Julio César, 230-231

R

Range, Athalie, 172-175, 248
Rasco, José Ignacio, 207
Reagan, Ronald, 130, 239, 241, 243-245, 248, 252, 257, 263, 266-267, 277
Reboso, Ali, 285
Reboso Balido, Noreen, 169, 285-286

Reboso Brito, Manuel, 21-26, 30, 34-35, 43, 49-52, 64
Reboso Brito, Maximina, 21-22
Reboso Lombard, Melissa, 169, 285-286
Reboso Padrón, José, 21-22, 26, 70
Reboso Solares, Irma, 46, 285
Reboso, Alex, 46, 70, 73, 110, 285
Reboso, David, 285
Reboso, Eva, 286
Reboso, Gavin, 285
Reboso, Kiki, 285
Reboso Jr., Manny, 286
Reboso, Manny, 169, 286
Reboso, Michelle, 26
Reboso, Mila, 285
Reboso, Roberto Luis, 46, 285
Reboso, Roberto, 25-26, 29-30, 43, 51, 64, 189, 284, 302
Reese, Melvin, 166
Regalado, Tomás, 297, 305
Reich, Otto, 149
Reno, Janet, 189
Rey Pernas Santiago, 71
Riera Gómez, Eliseo, 172
Rivero Agüero, Andrés, 45, 107, 227
Rivero, Felipe, 71-72
Rivero, Jose Ignacio, 207, 235
Roa García, Raúl, 69
Roberts, Tomás, 250
Rodríguez Tejera, Roberto, 11, 297, 305
Rodríguez, Carlos Rafael, 72, 257
Rodríguez, Héctor, 55, 58
Roig, Pedro, 254-255, 300, 302
Rojas, Mario, 66
Romney, Mitt, 326
Roosevelt, Franklin Delano, 277
Ros-Lehtinen, Ileana, 264, 279

Rothstein, Alan, 177
Ruiz Williams, Enrique, 118
Rusk, Dean, 106
Ruvin, Harvey, 26, 243, 297-298

S

Sabines, Luis, 149, 183-184, 226, 290, 292-293, 295
Saiff, Joseíto, 34
Salazar y Espinosa, Manuel, 233
Salmán, Carlos, 252-253, 279, 297
San Antonio, Laura, 67-68
Sánchez, Aldo, 55, 58
Sánchez, Álvaro, 118
Sánchez, Celia, 118
Sánchez, Joe, 297
Sansores, Carlos, 298
Senseman, Ronald, 110
Sevilla, Ninón, 71
Silva, Eddy, 301
Silveira, Silvio, 40
Silvertooth, Lynn, 186
Sinatra, Frank, 301
Sirhan, Sirhan Bishara, 131
Skakel Kennedy, Ethel, 112, 119
Skakel, George, 112
Smith, Earl E. T., 19
Smith, Leroy, 196
Solares Cirera, Gabriela, 285
Solares, Mario Luis, 285
Solares, Mario, 285
Soler Puig, Emilio, 115
Somoza García, Anastasio (Tacho), 227
Somoza Debayle, Anastasio (Tachito), 14, 225-236, 238-239, 242, 267, 269
Somoza, Jose R., 234
Sorí Marín, Humberto, 83
Sorzano Jorrín, Leonardo, 36

Stevenson, Adlai, 43
Suárez, Francis, 315
Suárez, Roberto, 206
Suárez, Xavier, 251, 253-254, 258, 260, 264
Sueiro, Hugo, 68-71, 109, 124

T

Tabernilla Dolz, Francisco, 117
Tabernilla, Carlos, 61, 117
Tapia Ruano, Alberto, 83
Taylor, Maxwell, 115
Teele, Arthur, 260, 262-263
Theberge, James, 227, 272
Tobin, Gerry, 297
Torres, Hugo, 233
Trujillo, Mario, 298
Trujillo, Rafael Leónidas, 59-61
Trump, Donald, 266, 277, 311, 321, 323, 325-331
Tse-tung, Mao, 128, 330
Turner, Jack, 169-170

V

Vadía, Alberto, 54, 58
Valdés, Jorge, 208, 259
Valls Jr., Felipe, 288, 297
Valls Sr., Felipe, 261, 287-289, 297
Valls, Aminta, 287
Valls, Jeannette, 287
Valls, Lety, 287
Valls, Lourdes, 288
Valls, Natty, 261
Vals, Willy, 40, 66-67
Varona, Tony, 14, 100, 116, 299
Vera, 111
Verdeja, Sam, 206
Villafaña, Manolo, 83
Villalobos, Pepe, 142
Villalón, Mitch, 302
Villoldo, Gustavo, 119-120, 297

W

Walters, Vernon, 257
Wright, Rev. Temperance, 169-170
Wynton, Ed, 184
Xirau, Gustavo, 40

Z

Zambrano Velasco, José Alberto, 231
Zamora, Guillermo, 196

www.ingramcontent.com/pod-product-compliance
Lightning Source LLC
Chambersburg PA
CBHW030510080526
44586CB00011B/139